P9-BJU-076

SEVEN PILLARS OF POPULAR CULTURE _____

Matthew Kahle, who fought under General George Washington, carved this statue from a single pine log around 1800. Now it tops Washington Hall on the campus of Washington and Lee University in Virginia. Decorated, painted, and parodied by generations of students, "Old George" is the very embodiment of *Seven Pillars of Popular Culture*. *Courtesy of Washington and Lee University.*

Seven Pillars of Popular Culture

MARSHALL W. FISHWICK

Contributions to the Study of Popular
Culture, Number 10

Greenwood Press
WESTPORT, CONNECTICUT
LONDON, ENGLAND

Library of Congress Cataloging in Publication Data

Fishwick, Marshall William.
  Seven pillars of popular culture.

  (Contributions to the study of popular culture,
ISSN 0198-9871 ; no. 10)
    Bibliography: p.
    Includes index.
    1. United States—Popular culture—History—20th
century. I. Title. II. Series.
E169.12.F645 1985   306'.4'0973   84-8994
ISBN 0-313-23263-6 (lib. bdg.)

Library of Congress Catalog Card Number: 84-8994
ISBN: 0-313-23263-6
ISSN: 0198-9871

First published in 1985

Greenwood Press
A division of Congressional Information Service, Inc.
88 Post Road West
Westport, Connecticut 06881

Printed in the United States of America

10 9 8 7 6 5 4 3 2 1

Two Jamies, two Marshalls, Will, Charlie, and Wick
Seven Grandsons—Seven Pillars—but let me add quick
Elise, Ann, and Farley make it Grandchildren ten
May good things await them—again and again.

Wisdom hath builded a house; she
hath hewn out her seven pillars.

Books of Proverbs

How reverend is the face of this tall pile,
Whose ancient pillars rear their marble heads,
To bear aloft its arch'd and pond'rous roof
By its own weight made stedfast and immoveable.

William Congreve, *The Mourning Bride*

With antique pillars massy proof
And story windows richy dight,
Casting a dim religious light.

John Milton, *Il Penseroso*

I charge you by the law,
Whereof you are a well-deserving pillar,
Proceed to judgment.

William Shakespeare, *The Merchant of Venice*

CONTENTS ⸻

ILLUSTRATIONS ————

SEVEN PILLARS OF POPULAR CULTURE ─────────────

PRELUDE _____

"Eat your heart out, Tom Swift! Roll over, Rover Boys! Now it's my turn to tackle the Head Hunters of Borneo!"

Thus my jubilant thoughts last summer as I landed in the airport of Sarawak, taking a side trip from an Asian lecture tour; fulfilling a childhood fantasy; going back into the primitive jungle.

Where was the primordial forest, where still dwell the black-crested baboon, proboscis monkey, charging rhino, and dwarf buffalo? What strange beasts might be munching on the rafflesia, whose flowers measure a yard in diameter? And where might the adders, cobras, and scorpions be waiting, quietly, to administer their death blows?

Never mind that modernity had partly overtaken my fantasy. On today's maps there is no Borneo—the Indonesians have renamed it Kalimantan. The airport has the standard electronic gadgets; and the employers are more concerned with radar than ritual. But the old history, legends, and places: they are all in place. Behind us lurks Makassarese, proud old kingdom toppled finally by the Dutch; ahead, the land of the fierce Toraja—never toppled by anyone. And who can discredit tales still told in villages like Nangapinah, Sunaipinang, or Kualamandjual—or not admire the teeming Sampit River, flowing majestically into Bandjarmasin?

Nor can anyone deny that for centuries on this wild and overgrown island, heads were hunted and severed: a kind of fertility ritual, to assure the survival of the crops and the people. All this has past, the American Embassy staff assured me; if I wanted to make the trip, I would be adequately guided and protected. In fact, like Bali, Kalimantan is becoming a routine tourist venture, with on and off seasons. To see one of the few unspoiled orangutan preserves on earth, one of the last preserves of the tropics, is well worth the effort. So I went.

Two hours later, we were following a narrow path miles from a settlement, let alone a city. My guides explained that the Old People had built their villages on hilltops, so they could wall and protect them from man and beast. Tribes warred constantly, seeking heads and slaves. Headhunting was a religious, social, political requirement; enemies' heads must be offered to ancestral spirits at burials and temple consecrations. When sorcerers were discovered, they were sold to other villages for beheading. Some people said that far back into the jungle, where no roads led and no government troops patrolled . . . .

We continued to walk, I continued to sweat. With my hand I wiped the moisture from my neck—pleased to note that all the necessary parts were intact. Was it Tarzan or Tom Swift whom I thought I heard wailing out there somewhere? I smiled bravely at my guides, and told myself all this was fun. Inside, I had another feeling. I was scared.

Fear breeds fear. Suppose something *were* to happen: how would we get back? Who would know just where we were, and how to locate us? Of course, the guides knew the local customs and cures . . . but to try a local cure on a scorpion bite?

Up ahead, a sharp turn in the path, leading down to a natural stone tunnel carved out by a tiny stream for over a million years. Vegetation had grown up so dense on both sides that we had no choice but to walk through. How many people had hidden or lived here, over the centuries? Twentieth-century man going back into the cave, the womb. What a splendid idea it had been to come!

Slowly, cautiously we walked through the semi-darkness, heard the trickle of relentless water, emerged back into the light. As my eyes adjusted, I heard a rustle in the bushes, and saw a figure moving towards me. I froze in my tracks, clenched my fists. A guide's hand moved quickly towards his pistol. Then she was standing just ahead of us in the path: a native child, perhaps six or seven years old, dark brown with white teeth, scantily clad, holding an object in her right hand. Unhesitatingly she walked straight up to me, thrust forth the object, spoke: "Coca-Cola, Meester? You wanna Coke?" Pop goes the world.

How she or the Coke got there remains a mystery. All I know is that I grabbed it, gulped it, and knew it was the Real Thing. Nothing else I did or saw was more satisfying. Not King Kong, but King Coke, had captured me in the heart of the jungle.

American pop in Paris or Peking, New York or New Delhi—a well told tale. But the rain forest of Kalimantan? How did this episode occur—not just physically, but psychologically? What are the cultural forces (predicted but often mispredicted in George Orwell's novel) that confront us in 1984? Not only Big Brother but Big Bottle and Big Bird are on the move. Folk, fake, elite, and popular culture form patterns that elude and intrigue us. Both inner and outer space—microcosm and macrocosm—present a host of new problems and possibilities.

We need not go to Borneo to confront culture shock and untamed territories: America itself is also a wilderness, our society a wilderness shared. We insist on fences, dogs, guns. Even in suburbia, we are fearful of neighborhood intruders. On a gun rack in our ranch is a rifle; the horse(power) rests in the garage, and the villains are out there somewhere, in black hats.[1] But the gods will come and save us. They will, they must. That is part of our *mythos*, to sustain us as we die, just as it succors us while we live.

In between, we are confused. The air is full of static and sounds—but where is the melody? Words, words, words—but where is the wisdom? Our journals are bulging with monographs—but where is the meaning?

Three and a half centuries after Rene Descartes published his monumental *Essay on Method*, popular culture specialists can't agree on any method—or indeed, if they even need and want one. To Descartes's ringing conclusion—*cogito ergo sum*—we can only reply *dubito ergo sum*. We are not sure we know—instead, we doubt. The Age of Information increases not only our data but dilemmas.

To make it worse—for those in the humanistic tradition—many of our colleagues seem to have given up not only Latin but also English. They speak science, mathematics, and (all too often) jargon. To admit that one doesn't understand the meaning of

$E = MC^2$, atomic fission, or DNA chains is enough to disqualify one from the Club. So we try to keep up, envy our scientific colleagues their enormous grants and prestige, and mutter to ourselves as we fall asleep: *Dubito ergo sum.*

Some doubts about popular culture are well founded. How can we describe it if we have no definition?[2] There is not even a consensus on where to locate it: for it is either everywhere or nowhere, depending on your criteria. Distinguished scholars and poets, like Ezra Pound, T. S. Eliot, Ortega Y. Gassett, F. R. Levis, and Richard Hoggart have been repulsed by what Hoggart calls (in *The Uses of Literary*) the candy floss culture, where sex comes in shiny packets, "and the world is largely a phantasmagoria of passing shows and vicarious stimulations." Critics rightly say much that passes for popular scholarship is trivial and faddish, lacking any systematic approach, based on borrowed or improvised methods. By and about situations which are not academic to begin with, the quarry is like the flying butterfly which dies when one tries to pin it to the wall.

Because much popular culture utilizes mass media, some equate the two things. This is misleading, since each epoch of history has its own unique forms. Ours is a flashy electronic variation of something that has existed throughout human history. We need to study the evolutionary process of popular culture: to show that it is not the enemy of, but the adjunct extension of what is variously described as academic, "high," or elite culture.

Bringing advocates of elite and popular culture together is like the mating of tarantulas. Attraction and desire may be there—but suspicion lurks—for consummation carries the risk of being stung—or eaten up! We should take the risk—and hope to find a way to make the mating a pleasurable (or at least satisfactory and credible) undertaking.

To start with, there should be some show of mutual self-respect and allowances for differences. There are academics and critics who view anything labeled *popular* the way some white Southerners once viewed anything *black*, and the way some males (here I specify no region or time span) view anything *feminine*. If we start with Dwight Macdonald's axiom—not only is what he calls "Mass-Cult" dreadful, it doesn't even have the capacity of being any better—there can be no mating or under-standing. There is plenty of reverse snobbery, too—"any girl who doesn't wear blue jeans to class," one of my students said scornfully, "should be expelled." To prefer Béla Bartók to the Beatles is certainly defensible: but might it be debatable? Can popular culture (at its best) be understood as a new and au-thentic manifestation of modern electronic society—not just as a faddish response, but a genuine product? Will the new dem-ocratic ways of communication produce something which matches the fine books that came from movable type, the great films from celluloid? Such intriguing and intricate questions should not be dismissed, or answered quickly in a monosylla-ble. The new energy brought to our world by film art, jazz, the musical comedy, and comics has had an incredible historical development and has reenergized the world stage.[3]

They are not, of course, *sui generis*-most of our popular expressions are extensions of traditional (elite) forms and for-mulas. Films learned much from the stage, jazz drew from clas-sical music, the musical comedy had one ear tuned to the op-era, and comic strips have ancestors stretching back to early cave drawings and medieval illuminations. But they have become forms in *their own right*: they have left the nest and soared. Hurrah!

Might not the American musical at its best—say, *Oklahoma*, *Guys and Dolls*, *West Side Story*, and *Chorus Line*, to name four of my favorites—fill the same function for audiences in New York that the Greek drama 2,500 years ago had for those in Athens? Might not theater art since Aristophanes have swung full cir-cle, to arrive back to its original form? Have we not again ac-quired a popular and national drama combining topical com-ment, satire, song, dance, and folklore, resplendent in appropriate settings and trimmings? And must we always sneer at a Hollywood that could produce, within the span of a few years, three films as different and enduring as *Citizen Kane*, *Gone with the Wind*, and *The Wizard of Oz*?

Even those who would concede some validity to the exam-ples I use—best of breed—would caution against what John M. Phelan, in his brilliant study *Mediaworld*, called "melodoxy." Like me, he goes back to Greek roots. Plato used the word *doxa* for uninformed opinion, unexamined folklore, and prejudice. *Melos* (Greek for "song" or "melody") was placed before seventeenth-century French popular dramas that featured sweet sentimental songs; hence the word *melodrama*. Melodoxy, then, combines ignorance and sentimentality, resulting in "the universe of discourse made possible—and perhaps required—by the mass communication systems of the production and distribution of ideas and sensibilities."[4]

Choosing an area where his case is easiest to make—modern advertising, where transparent subterfuge is permitted and expected—Phelan even conjures up "the melodoxical world," where mental and physical health comes from effortless application of secret formulas available at a local drugstore. We know all too well this world of tinsel wrappers, big breasts, and happy ethnics, where people who hunger for real food are given only cotton candy. Melodoxy is a clear and present danger. Scraping off the rough edges of ethnicity, Mediaworld markets millions of repeatable units. It is the mechanization and modernization of the art and knowledge of mankind. "In the old days," Phelan says, "folks had to handle well-wrought urns and sensate cultures. Now they can deal with hot and cool messages, zero degree, and metamyths." Yet even Mr. Phelan goes on to admit that "the miracle of the electronic distribution of film and tape has brought to millions the Mountains of the Moon . . . brilliant artists have been given the technical means to recreate past periods vividly."[5] So the answer to that famous Biblical taunt—"Has anything good ever come out of Nazareth?"—is an emphatic YES.

There is a rawness, even a savagery, to our culture and its popular portrayal which we might try both to understand and to acknowledge. A violence that often verges on the psychopathic is never far away. The Saturday Night Special pistol may be in the hands of the next man we meet, and it may be our death warrant. What we insist on calling exciting and dynamic may also be satanic. (Punk rock comes to mind.) Why can we find no rest, no peace? Why are we always breaking in and breaking out . . . going west and coming east . . . moving up and moving out? In European cities, buildings snuggle and cluster, protecting one another against a hostile world. But in

America, Jean-Paul Sartre has observed in *Essays on Aesthetics* (1966), streets are not winding walks closed in between houses, but national highways. The moment you set foot in one of them, you understand that they go on to Boston or Chicago. What is basically "American" is the concern with process as reflected in the word of heads, hearts, and hands. By what process do we create instant slums, colonial villages, neon nudes, silicon valleys, Jesus freaks, Watergates, Sewergates? What have we here?

A land of atomic reactors, foot-long hot dogs, Charles Addams Gothic, Hopi Indians, imitation castles, guided missiles, block slums, glass domes, mobile homes, little magazines, big sells, wetbacks, flashbacks, comebacks.

We have been so busy presenting all this as "uniquely American" that we have overlooked the fact that much that is involved is basically human. Our chauvinism, abundance, and prosperity have combined to separate us from the very cultures that sponsored and sustain us. We must reclaim our proper place sitting alongside (and not above) the rest of the human race. Nothing else can or will save us.

Yes, there is reason for alarm, amidst the profusion and confusion in popular art products—shifting and vanishing lines between once-clear categories, unreliability of data and labels—the over-serious attention to what was, until very recently, scorned. We saw the seventies as the "Me Decade"—a phrase that has become fashionable among the disenchanted, who were hardly enchanted to begin with. But there are stirrings in the land. Studs Terkel is right: "Those who were silent are no longer silent, no longer accept the word from on high. There is a flowing of juices that has not been covered on the Six O'Clock News."[6]

Still, the "Six O'Clock News," and an ever-increasing flow of video-culture through an ever-enlarging number of channels, is a basic fact of modern living. Shouting at our idiot boxes, and those who put on them what some find idiotic, will not shut them down.[7] Instead of condemning, we might try questioning all the mass media. Who puts what on, and why? Where are the new needs, markets, loyalties? Who are the viewers and how do we assess them? Just what is a mass audience? Why are millions of human beings willing to put aside everything in their lives to see a Super Bowl game, or a mini-series like "Roots" or "Mystic Warrior?"

Answers may require us to ponder the most revolutionary aspect of the new arts: their continuous availability, even more so than their ubiquitousness. Martin Esslin puts it in historical perspective:

Never before in the history of mankind has there been a continuous stream of collective consciousness into which—in the advanced Western societies—every member of the community can at will at any time of the day or night plug himself in—thus filling his individual consciousness with the thought and emotional content shared at that instant by millions of his fellow citizens.[8]

"That instant," which has become a cliché of the 1980s, was envisioned over half a century ago by two remarkable men who (with quite different insights and styles, but similar prescience) inspired the title and format of my book. The first was Thomas Edward Lawrence (alias Ross, Shaw, and Chapman) whose *Seven Pillars of Wisdom*, privately printed in 1926, was first published for general circulation in 1935. "The seven pillars of wisdom," the "Preface" notes, "are first mentioned in the Book of Proverbs: 'Wisdom hath builded a house; she hath hewn out her seven pillars.' "

Going back to the Biblical lands from whence the proverbs came, "Lawrence of Arabia" (1886–1935) became a popular then a legendary figure, raising the Arab Revolt against Turkey during World War I and writing a masterpiece which becomes ever more pivotal as Saudi Arabia (the world's largest oil producer) has moved center stage of world politics.

What interests me is not so much the military and political exploits, amazing though they be, but the point of view expressed in Lawrence's own "Introduction." He was not hampered by false modesty. "In these pages the history is not of the Arab movement," he writes, "but of me in it."[9] He then goes on to suggest why the book is not only an epical study of guerilla warfare, but a pioneer study in popular culture:

It is a narrative of daily life, mean happenings, little people. Here are no lessons for the world, no disclosures to shock peoples. It is filled with trivial things, partly that no one may mistake for history the bones from which some day a man may make history . . . . We were bound together, because of the sweep of the open places, the taste of wide winds, the sunlight, and the hopes in which we worked. The morning freshness of the world-to-be intoxicated us. We were wrought up with ideas inexpressible and vaporous, but to be fought for.[10]

I have read those lines again and again—and like them better with each reading. There is real wisdom in them. Daily life, daily bread, little people, trivial things: is not this the stuff and substance of culture, when all the fat is stripped off? What keeps us going in a life which (to quote Samuel Butler) is one damned thing after another, except the open places, the chance encounters, the sunlight, and the morning freshness? How many writers have the courage to stand beside Lawrence and admit they were and are wrought up "with ideas inexpressible and vaporous?" I, for one. Count me proud to join his legion and struggle to sustain his Seven Pillars.[11]

Not only the Seven Pillars, but also the Seven Lively Arts, a phrase coined by a contemporary of Lawrence who was a very different kind of pioneer in a different culture. In 1924 the New York critic Gilbert Seldes published *The 7 Lively Arts*—four words put together, he later recalled, on a winter evening in 1922 at the corner of 54th Street and Broadway. Harking back to the long-sacred number 7, and the "Seven Arts of the Greeks," the catchy title provided a sort of shorthand for any number of phrases and has become a part of the American language. Briefly put, Seldes argued that Krazy Kat, Charlie Chaplin, the Keystone Cops, and the circus were lively arts in the full sense of the word, as worthy of careful scrutiny as dance, theater, and painting. "There were those who felt (stuffily) that the seven were not arts," Seldes reminisced in "A Personal Preface" when the book was reprinted in 1957. "Lively was for the most part unchallenged."[12]

They have become much more lively, popular, and pervasive in the half-century between his *7 Lively Arts* and my *Seven Pillars of Popular Culture*—due in part to Seldes's own later works (especially *The Public Arts* and *The Great Audience*) and those of Van Wyck Brooks (who first described the high-middle-and-

lowbrow phenomenon), H. L. Mencken, Edmund Wilson, Lewis
Mumford, and Tom Wolfe. John Kouwenhoven helped by examining "the unselfconscious efforts of common people to create satisfying patterns, imposed by the driving energies of an
unprecedented social structure."[13] Sigfried Giedion showed that
molded plywood forms which revolutionized twentieth-century elite art were conventional material for ferryboat seats in
the 1870s; that certain highly acclaimed Bauhaus designs had
been standard equipment on American reapers and mowers
since the 1850s. The vivacious Pop artists and critics drew material from the supermarkets, filling stations, and neon-lighted
streets on which Everyman makes his contemporary pilgrim-
age.

Most interdisciplinary work of this type met with icy disdain.
The Big Thaw got under way in the Kennedy Years, affecting
films, literature, art, politics, journalism, and finally the academic Establishment itself. Significantly, the heading "Popular
Culture" didn't appear in *Reader's Guide* until 1960. The "silent
generation" and the gung-ho "organization man" passed. Emphasis moved from silence to uproar; from negative to positive
values; from turned off to tuned in. This recognition of ines-
capability, on a private and public level, moved modern thought
from existentialism to social realism. (What happened, for example, to David Riesman's *Lonely Crowd*?)

A number of scholars came to recognize popular culture as a
barometer, mirror, and monument of the world around them;
the cutting edge of American Studies, expanding further the
inquiry into and between subjects that began a generation ago.
Those over thirty must acquire its idiom and flavor; those under have been unable to avoid this *lingua franca* of their generation. Popular culture is their culture, norm, mode. Perhaps we
are not ex-elitists but post-elitists. Neat categories and barriers
are disappearing. Hard becomes soft, drama becomes audience, small becomes large, silence becomes music. Men like John
Cawelti are both fascinated and frightened by the new radical
cultural transformations. "At times they seem to hold out the
promise of a revitalization of our culture," he writes. "At other
times I wonder whether it is not simply an evasion of cultural
responsibility."[14] Meanwhile Peter Haertling, viewing the 1970

international Book Fair in Frankfurt, reported: "This has been a fair of pop singers and comic strips."[15] By 1984, pop singers were even included in the hundredth anniversary of the Metropolitan Opera House; Gilbert Seldes's ghost must have chuckled when the gala televised event was labeled "A Celebration of the Lively Arts."

Susan Sontag, in *Against Interpretation*, argues that the novel is dead. Interpretation is the revenge of the intellect upon art. "Even more, it is the revenge of the intellect upon the world." There are new standards of beauty, style, taste: pluralistic, high-speed, hectic. "From the vantage point of this new sensibility, the beauty of a machine, of a painting, of a film, and of the personalities and music of the Beatles is equally accessible."[16]

Nineteen seventy was also the year Gilbert Seldes died—fully aware by then that "the lively arts had turned into the mass media." The media had become the message, the massage, the money, and (in the eyes of many) the monster. People thought of our very atmosphere as a mediatmosphere, our planet as a global village; in one lifetime, the word and the world had been wired for sound.

Not only commmunication, but also Media Studies and Popular Culture had become recognized fields of study. Brilliant work by scholars like Harold Laswell, Carl Hovland, Paul Lazarsfeld, and Wilbur Schramm had opened up whole new vistas.[17] What an earlier generation had been content to call the Atomic Age or Age of Electronics was rechristened the Age of Information. In this soil I erect my own Seven Pillars.

In so doing, I am drawing more from the flavor and style of *Seven Pillars of Wisdom* and *The 7 Lively Arts* than from the material itself. Having chosen my title, I found that many other authors, including the Great Bard himself, have a penchant for pillars. Recall Shakespeare's words in *The Merchant of Venice*:

> I charge you by the law,
> Whereof you are a well-deserving pillar,
> Proceed to judgment.

John Milton spoke of "antique pillars massy proof" in *Il Penseroso*, and William Congreve caught in a clear memorable passage from *The Mourning Bride* the kind of "pillars" I mean to evoke:

> How reverend is the face of this tall pile,
> Whose ancient pillars rear their marble heads,
> To bear aloft its arch'd and pond'rous roof
> By its own weight made stedfast and immoveable.

The "pillar metaphor" is popular with a number of contemporary writers, icluding theologian Harvey R. Cox. His 1965 bestselling book *The Secular City* suggested that people had lost interest in the sacred; but his 1984 volume called *Religion in the Secular City* found him reversing his position: since our secular gods have failed, we are viewing more traditional gods with a new curiosity.[18] "Modernism," according to Cox, means the attempt to come to terms—in art, poetry, religion, or anything else—with the modern world, which he conceives as being supported by pillars: the national state, science-based technology, bureaucratic rationalism, the quest for profit maximization, and the secularization and trivialization of religion. "These are the five pillars," he writes in his 1984 book, "once proud, now leaning, of modernity. Together they support an imposing edifice of art and music, literature and theology."[19]

This passage in turn conjures up Biblical images, like Samson destroying the pillars of the temple and Lot being turned into a pillar of salt. All these are meant to converge in my title: my seven Pillars are both verbal metaphor and visual structure; they are literary, architectural, archetypal, and mystical. They are designed to describe a world which is neither logical nor illogical but alogical; a structure built partly on chance and serendipity, interpreted by "closed circuit" scholarship in an open circuit culture.

Yet I would not lose my Pillars in clouds of ambiguity. I invite the reader actually to *see* them, in his or her mind's eye, as a white Greek temple against a blue sky, in which fluted columns act separately yet work together to support a unified structure—a functioning culture.

Why seven? Seven has fascinated us since Creation (God made the world, says Genesis, in seven days) and ever since seven has been sacred. There are Seven Deadly Sins, Seven Wonders of the World, and Seven Beauties. Christ spoke "Seven Last Words from the Cross," Jakob and Wilhelm Grimm evoked Seven Ravens, Maurice Maeterlinck Seven Princesses, and John Buskin Seven Lamps of Architecture. We must forgive our enemies seventy times seven. Learned scholars long believed there were seven metals and seven planets, as well as seven names of God. Rome was built on seven hills. In the Age of Discovery bold men sailed the Seven Seas, "to set all at seven" (that is, to make a desperate adventure or attack). One constellation which guided them was the Seven Sisters. The English, from whom I am proudly descended, have always had a penchant for seven. There are Seven Champions (the national saints of England), seven-day fevers, and William Wordsworth's "We Are Seven." In cricket, seven runs may be made from one hit. What was distinctive about Dante Gabriel Rossetti's Blessed Damosel? "And the stars in her hair were seven."

Blessed Damosels are in short supply, but Snow White still has Seven Dwarfs, and many friends the Seven Year Itch. Historians write of the Seven Years' War; others of Seven States of Consciousness, Seven Types of Ambiguity, and the Seven Storey Mountain.

There are Seven Planets Governing Italy (Lodovico Ariosto) and Seven Lucky Gods of Japan. Seven Matched Hollow Gold Jaguars adorn Peru and Jacques Piccard's bathyscaph Trieste went Seven Miles Down. And what about Seven Who Slept (A. K. Porter), Seven Who Were Hanged (Leonid Andreiv), and Seven Women Against the World (Margaret Goldsmith)? Why not Seven Pillars of Popular Culture? the Greeks had seven crucial words, which is what my book is about. I hope my seven columns hold up.

NOTES

1. See Luther S. Luedtke, The Study of American Culture: Contemporary Conflicts (DeLand, Fla.: Everett Edwards, 1977); and C.W.E. Bigsby, ed., Superculture: American Popular Culture and Europe (Bowling Green, Ohio: Popular Press, 1975).

2. The frantic search for a suitable answer began in 1957, when Bernard Rosenberg and David Manning White raised the question in

Mass Culture: The Popular Arts in America (New York: Macmillan, 1957). Rosenberg gives a radical critique, White an impassioned defense.

3. This is documented by Alan Gowans in *The Unchanging Arts* (Philadelphia: J. B. Lippincott, 1971).

4. See Deric Regin, *Culture and the Crowd: A Cultural History of the Proletarian Era* (Philadelphia: Chilton, 1968), p. 286. There is a fine "Selected Booklist," pp. 488–502.

5. John M. Phelan, *Mediaworld: Programming the Public* (New York: Seabury World, 1977), p. 8.

6. Studs Terkel, "The New Mood," in *Parade*, October 11, 1981, p. 15.

7. Books like Milton Shulman's *The Ravenous Eye* (1973), Edward Epstein's *News from Nowhere* (1974), Bruce Herschensohn's *The Gods of the Antenna* (1976), and Robert Cirino's *We're Being More than Entertained* (1980) indicate how emotional and myopic much writing about television has become. They are outdone by Malcolm Muggeridge, whose *Christ and the Media* (London: Collins, 1977) urges us to "laugh at the media as Rabelais laughs at the antics of carnal men" (p. 77).

8. Martin Esslin, "The Television Series as Folk Epic," in C.W.E. Bigsby, ed., *Superculture*, pp. 190ff.

9. T. E. Lawrence, *Seven Pillars of Wisdom* (London: Jonathan Cape, 1973), p. 22.

10. Ibid.

11. There were a series of largely hagiographic biographies during Lawrence's lifetime, such as Lowell Thomas's *With Lawrence in Arabia* (1924), Robert Graves's *Lawrence and the Arabs* (1927), and Liddell Hart's *T. E. Lawrence: In Arabia and After* (1934). Among recent studies see Philip Knightly and Colin Simpson's *The Secret Lives of Lawrence of Arabia* (1969) and Peter Prent's *T. E. Lawrence* (1975).

12. Gilbert Seldes, *The 7 Lively Arts* (1924; reprint New York: Sagamore Press, 1957), p. 14. Seldes's book was no youthful indiscretion. By 1924 he had voted for President (twice), served in the Army (once), and paid taxes (often). Despite his case for Popular Culture, that term did not appear in the standard *Reader's Guide* until 1960.

13. John Kouwenhoven, *Made in America* (New York: Dutton, 1948), p. 77.

14. John Cawelti, "Beatles, Batman, and the New Aesthetic," in *Midway*, Autumn 1966, p. 68.

15. *New York Times*, October 11, 1970, p. 88.

16. Susan Sontag, *Against Interpretation* (New York: Farrar, Straus & Giroux, 1969), p. 104.

17. See Joseph Klapper, *The Effects of Mass Communication* (New York: McGraw-Hill, 1960); and Melvin DeFleur and Otto Larsen, *The Flow of*

Information (New York: World, 1958). How this effects popular culture is discussed in my *Man-Media-Mosaic* (Bowling Green, Ohio: Popular Press, 1980); and C.W.E. Bigsby, ed., *Approaches to Popular Culture* (Bowling Green, Ohio: Popular Press, 1976).

18. Harvey R. Cox, *The Secular City: Urbanization and Secularization in Perspective* (New York: Macmillan, 1965). The latter book is *Religion in the Secular City: Toward a Postmodern Theology* (New York: Simon and Schuster, 1984). The same themes of Cox's new books are developed by James Davison Hunter in *American Evangelicalism: Conservative Religion and the Quandary of Modernity* (New Brunswick, N.J.: Rutgers University Press, 1984).

19. Cox, *Religion in the Secular City*, p. 183.

DEMOS _____ 1

And now to conceive and show to the world what your children en-masse really are.

Walt Whitman, *Democratic Vistas*

Popular culture is people's culture—"your children en-masse." The First Pillar is *demos*: Greek for common people.[1] If much of Western tradition stems from Greece, *demos* goes far back and beyond in space and time. Man is the end result of a process of change characteristic of all living creatures; when, where, and how he evolved is still a mystery. *Homo sapiens* remains the glory, jest, and riddle of the world.

Origin myths (like the Garden of Eden) abound. The science of paleo-anthropology blossomed in 1891 when the Dutch physician Dr. Eugene Dubois discovered "the erect ape-man of Java" (*Pithecanthropus Erectus*) which in the 1890s became the "missing link" between man and ape. When another Dutchman, Jan von Koenigswald, found huge molars in a Chinese apothecary shop (1935), scientists assumed it was in China, not Java, that our species emerged. Then evidence pointed to North India; in our own day, to Africa.

In 1972 Dr. Richard Leakey unearthed in Kenya the nearly complete skull of *Homo habilis* with a brain half again as big as earlier primates. Dr. Leakey speculated that *habilis* passed his genes along to *erectus*, who eventually evolved into modern man—Shakespeare's "paragon of animals."[2] A few years later another expedition found remains of a female in Ethiopia (her assigned name was Lucy) who might have existed much earlier, going back three million years. As if that weren't enough, science-popularizers like Carl Sagan spoke not of millions but billions of years of cosmic change, and our evolving from the stars on "the edge of forever."[3] Who knows where the scientific imagination, weighing so many imponderables with such sophisticated new technology, will go in the years ahead? *Demos*, our First Pillar, is incredibly ancient and complex, still only dimly understood.

Our task is not to trace the evolution of man, but to note that the process of culture-building goes far beyond the current definition of "popular." The proper stage on which to work is the great globe itself—and beyond that, the cosmos. Our task will not be so much to answer questions, as to raise them.

How, for example, did *habilis* and Lucy live? Without such artifacts as stone tools, cave paintings, or burial mounds, we have few solid clues. But Dr. Leakey, an acknowledged leader in the field, thinks the fossil record provides a skeleton key. These gatherer-hunters, he speculates, led a shrewd, uncompetitive life and spent little time on the hunt. Did they, in their leisure, invent what we would now label popular culture? Was it—as Leakey insists—not hunting or gathering but sharing that made us human? Were our primitive ancestors far more prone to cooperate than to annihilate? How did we get from Ape Man to Homer?[4]

Meanwhile other scientists gathered information on the lifestyles of primates and modern-day primitives like the !Kung, Bushman, and Eskimo. Then, a major breakthrough. In 1967, on the tip end of the Philippine Island of Mindanao, a native of the Manubo Blit Tribe walked through remote rain forests setting traps for deer and pigs. He stumbled on a frightened band of food-gatherers still using stone tools, with no knowledge of agriculture, unaware that other societies existed. After several years of visits and talks, he persuaded them to meet with outsiders. In the Atomic Age, we actually had found people living in the Stone Age.

Led by Manuel Elizalde, Jr. (a Philippine cabinet member and president of the Private Association for National Minorities), official contact was made on June 7, 1971. Communication was extremely difficult, requiring a team of translators. The Tasadays, as the tribesmen were called, lived on tadpoles, frogs, wild yam, and grub worms dug from rotted logs. Gentle and playful, they enjoyed making up tunes. Slim, muscular, and monogomous, they had no words for war, kill, fields, or phases of the moon. But they did have an explanation for having stayed here, and now welcomed the outsiders: "Our ancestors told us never to leave this place. They told us the gods would come if we remained here. Now this is true. You are *momo dakel diwata Tasaday*" (great bringer of good fortune of the Tasaday).[5]

Although a seventy-five-foot high treetop perch for a helicopter was built, allowing an NBC news team to visit and produce a television program on the Tasadays, we are only beginning to assimilate the meaning of this culture. Crucial questions remain unanswered. Did these people flee into the forest and retrogress? How long ago? Do agricultural people forget agriculture? Do they reinvent long discarded arts (like making fire with a fire drill)? What happens to an isolated language? An isolated popular culture?

Awaiting answers, we ponder the comment of Kenneth MacLeith, an American anthropologist who knows a great deal about them. "Our friends have given me a new measure to man. If our ancient ancestors were like the Tasadays, we came of far better stock than I had thought."[6]

If the living Stone Age Tasadays fascinate us, and give us reason to rethink the premises on which many assumptions rest, so have people long dead but resurrected. Archeological gravediggers have changed many attitudes of the living. Consider the recent case of Egypt and the rediscovered tomb of Tutankhamen—known in the popular press as Egyptian fever, Tutmania, the Tut glut, Mummy madness. The great obsession over King Tutankhamen peaked in the fall of 1978, when thousands wore a "Love My Mummy" T-shirt.

Why this particular popular outburst, at this moment in time? No one can say—the *demos* act, and scholars try to explain, after the fact. The English archeologist Howard Carter discovered Tut's tomb in 1922. When the contents toured the United States over half a century later, they broke all records for museum attendance.[7] Entertainer Steve Martin released a hit record lamenting that he wished he'd put all his money into buying a museum.

Surely this is Popular Culture; but just what do you *mean* by *popular culture*, and how does it connect King Tut and Steve Martin? The honest answer is embarrassing: we can't hope to describe it, because we have never defined it.[8] We cannot agree just where to look for popular culture, which is either everywhere or nowhere, depending on your assumptions. Lacking both a consensus on meaning and a systematic approach on collecting, we borrow methods of historians, anthropologists, folklorists. We seek the ribs of a universal human grammar but have no anatomy book to guide us.

The Greeks, who had words for so many things, had no word for *culture*. That came later, with the Romans (from *colere*—to till, cultivate). From the cultivation or rearing of a particular crop (oyster culture, corn culture, bee culture), to farming in general (agriculture, horticulture) the word has come to mean people's total "way of life." Roman law, architecture, and engineering were widely exported throughout the ancient world, along with popular culture (from *populus*—of or relating to the common people, suitable for the majority, easy to understand). With their numerous holidays and burgeoning Colosseum, the Romans emphasized what we now call the "entertainment industry." *S.P.Q.R.*—the Senate and the Roman people—gave the world its greatest empire, of and by the people, from the earth they inhabit and cultivate.[9]

The *demos* have a long, complex, and crucial history, predating words and concepts now used to describe it. The Sumerians were mass producing funeral effigies centuries before the Greeks and Romans flourished; so were the Egyptians, Tibetans, and Chinese.[10] Duplication and multiplication of sights and sounds took place when history was still blind. The popular arts stretch back to an unknown dawn.

The remarkable thing about culture is not the multiple differences but the inherent similarities. These elements, coming in part from the least educated and sophisticated, are the building blocks of community. For millenia their method of transmission (on *media*, plural of the Latin *medium*—intermediate, between) was the human voice. Media are extensions which allow us to share and store information.

We know little about the majority of mankind, especially in the premodern period. Of course, we get bits and snatches about "the people" from documents, narrative histories, letters, sermons, and council minutes. By far the most common reference in such sources is to riots or disturbances—not a collection of individuals but "the mob." Even in American democracy, committed to the notion that we are all born with inalienable rights, such a prominent early leader as Alexander Hamilton was frank to say, "The people, Sir, is a beast."

Whatever their disposition, Mr. Hamilton, how would you propose to have a democracy without *demos*?

Hamilton's charges have echoed throughout history. Both Thucydides and Tacitus assumed it was the nature of common people to be irresponsible and violent. The sordid plebs or dirty commoners were scorned by most writers—invariably upperclass literary observers, removed both physically and emotionally from the masses.

In fact, *demos* has never meant *all* the people, in ancient, medieval, or modern societies.[11] The Helots in ancient Greece had no rights or political position. In *The Republic*, Plato contends that democracy—which he defines as the rule of the mob—is the worst form of government imaginable. This startles those of us living in a government proud to be "of the people, by the people, for the people." We seldom challenge that sacred cow of democracy—or ask just who "the people" are. When "We, the people of the United States" wrote a Constitution, just how many of "the people" were consulted—or allowed to vote for those who ran the country?[12]

In this, America follows the pattern of the ages. Only recently—because of Marxist scholarship—have historians paid serious attention to the ordinary people (the Marxists' proletariat) throughout history. Ecclesiasticus wrote their epitaph centuries ago, "And some there be who have no memorial."

Little wonder: evidence for the attitudes and values, hopes and fears of Everyman are fragmentary and fleeting. Much of his culture is oral and "words fly by." His feasts and festivals, so central to life, are equally impermanent. The little we know about his activities (he being illiterate) are through the eyes of literate outsiders.[13] The historian, as Peter Burke points out, "is a literate self-conscious person who finds it difficult to comprehend people unlike himself."[14]

Many other historians have themselves pointed to the real dilemma. "It is next to impossible," George Dorsey writes, "for a man set above his fellow-man to think clearly about social justice, or to feel humanely about his fellow-man. If history shows anything, it is that power over man, like a habit-forming drug, leads to lust for power."[15]

So it has come to pass that most of us trained in the chronological disciplines—American Studies, literature, history, art history—deal mainly with the great and the obvious. Social scientists are generally attracted to selected areas of oral retention, preliterate cultures, ethnic groups, the progressive mainstream—and leave vast areas of life unexplored. Admittedly, these areas are hard to travel. But as Henry Glassie has pointed out, "Until they are studied and understood, our generalizations about both culture and the programs based on these generalizations can be correct and workable only by accident."[16]

Even if much of premodern culture was oral, we do have some documents and texts: the story cycles of India, the Buddhist canons, Aesop's *Fables*, *The Arabian Nights*. Various bibles and sacred texts have come down, along with secular myths and apocryphal books. We have fragments of Greek epics, German sagas, saints' tales, and actual compilations by authors like Ovid and Apuleius. Who produced, preserved, read them? Just what do we mean by literacy? Is it the ability to read, to write, or both? How can we assess the strength or significance of attitudes and patterns of feeling? There are many things the historian can never know; and as Aristotle said, poetry is more philosophical and of graver import than history.

With the advent of printing, popular literature abounded (broadsides, jestbooks, narratives, almanacs), but most of it was ephemeral.[17] There are early examples of romance, demonology, ballads. We have only a few bits and pieces to work with; in addition, we must remember that printed popular literature represents only a small part of a total popular culture.[18] The same can be said for archeological findings such as tools, artifacts, cave paintings. All told, the past has covered its tracks very effectively.

If we are ever to have a more adequate picture of the *demos* over the centuries, we must reexamine what we already have.

We need scholars who will search well-known writers for new clues—like W.M.S. Russel, in his study of "Plutarch as a Folklorist,"[19] or Timothy E. Gregory in *Vox Populi: Popular Opinions and Violence in the Religious Controversies of the Fifth Century A.D.* Focusing on the way theology appeared to ordinary people, Gregory shows how popular opinion was affected by events and how this, in turn, played a role of its own. Did people really believe what their leaders said? Why did peaceful protest become violent? What was the role of "outside agitators"? Who hears the voice of the people? No matter how we answer such questions, Gregory concludes, the action and influence of the crowd was a significant ingredient which cannot be ignored.[20]

Strongly influenced by socialism in general and Marxism in particular, many young post-war European intellectuals approached the whole *demos* question with new critical attitudes. To many, America was the arch-villain, the land of rootless vacuity, inhuman scale, failure of organic cultural life, antihuman reductionism "that favors the American neo-imperialism of the computer."[21] Groups like the Society for the Study of Labour History began to look closely at Working Men's Clubs, music halls, alehouses, working class movements, and the rise of popular church music.[22] Here was the *demos* in a new light. Deric Regin's *Culture and the Crowd: A Cultural History of the Proletarian Era*, tackles some of the semantic confusion which has hampered understanding. The proletariat, he insists, is not the factory worker, the slum-dweller in capitalistic cities, destined by an abstract formula of history to generate the violent overthrow of the bourgeois. He is chiefly marked by being cut out from the vital functions of his own society.[23] He is the aggregate of outsiders, the fringe-dwellers. Proletarian culture is the self-expression of the modern mass-consciousness, which identifies itself with those who in earlier times were at the margins of society, having no part in the shaping of its configurations. One result is *anomia*—social or political apathy. One way to combat it is to join the crowd—for there is warmth and comfort in being "part of something." The proletariat clings and swears allegiance to his last security—he is one of the crowd. He is a nonperson.

The Marxists stress what they like to call mass-consciousness, which is winning out over self-consciousness and thus transforming civilization. Undoubtedly there has been some leveling of values in social relations and ethics—but does this mean a diminishing of self-consciousness? Anyone can see that systems of thought (including Christianity) are viewed by some as general commodities, to be sold by the most effective media, but does this prove that people are less sincere or effective Christians? Who can say that "profound scholarly discovery and religious intensity" are becoming losing propositions?[24]

And is not the "Age of the Masses" a misnomer? Just where do the masses rule? Surely not in Russia or the other Marxist states. Is ours not instead the "Age of the Leader"? And do not the leaders get their cues and their power from popular culture? Are not the masses neither "good" nor "bad," but neutral—like the media and machines which entertain them? The *demos* are what they are not because of choice or intrinsic development; but because the development of Western culture has made them thus.[25]

George Rude comes to quite different conclusions in *The Crowd in the French Revolution*. This meticulous study, supported by statistics and maps, concludes that crowds are active agents in the revolutionary process, composed of social elements with their own distinctive identities, interests, and aspirations.

Evidence in this and many outbreaks does not support the widespread assumption that the *demos* were the passive agents of educated leaders; nor were they inchoate mobs without any social identity. Crowds were and are composed of people with varying social needs who respond to a variety of impulses, in which economic crisis, political upheaval, and the urge to satisfy grievances all play their part. Let those who are so quick to speak of the urban poor, the lower classes, the inferior set of people, or the *menu peuple*, take note. Such phrases are often terms of convenience, or frank symbols of prejudices, rather than a verifiable historical phenomenon.[26] The people, Mr. Hamilton, is not "a beast."

Crowds, like history, are constantly changing and regrouping. Just when Western Europe's traditional popular culture was beginning to disappear, and the Industrial Revolution to prevail, European intellectuals "discovered" the people and the "folk." Part of the romantic movement and nostalgia which swept over the continent, this discovery greatly influenced what we think about the people, crafts, and popular culture.

Among the leaders were Gottfried von Herder (1744–1803), who popularized the idea of a *Volksgeist*—the spirit of the people. This spirit is the result of tradition, environment, and the times: tradition being the peculiar history of the people, environment the physical conditions under which they lived, and the times (*Zeitgeist*) being the spirit of the times. Putting his philosophy into practice, Herder began to collect and publish *Volkslieder*—songs of the people—and *Volksmärchen*—folk tales. The idea spread throughout Europe, as Swedes collected *folkviser*, Italians *canti populari*, Hungarians *nepdalok*, and Russians *narodnye pensi*.[27]

Saying that folklore became crucial to preserving and understanding popular culture doesn't make folklore any easier to define. There is no universally accepted definition. Alan Dundes, in *The Study of Folklore*, comments on the proliferation of such definitions.[28] One wonders if there might not be as many definitions as folklorists. Five key words emerge: oral, transmission, tradition, survival, and communal. One central idea is inescapable: The vitality of life does not flow from the top to the bottom, but like a great tree, from the soil up.[29]

It is part of contemporary folklore to say that folk culture is finished. This vast body of knowledge, handed down by mouth, practice, and custom, is still very much with us. Folklore is first cousin to mythology. Patterned on common experience, indigenous and indelible, it feeds and sustains popular culture. The *demos* are all individuals, despite massification; each has his or her pride and prejudice, customs, songs, and idiom; the sap and savor of a people endures.[30]

That is why our young, strumming their electric guitars, yearn for attachments the industrial urban environment has denied them. They dream of pink cherry blossoms and a sow that got the measles and died in the spring. Amidst the siren screeches they reaffirm that "never did hoof of beast go down on a lark's nest." The Ecology Crusade is another manifestation of our folk longings. One of the Old Boys who keeps attracting the young is Henry David Thoreau.

What then do we know about "the people"—the plebs, commoners, masses, *demos*? Surprisingly little. When they have risen from the ranks, become generals, leaders, or rebels like Sparticus, Gracchus, Nat Turner, or Che Guevera, we deal with them as persons. Our information system is like a fishnet, which catches the big ones but misses the myriads of anonymous minnows.

For centuries there was no lack of comment by the big fish on the minnows—much of it scornful and derogatory. Then the Romantic Movement and Socialism swept over nineteenth-century Europe. The Romantics idealized the people, finding in them virtues that industrialism was destroying. Wordsworth defined poetry as "man speaking to man," and even managed to romanticize the poverty which had plagued the poor for centuries. Poverty was somehow pure, renewing, almost holy. "Getting and spending," we lay waste our powers. This romantic notion was still strong during the "Youthquake" of the 1960s.

Socialists, especially Marxists, idealized "the people" as proletariat and made them the basis of ideology. They were the workers; and since labor was wealth, they were the hope of any brave new world. In all this, abstractions were obscuring reality. Ralph Waldo Emerson, that clear-eyed Yankee philosopher, understood this danger when he advised us in "The American Scholar" to understand people by examining "the meal in the firkin; the milk in the pan; the ballad in the street; the news of the boat; the glance of the eye; the form and gait of the body." Walt Whitman insisted that a mouse is miracle enough to stagger sextillions of infidels. His brilliant nineteenth-century contemporary, Soren Kierkegaard, couched the same thoughts in more philosophical language, suggesting that system-builders liked to construct great castles—even when they had to live in cabins or barns.

Each of these three quotations is close to the earth; they deal with firkins, mice, and barns. Much twentieth-century scholarship, produced in urban areas and library stacks, is far removed from the earth which is the womb and hub of man's existence. It is the earth alone, as A. C. Spectorsky reminds us in *The Book of the Earth*, that man may touch, probe, pat, smell, work with—and upon which he lives, toils, and dreams. Culture and land surface are interwoven, and interact in countless directions. The story of man—land use, pieced together and understood—furnishes a commentary more accurate than all the histories ever written. But only fragments of that commentary exist; and many of us do not know even them.

Seeking a methodology which will succeed academically, we have favored the abstract over the earthy.[31] Worse yet, we have insisted on explaining culture from the top down, rather than from the bottom up. Very few have been willing or able to discover just how people have lived and thought, as individuals and members of communities, in specific eras and places. Speculative schemes have seemed more important, and shopworn cliches have been accepted without question.

We should read David Cort's *Revolution by Cliche* (1970). Clichés, he says, have no certifiable meaning; they are signals, not meaning. They suppress the word's history in depth, and send only a contemporary cue. Clichés do not show us reality; they exclude it.[32] Popular culture is a haven for clichés. So are some modern societies, in which human beings become a cliché, a stereotype, a nothing. Easy enough to say about "Them"; is it becoming increasingly true of "Us"?

We have begun to synthesize and generalize too soon, conjuring up forests in which many trees have no place. Thus have scholars demonstrated a major shortcoming: our love affair with simple solutions. We are prone to look for the secret trap door that will make the tedious trip unnecessary; the blanket formula which will prevent struggling and agonizing over ambiguities.

We do not always couch simple solutions in simple language; on the contrary, we often prefer multisyllabic jargon. This was the case in F.S.C. Northrop's famous study, *The Meeting of East and West*. Northrop spoke to the basic problem underlying the issue of our times: "The answer to the basic problem underlying the ideological issues of these times is as follows: the aesthetic, intuitive, purely empirically given component in man and nature is related to the theoretically designed and indirectly verified component by the two-termed relation of epistemic correlation."[33]

Perhaps we can find more substance, and surely more challenge, in a poem like Walt Whitman's "By Blue Ontario's Shore":

> Who are you indeed who would talk or sing to America?
> Have you studied out the land, its idiom and men?
> Have you learn'd the physiology, phrenology, politics, geog-
> raphy, pride, freedom, friendship of the land? its substra-
> tums and objects?
> Are you faithful to things? do you teach what the land and sea,
> the bodies of men, womanhood, amativeness, heroic angers
> teach?
> Are you really of the whole People?
> Have you vivified yourself from the maternity of these States?

So far as "the people" are concerned, most scholars and disciplines have not yet "vivified" themselves. Popular culture has
been overused in a flattened, one-dimensional way, to denote
either commercially-provided culture or cute-and-quaint fragments of plebian culture. Data and documents continue to accumulate, but connections and patterns elude us. We are like
those working in folklore before Antti Aarne devised a Type-
Index, and before Archer Taylor and Stith Thompson applied
it to America. We are still borrowing methods, materials, and
manpower from other cultures and disciplines.

Some have recognized the folk-popular culture connection and
examined aspects of it. Joseph Janeti has written on "Folk Music's Affair with Popular Culture,"[34] and R. Serge Denisoff has
linked labor songs and popular attitudes.[35] During the 1930s and
1940s cultural, political, and economic factors popularized "the
people's music." Artists like Aunt Molly Jackson, Leadbelly,
Woody Guthrie, Pete Seeger, and Burl Ives combined folk and
pop, introducing millions to union meetings, rallies, protests,
and picket lines.

Still the majority of folklorists would not or could not make
the connection. As traditional folk material in rural hamlets disappeared, they did not seek it in urban ghettoes. They la-
mented the disappearance of zithers—but did not hail the electric guitars, which took over with a vengeance. Folklore's plight
was reflected in the work and pronouncements of Richard Dor-

son: "The cavernous maw of the mass media gobbled up end-less chunks of folksiness, and a new rationale appeared for the folklorist: his mission is to polish up, revamp, and distribute folklore to the American people . . . . We cannot tarry with folklore performers and popularizers . . . ."[36]

Nor can popular culture tarry with the Richard Dorsons. It has—and will—evolve with the dynamic culture it mirrors. "Popularizers" do not threaten folklore: they provide material, arguments, trends. In their own day Homer, Dante, Shake-speare, and the man who added new verses to "Barbara Allen" were popularizers. Their spiritual descendents appear on film and tape today. They and their followers—not the archivists—keep folklore alive.

The creative thrust in folklore studies in the 1980s is the "folklife movement." Adapted from the Swedish *folkliv*, the word implies an analysis of folk culture in its entirety. By limiting themselves largely to literary aspects of folklore, scholars have tended to slight other aspects and to take the material studied out of context. In Sweden today over four hundred communities maintain "outdoor museums." The first such venture in America was in Decorah, Iowa, in 1925. The most spectacular was Williamsburg (begun in 1926). Despite good work at Coop-erstown, Sturbridge, Shelburne, and Dearborn, we still know and see far too little of folklife. Professor Don Yoder, a leading advocate of the folklife movement, lists things we should study: folk names, agriculture, architecture, cookery, costume, crafts, medicine, music, recreation, religion, speech, transportation, the folk year. Back to the plow and the flail, the husking peg and hominy block, the schoolhouse and meetinghouse!

Knowing more about settlement patterns, games, song, dance, clothing, and customary behavior, we might see folklore as an integral part of the total range of traditional behavior—and hence of popular culture. To illustrate: long isolated Scotch-Irish farmers in the Ozarks are so deeply Calvinistic that they still refer to bulls as "gentlemen cows" in mixed company. Yet they send maidens to dance in apple orchards each spring, and encour-age couples to "jolly themselves" in newly planted fields, thus helping seeds to germinate. In the ritual for sowing flax, Vance Randolph reports, the farmer and his wife appear naked in the field at sunup. The woman walks ahead as the man sows. They chant a rhyme which ends, "Up to my ass, and higher too!" Every few steps the man throws seeds against the woman's buttocks, singing and scattering until the planting is done. "Then they just lay down on the ground and have a good time," Randolph concludes in *Pissing in the Snow and Other Ozark Folktales*. A less delicate informer has this to say of turnip planting:

The boy throwed all the seed, and the gals kept a-hollering Pecker deep! Pecker deep! and when they got done, the whole bunch would roll in the dust like wild animals. Ain't no sense to it, but they always raised the best turnips on the creek![37]

Not only scholarly folklorists but also leading critics and literati have found little to admire in the new "people's culture." They want nothing to do with the world that mass produces pop-rock records and nuclear weapons. Listing charges against contemporary popular culture is a favorite indoor sport: the *demos* trivialize, vulgarize, distort, seduce, homogenize, distract from serious events, manipulate people. Complaints about the new and unknown echo in every age. "Without the taste and manner of the Ancients," John Dryden wrote in "An Essay on Dramatic Poesy" (1668), "all is nothing but a blind and rash barbarity." The issues haven't changed—only the media.

This kind of argument tends to be a wasteful activity on the contemporary intellectual scene. What's needed is a way of studying high culture and popular culture in terms that focus not only on the gap between them, but also on likenesses among the activities that make both possible. Not so, insist Ortega Y. Gassett, Dwight Macdonald, R. F. Blackmuir, and Ezra Pound, who suggested that if the 243 Americans who understood civilization would get together, that would be a start.

The 243 have not prevailed. Instead, an impressive group of writers and scholars, working in different fields and nations, have turned the tables on the elitists. No ideology or strategy in writing history is "nobler" or "better" than another, they suggest. All cultural data have precisely the same value as evidence of a culture's fundamental form. The people we have called "common" or "primitive" are complex, sensitive, and adaptable.

I speak of structuralists like Claude Levi-Strauss and Jean Piaget; theorists like Noam Chomsky, Northrop Frye, and Marshall McLuhan; critics like Paul de Man and Geoffrey Hartman; social scientists like Hayden White and Dell Humes. The area known as metahistory has been successful in stressing and documenting the potential equality of all mankind.

Andrew Levison's 1974 book, *The Working Class Majority*, suggests that many of the widely held stereotypes are not true. Recent studies indicate, for example, that the working class are not more conservative and racist than other classes of society. Clichés and stereotypes are often strongest with the college-educated middle class. Writing to the French aristocrat Eleuthere duPont de Nemeurs, who did not think much of the masses, Thomas Jefferson insisted that if we give the people light, they will find their way.

I believe he was right. So did Horatio Greenough, who wrote in the *Democratic Review* (1843): "It is the great multitude for whom all really great things are done, said, suffered. The multitude desires the best of everything; and in the long run is the best judge of it."

There is a quiet but constant struggle between *demos* and elite; plebian and patrician. What one likes, the other often tries to usurp. Consider, as a recent example, Marilyn Monroe, the illegitimate, frightened girl who went to Hollywood, made good, and became not only a sex symbol but a film goddess. "In 1983," Lesley Dick could report, "she is being picked up by the elite, being made the subject of *haute couture*, with gowns designed for the beautiful people, sold in thirty exclusive shops. There was also a new "Marilyn Monroe Doll" on the market—priced at $2,600. But the *demos* don't give up without a fight. "Monroe is the hero of the people," Ms. Dick concludes. "The elite can crowd in front of the people but they can never take Monroe from the masses."[38]

Behold, then, the people; or rather, the persons who make up the people, individuals all; despite their rank and station, age or sex, each has his or her pride and prejudices, customs and convictions. Together, the people are like the giant Atlas, who carried the world on his shoulder. The people are the pillar: to understand and interpret them will always be popular culture's first task.

NOTES

1. *Demos* also means a deme—one of the hundred townships into which Cleisthenes divided Attica (about 508 B.C.). *Demos* is the root word of democracy (*demos* the people + *kratos* authority).

2. Richard Leakey and Roger Lewin, *People of the Lake* (New York: Anchor, 1978). See also Joan Marble Cook, *In Defense of Homo Sapiens* (New York: Dell, 1975). Books on astronomy, archeology, and ethnography have become best sellers, part of today's popular culture.

3. Carl Sagan, *Cosmos* (New York: Random House, 1980). His ideas are presented not only in books and television programs, but also in maps and trinkets which he markets on a grand scale. See also Harlow Shapley, *The View from a Distant Star* (New York: Basic Books, 1963).

4. H.E.L. Mellersh chose this question for the title of a book, *From Ape Man to Homer: The Story of the Beginnings of Western Civilization* (New York: Greenwood Press, 1962). An excellent historical summary, it deals mainly with the elite, not the *demos*. In August, 1984 a joint U.S.-Kenyan team of archeologists (including Dr. Richard Leakey) found an "unprecedented" Kenyan fossil site where they recovered five rare partial skeletons of 18 million-year-old ape-like creatures. These animals, belonging to the Proconsul species africanus, may be the common ancestor from which apes and humans came.

5. Of the many articles and reports, the best introduction is the August 1972 issue of the *National Geographic*. The text is by Kenneth MacLeith and photographs by John Laurnois.

6. This quote is from Kenneth MacLeith's *National Geographic* article, August 1972, p. 248. There is reason to believe there are other Stone Age people thriving today, still out of touch with the modern world. In December, 1982, an Indian army expedition encountered some at the foothills of the Himalayas. The tribespeople ate raw meat, wore no clothes, lived in caves, and didn't know how to kindle a fire. No one could explain how they survived in the bitter cold when the ground was covered with sixteen feet of snow.

7. To accommodate unprecedented crowds, the Metropolitan Museum in New York stayed open seven days (82 hours) a week. Tut broke attendance records everywhere. See Kamal El Mallakh and Arnold C. Brackman, *The Gold of Tutankhamen* (New York: Newsweek Books, 1982). Far more than museum attendance was involved in Tut fever—styles in clothing, jewelry, and even architecture. And who can say how much it affected political and cultural attitudes towards Egypt, then passing through a period of great crisis?

8. Not that we haven't tried—again and again. See Russel B. Nye, "Notes on a Rationale for Popular Culture," in Jack Nachbar, Deborah

Weiser, John L. Wright, eds., *The Popular Culture Reader* (Bowling Green, Ohio: Popular Press, 1978). My own efforts are set forth in *Parameters of Popular Culture* (Bowling Green, Ohio: Popular Press, 1977).

9. See C.W.E. Bigsby, ed., *Approaches to Popular Culture* and Ray Browne, Sam Grogg, Jr., and Larry Landrum, eds., *Theories and Methodologies in Popular Culture*. In the latter volume, Roger B. Rollin (pp. 3–5) argues fellow scholars have inadvertently proposed an impossible mission—to devise an aesthetics of popular culture that would incorporate a value theory. In my essay in this volume (pp. 143ff.) I suggest we should concede that the real meaning of popular culture lies not in some precise method, but in a search for new ways to understand the world which people inhabit and relish.

10. See Fred Schroeder, *Five Thousand Years of Popular Culture* (1980) and his earlier article, "The Discovery of Popular Culture before Printing," *Journal of Popular Culture*, 11, Winter 1977. Schroeder believes we have a technological connection to Sony radios, Coke bottles, the Bay Psalm Book, and the Gutenberg Bible.

11. George Boas, "The People," in *The History of Ideas: An Introduction* (New York: Charles Scribner's, 1969).

12. Morris D. Forkosch, "Who Are the 'People' in the Preamble to the Constitution?" in *Case Western Reserve Law Review*, 19, 3, April 1968, pp. 644–712.

13. For more on these problems, see E. J. Hobsbawn, *Primitive Rebels* (Manchester, U.K.: University Press, 1959); Richard Samuel, *Village Life and Labour* (London: Unwin, 1975); and M. de Certeau, *L'Ecriture de l'Histoire* (Paris: n.p., 1975).

14. Peter Burke, "An Elusive Quarry," in *Popular Culture in Early Modern Europe* (New York: Harper & Row, 1978), p. 86. See also Peter Laslett, *The World We Have Lost* (New York: Scribner's, 1965).

15. George Dorsey, *The Story of Civilization: Man's Own Show* (New York: Haleyon, 1931), p. 197; and A. C. Spectorsky, *The Book of the Earth* (New York: Macmillan, 1957).

16. Henry Glassie, ed., *Folksongs and Their Makers* (Bowling Green, Ohio: Popular Press, 1979), p. 54. See also Richard Dorson, *American Folklore and the Historian* (Chicago: University of Chicago Press, 1971).

17. Victor E. Neuberg, *Popular Literature: A History and Guide* (Middlesex, U.K.: Penguin Books, 1977). For a very different interpretation, see Marshall McLuhan, *The Gutenberg Galaxy: The Making of Typographic Man* (Toronto: University of Toronto Press, 1965).

18. Neuberg, *Popular Literature*, p. 235.

19. W.M.S. Russel, "Plutarch as a Folklorist," in Venetia J. Newhall, ed., *Folklore Studies in the Twentieth Century* (Bury St. Edmunds, U.K.: St. Edmundsbury Press, 1980), pp. 371 ff.

20. Timothy E. Gregory, *Vox Populi: Popular Opinion and Violence in the Religious Controversies of the Fifth Century A.D.* (Columbus: Ohio State University Press, 1979), p. 226.

21. F. R. Leavis, *Nor Shall My Sword* (New York: Macmillan, 1972). Leavis had begun his attack much earlier with *Mass Civilization and Minority Culture* (Cambridge: Cambridge University Press, 1930).

22. All these topics are included in Eileen and Stephen Yeo, eds., *Popular Culture and Class Conflict, 1590–1914: Explorations in the History of Labour and Leisure* (Sussex, U.K.: Harvester Press, 1981). See also Terry Eagleton, *Marxism and Literary Criticism* (New York: Methuen, 1976). Of many recent Russian studies, Gregori Oganov's *Genuine Culture and False Substitutes* (Moscow, U.S.S.R.: Novosti Press, 1979) is perhaps the most comprehensive.

23. Deric Regin, *Culture and the Crowd.* See also Raymond Williams, *Culture and Society, 1870–1950* (New York: Harper, 1959) and Hannah Arendt, *The Human Condition* (Chicago: University of Chicago Press, 1958).

24. The matter is discussed in "The Average Way of Living," in Regin, *Culture and the Crowd.* See also "Mass Culture and Mass Media," in *Daedalus*, Spring 1960.

25. So argues Robert Strausz-Hupe in *The Zone of Indifference* (New York: G. P. Putnam's Sons, 1952), p. 64.

26. George Rude, *The Crowd in the French Revolution* (Oxford, U.K.: Clarendon Press, 1959), p. 232. See also Rude's *The Crowd in History: A Study of Popular Disturbances in France and England, 1730–1848* (New York: John Wiley & Sons, 1964). Rude builds on the earlier work of Gustave Le Bon whose study *The Crowd* appeared in 1909. See also Hobsbawn, *Primitive Rebels*; Ernesto Canetti, *Crowds and Power* (New York: Viking, 1962); David Riesman, *The Lonely Crowd* (New Haven, Conn.: Yale University Press, 1950); and M. J. Smelser, *Theory of Collective Behavior* (New York: Knopf, 1963).

27. For a full account, see Burke, "The Discovery of the People," in *Popular Culture.* See also William A. Wilson, "Herder, Folklore, and Romantic Nationalism," in *Journal of Popular Culture*, 6 (1973), pp. 819–835.

28. Alan Dundes, *The Study of Folklore* (Englewood Cliffs, N.J.: Prentice-Hall, 1965), p. 2.

29. Richard Dorson, "The Founders of British Folklore," in Newhall, ed., *Folklore Studies.*

30. Robert Spiller et al., eds., *Literary History of the United States*, 1 (New York: Macmillan, 1963).

31. Most of the subjects on which our Seven Pillars rest—mythology, folklore, cultural studies, ethnic studies, popular culture, Amer-

ican Studies—are constantly challenged by the "established" academic disciplines for "lack of methodology." Do old methods, like old technologies, need to be updated—or even abandoned?

32. David Cort, *Revolution by Cliché* (New York: Funk & Wagnalls, 1970).

33. F.S.C. Northrop, *The Meeting of East and West* (New York: Macmillan, 1945), p. 443.

34. Joseph Janeti, "Folk Music's Affair with Popular Culture: A Redefinition of the Revival," in Russel B. Nye, ed., *New Dimensions in Popular Culture* (Bowling Green, Ohio: Popular Press, 1972). See also Donald K. Wilgus, *Anglo-American Folksong Scholarship Since 1898* (Brunswick, N.J.: Rutgers University Press, 1959); Harvey Swados, *The American Writer and the Great Depression* (New York: Bobbs-Merrill, 1966); and Jan Harold Brunvand, *The Study of American Folklore: An Introduction* (New York: Norton, 1968).

35. See R. Serge Denisoff, "Urban Folk 'Movement Research:' Value Free?" in *Western Folklore*, 27, no. 3, July 1969, especially pp. 192 ff.

36. Richard Dorson in *Journal of American Folklore*, 72, September 1959, p. 202. Not all folklorists side with Dorson, of course. Jan Harold Brunvand believes that "from a practical point of view, the folklore/poplore area offers almost limitless, untouched, and ever-changing opportunities." Brunvand, *American Folklore*, p. 55.

37. Vance Randolph, *Pissing in the Snow and Other Ozark Folktales* (Urbana: University of Illinois Press, 1976), p. 214.

38. Lesley Dick, "Marilyn Monroe: Cult Heroine," in Ray Browne and Marshall Fishwick, eds., *The Hero in Transition* (Bowling Green, Ohio: Popular Press, 1983), p. 284.

ETHNOS _____ 2

The black man's one great and present hope is to know
and understand his Afro-American history.
                    Harold Cruse, *The Crisis of the Negro Intellectual*

Demos deals with the unity, the communality of people. *Ethnos*
confronts their divisions into groups, races, and language. An
ethnic, while still part of the *demos*, retains customs, myths, and
social views of his group. *Ethnology* is the science that deals with
mankind's divisions; *ethnicity* is one of the major issues and flash
points of the twentieth century. *Ethnos* is our Second Pillar of
Popular Culture.

Ethnos has to do with roots; one of the most popular American television mini-series ever produced—about Afro-Americans—was called "Roots." "You cannot be a people or love a
country," Woodrow Wilson wrote in *The New Freedom*, "if you
do not have the true roots of intimate affection which are the
real sources of all that is strongest in human life."[1] Wilson's
roots are, in essence, the same as our pillar.

Born and rooted in the snug Valley of Virginia, Wilson knew
that people inherit both folklore and placelore. Landscape, a state
of being derived from the inner mind, follows us wherever we
go. From our landscape, our soil, spring heroes, myths, archetypes, and memories that cement us together. This is the heart
of *ethnos*. We live not only from crops of the land, but from what
love and laughter and pride can make of those who work it.
Here is the sinew of the world, the stuff of popular culture.
People are first and foremost ethnic beings.

Every group wants a home and life of its own. People plus

nature equals *ethnos*. The relationship is primitive and primordial. From it comes our sense of space, and shape of time.[2] *Homo sapiens* must have had such instincts when he was first able to walk on two legs.

Attributed to the ancient Hebrews, the "chosen people" idea is neither original nor unique.[3] Throughout history, *demos* have set themselves apart through ties of kinship, faith, politics, tradition—real or imagined, separately or in combination. "We" are not like "them"—is there any concept more basic in human history?

The ancient Indians, Chinese, Egyptians, Greeks, Mongols, and scores of others made invidious comparisons between themselves and others. For five thousand years there have been stories about the Aryan invasion of the Indus Valley, where "dark-skinned barbarians" lived. When the Chinese confronted the first Westerners, they thought these "yellow-haired and green-eyes people greatly resemble monkeys from whom they are descended."[4] No one has to be reminded of what the Europeans said about—and did to—the ethnic American Indians.

The red-faced Egyptians made "lesser ethnic groups" their enemies—"whites" to the north, "blacks" to the south, and "yellows" to the east. The injunction of the Jewish prophet Ezra against mixing the seed of Israel with that of the Ammonite and Moabite is well known; while Jeremiah's rhetorical question ("Can the Ethiopian change his skin or the leopard his spots?") has been called by A. A. Roback "the first recorded slur against Negroes."[5]

Aristotle, like Hippocrates and other Greek physicians, believed in racial differences; Cicero advised his friend Atticus not to obtain British slaves "because they are so stupid and so utterly incapable of being taught that they are not fit to form a part of the household of Athens."[6] And so it went, century after century, conquest after conquest.

The effort to turn *ethnos* into a science, and substitute fact for fiction, we call *ethnology*. A branch of anthropology, it is relatively new. Attempting to explore culture growth scientifically and analyze sub-cultures, ethnologists have developed major schools (evolutionist, diffusionist, functionalist), the configura-

tion concept, and personality and culture analysis. Accultura-
tion—the special situation of diffusion of culture traits, patterns, values, and attitudes—has been studied on a global scale.
So has innovation—the conceptual and learning processes involved in the diffusion of culture. Inherent in all this is the idea
that "the truth shall set us free," and that nasty aspects of ethnicity—like those of polio and smallpox—will gradually disappear.

Robert E. Park went so far as to set forth an inevitable and
irreversible four-stage process of complete assimilation: contact, conflict, accommodation, and assimilation. This, he thought,
was a generalized law, universally applicable and at the same
time descriptive of the evolution of race relations in any particular society.[7] Once the racial cycle was completed, racial im-
pediments would disappear. Because this notion appealed to
Marxists—who saw class struggle as part of the "racial imped-
iments"—this notion of liberal and progressive reform colored
not only sociological theory and social reform but also practical
politics. The Melting Pot would work—not only in America, but
everywhere—and we would finally have One World.

While scholars filled their books, Adolf Hitler and Joseph Stalin
filled their concentration camps. A stunned world saw ethnic
and racial hatreds flare up, not only in Germany, but around
the world. A holocaust wiped out one-third of the Jewish population—merely because they were Jews. When surviving Jews
set up the state of Israel, they brought not peace but a sword
to the tinderbox of the Middle East. With every year, *ethnos*
tension has increased, not diminished. "It is no longer news
that in virtually every country ethnic differences have become
sharper, more salient," William Petersen wrote in 1979. "From
no matter what corner of the earth, every dispatch is likely to
tell us of another dispute between racial, religious, language,
or national groups."[8] That blacks slaughter whites in Rhodesia,
that Hausa kill Ibo in the Biafran war, that Catholics and Protestants stage blood-baths in Ireland, that Indonesians slaughter
Chinese, and that Uganda seems more intent on genocide than
even Nazi Germany—these are facts of life. And what about the
United States, where one might have supposed that all ethnic
distinctions were in the process of fading away? "The Bicenten-

nial in 1976," Petersen goes on to point out, "marked a revival
of ethnicity that a generation ago no social or political analyst
would have dreamed of."[9] All the rosy predictions had been
wrong. *Ethnos* is a permanent echo in the mind of man. If
underestimated or ignored, that echo becomes a scream.

Faced with new evidence and reality, scholars began to re-
trace their steps and restate their conclusions. Levic Jessel rejected Park's idea of ethnic process, defining it instead as "a
dynamic current of primordial origin flowing from pristine group
to modern society, taking on territorial, social, psychological,
behavioral, and linguistic forms."[10] In the history of human society it functions continuously as a social mechanism. The very
foundations of society are ethnic.

This, so the argument runs, is why mankind falls into distinctive tribes or groups—with their own territory, language,
traditions, customs, religion, heroes, and mythology. From cave
to clan to village to town to province to city to nation—the ethnic process is always at work. Nationalism is the form *ethnos*
takes under capitalism; there will be different forms under
communism or any other form of society, including a world society where, presumably, we would have a world of ethnic
neighborhoods.[11] Goodbye, universalism and dreams of One
World.

I do not intend to enter the Dark and Bloody Ground of current ethnicity—only to assert that it is indeed one of the pillars
on which Popular Culture rests. Goodbye, Melting Pot—hello,
Salad Bowl. *Ethnos* is no longer a black mark of shame, but a
red badge of courage. Hyphenated Americans (Irish-American,
Italian-American, etc.) want to emphasize, not diminish ethnic
differences. Instead of a curse, being part of a sub-culture is seen
as a blessing, sometimes even a stepping stone to preferential
treatment and employment. Instead of belittling and ridiculing
ethnic roots, we find politicians, leaders, and intellectuals af-
firming and reinforcing them in the interests of all humanity.

All this has occurred within my lifetime, and I should like to
examine, in a personal way, the one ethnic group with which
I have had continuous contact. I was born and raised in a Virginia in which segregation was the law of the land and the accepted mode. Black people (called Negroes in polite society,

Niggers elsewhere) "knew their place"—which was certainly not in the schools, toilets, or restaurants where whites went. This was not because that genteel world of white superiority had the mentality of the Ku Klux Klan. In college one read books like that of leading sociologist Frank M. Hankins on *The Racial Basis of Civilization*:

One cannot explain the general backwardness of the Negro by the lack of social opportunity. Had he been sufficiently gifted he would have made his opportunity in the culture. The cause is deeper and must be sought in differences of body and brain structure.[12]

And didn't I hear the respectable white girls, playing jump rope in the white school playground, chanting:

Eenie-meanie-miney-moe
Catch a Nigger by the toe
If he hollers, let him go,
Eenie-meanie-miney-moe.

Weren't black men (of whatever age) called "boy," and weren't black babies pickaninnies? And who but blacks were spoken of, at the local filling station, as coons, jigs, or jungle bunnies?

Teaching at one of the "better" (white segregated) colleges, where faculty members had "maids" (black women of any age) and "mammies" to rear their young in 1954, I arose one morning to read that the Supreme Court of the United States had thrown out the "separate but equal" doctrine and ordered integration in public schools.

How did our power structure (not only throughout the state, but also in the United States Senate, where Virginians held massive power and prestige) react? With massive resistance. How long ago this all seems; for now I teach in Virginia's largest state university, which actively recruits black students and faculty members as one of its top priorities.

In between these events, I spent six years as a professor in a predominantly black university, and many months travelling and teaching in nonwhite nations. All this has convinced me, more than ever, that pluralism, ethnic recognition, and cultural diversity offer the best possible way to survival; and that popular culture can and will foster them all.

Ethnos is the unique and creative aspects of one group inside a large society. To study the creative aspects of one such group—Afro-Americans—we must include a wide scope of materials worked by human hands and minds, shaped by popular belief, and guided by connected ideas.[13] We must seek a visible portrait of a collective identity; deal with the history of things, physical and psychic; and reunite ideas and objects under the rubric of visual form. Every kind of image-making produces its own kind of truth with a new type of beauty. The aesthetic impulse finds expression in terms of the standards of beauty laid down by tradition. Art and artifacts are not separated by any innate quality of value: only by the particular standards we choose to impose. Art, in the full sense, can never be encompassed by narrow canons of personal taste or nomenclature, but only as products of man the maker. As tool-maker, home-maker, image-maker, myth-maker, city-maker, nation-maker, man uses his hands, head, and heart to bring meaning out of chaos.

In the ethnic case study we have undertaken, part of the problem springs from terms and definitions. What, for example, is "black"? A color, a concept, a password, a taunt, a powerful image, a rallying cry, a major input into popular culture. People whose grandparents wished to be called "colored," and whose parents called themselves Negroes, now insist that they are Blacks; that "Black is beautiful." To some, pursuing theories of Negritude, soul power, and separatism, black has become not only beautiful but dutiful.

On this much most agree: "black" has become for many a strength, after generations of being a barrier; a shaper of both white and black popular culture; and a growing international force, in a world where most human beings are nonwhite.[14]

Other statistics, gathered inside the United States, are worth remembering as we probe *ethnos* in our Republic. In 1984, for example, thirty percent of the children born here were black, Hispanic, American Indian, or other nonwhite lineage. Over a fourth of our population consists of ethnic and racial groups classified as nonwhite; four-fifths of all blacks (long basically rural) now live in urban areas. Many of these cities are domi-

These young people are undergraduates at Lincoln University, a predominantly black institution. A part of yet isolated from two cultural
heritages, Afro-Americans struggle to find their place in predominantly white Anglo-Saxon Protestant society (Waspland). To which
culture does the amulet around the man's neck belong? Questions of
ethnos and *mythos* often merge. *Photo by the author.*

nated by black political figures; and many institutions—such as urban public schools, the penal institutions, and the armed forces—are made up predominantly of ethnic groups.

World War II was a catalyst that changed everything in the United States, including race relations. That so many black people were willing to fight racism in Europe, at the same time they were victims of it at home, did not escape the eyes of black or white leaders. The former felt that they could demand more from the country and many of the latter were determined that they should get it. The wartime president, Franklin D. Roosevelt, was instrumental in starting in 1944 the Independent Citizens' Committee of the Arts, Sciences, and Professions (I.C.C.A.S.P.), which took a strong stand against Jim Crow and all forms of discrimination. Lena Horne, Hazel Scott, Bette Davis, and Frank Sinatra were among its leaders.

That same year the International Film and Radio Guild (I.F.R.G.) was formed, with three announced basic aims and purposes:

1. To create an awareness of misrepresentations of minorities among theater, film, and radio audiences.
2. To influence producers, directors, writers, and performers towards creating truthful, realistic, and democratic presentations of minorities.
3. To watch carefully portrayals and presentations of minorities, and to guard against distortion of characters.

The distortions, or at least the unexamined platitudes, continued. The big difference was that black performers, whose alternative had been "accept stereotype or starve," began to demand and get other alternatives. Consider the case of Butterfly McQueen, the petite black actress with the squeaky voice who won acclaim for her "maid part" in Gone With the Wind (1939). Once the comic maid mantle was thrust upon her, she seemed destined to wear it forever. Her roles in The Women and Cabin in the Sky proved the point. But while working on Mildred Pierce, the diminutive McQueen announced that she would no longer accept the sort of parts she had been forced to play. She was determined to establish the right of her people to a just representation.

Since World War II, these five demands have been stated, restated, and implemented by many leaders, black and white:

1. America can never really lead the "free world" if she does not give real freedom (not only political, but economic and artistic) to all Americans at home.
2. There are not only moral but also economic reasons to open up a true black cinema.
3. More Negro capital should be invested in cinema ownership and management.
4. The near-monopoly of a few major Hollywood studios should and must be ended.
5. Blacks must get a more meaningful role in all the media, and should train black critics to handle such assignments.

Paul Robeson's films were the exceptions; stereotypes were still the rule. As a protest against stereotyping, the National Association for the Advancement of Colored People (N.A.A.C.P.) established a Hollywood unit to work with film makers in 1945. There were many gradual changes, some immediate ones. For example, Metro-Goldwyn-Mayer abandoned plans to screen *Uncle Tom's Cabin*, and Twentieth Century-Fox retitled a film which was planned as *Ten Little Niggers* to *Ten Little Indians*. Other black leaders, like William Grant Still, argued that all-Negro films (like *Cabin in the Sky* and *Stormy Weather*) tended to "glorify segregation," and forced studios to abandon them. A generation later blacks would argue *for* all-black films, and even "glorify segregation" under the new title of "black aesthetic."

In any case, American movies tended to break away from black stereotypes and present roles with much greater sensitivity and individuality in the 1950s. A new cycle of Negro-prejudice pictures was started with Stanley Kramer's *Home of the Brave*. The central character is a black soldier (James Edwards) who suffers a breakdown after a harrowing raid during World War II; but we later discover that his neurosis was caused by the racial prejudice of a comrade who called him "nigger." In quick succession such problem-films as *Lost Boundaries*, *Intruder in the Dust*, and *No Way Out* were receiving wide attention. In *Lost Boundaries*, a small New England town decides to accept a black doctor who has "passed" the color line, putting humanity above bigotry. *Intruder in the Dust*, based on a William Faulkner novel, tells the story of a proud, defiant black man who prefers lynching to crawling. In the end, he is not lynched, and the white lawyer who saves him says of black Lucas: "Lucas wasn't in trouble. We were in trouble."

No Way Out introduced America to a brilliant black actor, Sidney Poitier. Born in the Bahamas in 1924 and educated in Nassau, he came to New York at the age of sixteen. After military service he studied theater and made *No Way Out* in 1950. "Poitier is particularly good as the doctor who has to hurdle both his color and the exacting demands of his profession," critic Howard Barnes wrote in the *New York Herald Tribune* on October 12, 1950. Pursued by a psychopathic criminal-racist, Poitier has to show real strength to preserve his life. The black-white ghetto confrontation in the picture foreshadowed what would happen in American cities in the sixties. After outstanding performances in *Cry the Beloved Country*, *Blackboard Jungle*, and *Something of Value*, Poitier skyrocketed to fame in *The Defiant Ones* (1958). Centering on two prisoners chained together (one white, one black), the movie stresses faith in decency and brotherhood. For this role Poitier was nominated for an Academy Award and the Berlin Film Festival Award. Subsequent performances in *Lilies in the Field*, *A Patch of Blue*, and *Guess Who's Coming to Dinner* added to his stature.

A new poignancy and artistry, on the much-presented theme of racism, ws reached in Robert Mulligan's *To Kill a Mockingbird* (1962). By contrasting the deep prejudices of adults in a small town with the innocence of two children (those of the lawyer defending a black man accused of rape), the picture brought real drama where once there had been only cliché. Now the small-town south began to appear as the villain—not the blacks persecuted there. In *The Chase* (1966), Lillian Hellman shows a Texas town full of bigotry, fanaticism, and prejudice. *In the Heat of the Night* (1967) shows an equally wretched Mississippi town, with a redneck police chief who became a kind of white cliché in the sixties.

By now, however, the notion of brotherhood and reconciliation was being challenged, intellectually and physically, in

America. Both John F. Kennedy and Martin Luther King were assassinated, and black men decided that force must be met with force. "Black Power" became the new slogan. The cry of "Burn Baby Burn" was heard throughout the land. Once again, films reflected these changes. These same films also played an important role in the development of black consciousness.

"Non-violence is dead—it was killed in Memphis," a black militant says in *Up Tight*, produced by Jules Dassin in 1968. "You bled my Momma, you bled my Poppa—but you won't bleed me!" the black protagonist screams in Melvin Van Peeples's *Sweet Sweetback's Baadasssss Song*. The film indicates that America has come full turn since *Birth of a Nation*. In the 1915 film, every black man had been hopelessly stereotyped; now, in 1971, the same could be said of every white man.

Van Peeples's protagonist outlaw from the Los Angeles ghetto kills a number of whites (known collectively as the Man) en route to Mexico. "The message of *Sweetback*," Van Peeples was quoted as saying in the August 16, 1971 issue of *Time*, "is that if you can get it together and stand up to the Man, you can win."

By 1970 the idea of a black cinema was a reality. Al Freeman, Jr., directed and starred in *A Fable* (1971), an antiwhite movie based on LeRoi Jones's play *Slave*. *The Bus is Coming* (1971), produced in the Watts area of Los Angeles where some of the worst racial violence occurred in the 1960s, tells the story of the militant Black Fists, who resolve to revenge the death of a nonviolent black killed by a white policeman. The director, Wendell Franklin, was the first black admitted to the Screen Directors Guild.

Another black film produced in 1971, *Black Chariot*, was underwritten by the black population of California. Not only the investment of twenty-four limited partners, but also personal loans made to the producing firm through widespread soliciting of black communities, made the film possible.

International aspects of Negritude and black peoples was stressed by films oriented towards Afro-American ties. The outstanding black American actor and playwright, Ossie Davis, went to Nigeria to direct *Kongi's Harvest* in 1971. Americans played leading roles at the African Festival of the Arts in Dakar, Senegal, in 1966 and at many other such meetings. More and more American automobiles carried "Afro" bumper stickers with the red, green, and black colors of Black Liberation.

All this had wide economic as well as political implications. By 1970, it was estimated that Blacks comprised nearly one-third of American moviegoers; the purchasing power of the black population stood near $40 billion annually. In areas where white products couldn't succeed, black ones might. For example, *Look* and *Life* failed, but the black equivalent, *Ebony*, continued to flourish. This was a significant cultural phenomenum of the generation.

So was the rise of a successful New Black Cinema, heralded when the experimental *Cotton Comes to Harlem* was released in 1970. Directed by Ossie Davis and costarring Godfrey Cambridge and Raymond St. Jacques, the film grossed more than $9 million; within two years fifty black movies had flooded the market, often imitative of earlier white successes. Among them was a black *Dracula* (*Blacula*), the radical slave saga (*Legend of Nigger Charlie*), a black western (*Buck and the Preacher*), a black deejay story (*Melinda*), a black boxer story (*Hammer*), and a black thriller (*Slaughter*). A new vogue was also ushered in—the "Black Superstud" craze.

The outstanding example was *Shaft* (1971), which starred Richard Roundtree as an invincible, hard-hitting private detective who could laugh, love, fight, and prevail better than any man, black or white. He reminded some of the white superstud, James Bond—007 raised to a new (black) power.

Soon *Shaft* suits, watches, belts, sunglasses, decals, and aftershave lotion flooded the market. Director Gordon Parks, Jr., observed that if someone is going to put their money in a project, they expect a good return. In this case, they got it. *Shaft* grossed $15 million.

Equally successful was the 1972 film *Super Fly*—a slang term for the "best dope" or drugs around. The hero, portrayed by Ron O'Neal, is a cocaine seller named "Priest" who decides to leave the racket after a super-deal which will bring him $1 million. Aided by two mistresses (one white, one black), hired killers, and generous applications of drugs, he overcomes all opposition and gets his million.

Not all black leaders applauded. Some saw it as a film which portrays the black community as glorifying dope-pushers, pimps, and thieves. The Reverend Jesse Jackson, head of Operation PUSH (and later on a presidential aspirant), ordered a boycott of the film which glamorized a black man who exploits his own people and gets away unharmed. In moving from Stepin Fetchit to "Super Nigger," *Ebony* commented in a December, 1972 article, black folk portraits had come full circle. Moses Gunn, who costarred in both *Shaft* and its sequel, *Shaft's Big Score*, was quoted in that issue as saying: "I'm determined not to do another. I did the first two pictures because I thought my character (Bumpy) was real enough to portray; but one real cat in a movie full of caricatures isn't worth a damn."

What did this sudden upsurge in black film-making mean? Was it (in *Ebony*'s phrase) a "giant con game," or were we witnessing the birth of another creative chapter in film history? Are blacks once again victims of a white establishment bent on thought-control? Is *Super-Fly* in the final analysis more admirable than Uncle Tom? History suggests that "cultural explosions" can leave ditches as well as mountains. But we are too close to present-day affairs to make historical judgments.

The "magnolia myth" of smiling, contented darkies was well-rooted in American soil; it withered slowly, and even yet has not entirely died. Meanwhile, other myths have grown and flourished.

Can we balance the record without adding new and equally questionable distortions? The problem of Hegel's pendulum, moving from one extreme to the other, applies to film history as well as to economics. The pendulum swung wildly in the 1970s and 1980s. "There is a tendency born of neglect to over-emphasize the importance of the Negro in America," historian Alan Conway writes with perspective gained from living in New Zealand. "If this is a fault then it is a fault on the right side to compensate for years of neglect and underrating."[15]

If a single man emerges as "villain" in this rapid leap through many years and hundreds of movies, it is D. W. Griffith, who conceived and directed *Birth of a Nation*. Yet this is the same man who saw the cinema camera as the agent of democracy, leveling barriers between races and classes.

The use of the camera, and the other devices at our command, will continue to be one of the most sensitive and meaningful aspects of American civilization. What we see on the screen is ourselves, writ large. No one, black or white, can be happy with all that has taken place on the screen and streets of America—and is still going on. (The 1983 riots in Washington and Miami were painful reminders that "Burn Baby Burn" lingers on.) The perceptive and prophetic words of Norman Mailer, whose 1957 study *The White Negro* is a key document to students of *ethnos*, bear repeating. When the bohemian and the juvenile delinquent came face-to-face with the black, the result was a hipster. "If marijuana was the wedding ring, in this wedding of the white and the black, it was the Negro who brought the cultural dowry."[16]

In a remarkably prophetic passage, Mailer spoke of a "new breed of adventurers, adrift in the night, with a black man's code to fit their facts." The new revolutionary of the Counter-Culture, he decided, would be the White Negro.[17]

Martin Luther King, who "had a dream," is long in his grave; no leader of his stature has emerged to advocate his principles. Long-rooted ethnic prejudices and misconceptions—not only here, but around the world—must still be dealt with. Massacres keep cropping up: in Ireland, Uganda, Vietnam, Lebanon. There is some grounds for hope, but none for complacency.

Afro-Americans have been (and are being) welded into an *ethnos* not just because of color, but also because of the totality of historical, psychological, cultural, and political reasons that have persisted for centuries. Having lost his remote antiquity, he got the new black chauvinism—no more justifiable than any other kind of chauvinism. On the other hand, it brings great vitality and spontaneity to American life—the play motive (in music, drama, language, sports) that has benefited not only the nation, but the whole world. Sometimes vitality escalates into savage passion. As the English critic Deric Regin points out, "savage" is the key word for success acceptance in today's America—not only in gang life and contact sports, but also in much of our painting and writing. And has not *eros* plus play-expression helped dramatically to alter woman's role in modern civilization and popular culture?

Raised in a sub-culture that has stressed black pride and even suggested that we have a *black* Santa Claus and sing "I'm Dreaming of a Black Christmas," a new generation of Afro-Americans want to come to terms with blacks around the world. But the black American in Africa is in some ways just as much of an "outsider" as any tourist. There has been no major success in making "Negritude" a workable philosophy, at home or abroad. Efforts to unite the poor in our own nation—not only black but also Hispanic, Indian, and white—have not been very effective. A series of "Poor People's Marches" had little impact; and as social program after program was cut by the Reagan administration, the plight of the poor worsened. Social workers reported during the winter of 1983 that conditions were worse than they had been at any time since the Great Depression. Communication and compassion between the dominant culture and sub-cultures seemed to be getting worse, not better. Yet the feeling throughout the land was less one of indignation than of despair. "We meet disdain on one hand," an unemployed black man said, "and distrust on the other."[18]

In the eighteenth century, white American revolutionaries fired "the shot heard round the world." In the twentieth, it was black Americans who fired that shot. The future of our nation may well depend (in a world in which most people are nonwhite) on how we deal with our ethnic problems at home and abroad.

This raises many pragmatic and theoretical questions. One of them is central to us here: is there a separate black aesthetic, on which the black *ethnos* can draw and flourish in the twenty-first century? Can and should we give up the "Melting Pot" idea and move on to something else?

There is no clear answer. Claims and arguments, often arising from emotional confrontation, are blurred and confusing. The mystique called Negritude, black critic Saunders Redding points out, embraces a heavy, indeed, overriding emotional component referred to as "soul force." But "the advocates of this way of thinking have no corpus of cognitive knowledge to fall back on."[19] At the same time, the fact of blackness is not only a powerful inspiration and force for black writers today but also an intense force affecting nonblack thinking and writing as well. Being black is suddenly a strength and advantage after generations of acting as a barrier and handicap.[20] The consequences of wedding art and politics, black literature and black power, are uncertain.

The answer to my "central question" is not yet in. What *is* clear is that *ethnos* is indeed a Pillar of Popular Culture; any study which ignores it (in the United States, or anywhere else) is not really studying the popular culture at all.

The Afro-American condition—some would say plight—has produced a series of popular American stories which Leslie Fiedler aptly labels "inadvertent epics"—*Uncle Tom's Cabin*, *The Clansman*, *The Birth of a Nation*, *Gone With the Wind*, *Black Boy*, and *Roots*.[21] If they have not made their mark as High Art, they are known to millions around the globe. What explains the success of such literature as popular culture? Literary works which long endure, Fiedler concludes, do not (like philosophy or science) appeal to reason and logic, but to passion. At its most authentic, art releases dionysian, demonic impulses and permits us "moments of privileged madness, a temporary return to psychic states which we have theoretically abandoned in the name of humanity and sweet reason."[22] That is why *Uncle Tom*, Rhett Butler, and Kunta Kinte delight us, no matter what critics say. The work of Harriet Beecher Stowe, Margaret Mitchell, Thomas Dixon, Richard Wright, and Alex Haley may be inept in form and weak in ideas, but (like Shakespeare or Sophocles) they somehow have mythopoetic power. Thus does Fiedler suggest a new key to understanding not only what some have called "popular trash" but also the whole ethnic layer at the very heart of American culture.

How that layer is seen, by both blacks and whites, changes with time and circumstance. In *Black Boy*, Wright mulls over "the strange absence of real kindness in Negroes . . . how lacking we are in those intangible sentiments that bind man to man . . . ."[23] But myths of black brutalization, murder, and rape were out of style a generation later when Haley wrote *Roots*, stressing black community, gentleness, and such bourgeois virtues as piety, domesticity, and sexual fidelity. Thus did Haley become the first black writer to modify the mythology of black-white relations for the majority audience. Here finally was a book which would not only (like Stowe's *Uncle Tom's Cabin*) be "equally read in the parlor, the kitchen, and the nursery," but also be condensed for the *Reader's Digest* and assigned in every classroom in the land.

Meanwhile, *ethnos* prospers in the 1980s. Albert Murray's book *The Omni-Americans*, an iconoclastic collection of essays on ethnic politics, literature, and music, points to fresh approaches and themes.[24] Even the most conservative politicians take care to see that "special groups" are given their due. Talk of the "Hispanic Vote," the "Black Vote," and the "Jewish Vote" is heard from sea to shining sea. No one heats up the Melting Pot now. And yet the heat is always on.

Those who know how to deal with *ethnos* best, and translate local circumstances into universal meaning, are the ones whose words and work will endure. I believe Romare Bearden, the Afro-American artist, is such a person. His own statement on his work sums it up well: "I work out of a response and need to redefine the image of man in the terms of the Negro experience I know best."[25]

Such words are echoed by another American—this one a white Southerner who has already won a place in world literature. Of the black people he knew, and wrote of with such compelling power, William Faulkner said: "They endured."

Endurance and *ethnos* often go hand in hand. On February 7, 1983, the United States celebrated the one hundredth birthday of one of our finest song writers and entertainers, Eubie Blake. A black man who remembered the Spanish-American War, he wrote over two thousand songs and five hit Broadway musicals before he died. Let us now praise famous men. Happy Birthday, Eubie.

NOTES

1. Woodrow Wilson, *The New Freedom* (New York: Doubleday, 1913), p. 14. Wilson's inability to persuade his Allies to write some of his democratic and ethnic ideas into the Treaty of Versailles a few years later is one of the major tragedies of our time.

2. This is one of the profound points George Kubler develops in *The Shape of Time: Remarks on the History of Things* (New Haven, Conn.: Yale University Press, 1962).

3. Thomas F. Gossett, *Race: The History of an Idea in America* (Dallas:

Southern Methodist University Press, 1963), p. 4; and Carleton S. Coon, *The Origin of Races* (New York: Knopf, 1962).

4. Coon, *Origin of Races*, p. 16.

5. A. A. Roback, *A Dictionary of International Slurs* (Cambridge, Mass.: Sci-Art Publishers, 1944), p. 283.

6. Ruth Benedict uses this quotation in *Patterns of Culture* (Boston: Houghton Mifflin, 1959), p. 10. Cicero's letter to Atticus was dated October 1, 54 B.C.

7. Robert E. Park and Ernest W. Burgess, *Introduction to the Science of Sociology* (Chicago: University of Chicago Press, 1921); and Robert E. Park, *Race and Culture* (Glencoe, Ill.: Free Press, 1973). It should be pointed out that Park modified his position over the years, and that the whole matter is far more complex than my brief summary implies. See also Stanford M. Lyman, *The Black American in Sociological Thought* (New York: G. P. Putnam's Sons, 1972); Michael Banton, *The Idea of Race* (Cambridge: University Printing House, 1977); and William Petersen, *The Background to Ethnic Conflict* (Leiden, Neth.: E. J. Brill, 1979).

8. Petersen, *Ethnic Conflict*, p. 1.

9. Ibid.

10. Levic Jessel, *The Ethnic Process: An Evolutionary Concept of Languages and Peoples* (The Hague: Mouton Publishers, 1978), p. 18. See also Fredrick Barth, ed., *Ethnic Groups and Boundaries* (Boston: Little, Brown, 1969).

11. Barth, *Ethnic Groups and Boundaries*, p. 20. See also Rik Pinxten, ed., *Ethnic Groups versus Relativism in Language and Thought* (The Hague: Mouton Publishers, 1976).

12. Frank M. Hankins, *The Racial Basis of Civilization* (New York: Knopf, 1926), p. 307.

13. Books and articles on Afro-American life and culture continue to pour from the presses. Standard bibliographies include Elizabeth W. Miller, *The Negro in America: A Bibliography* (Cambridge: Harvard University Press, 1966); and Dwight La Vern Smith, *Afro-American History: A Bibliography* (Santa Barbara, Calif.: ABC-Clio, 1974). See also Charles D. Peavy, *Afro-American Literature and Culture Since World War II* (Detroit: Gale, 1979); Lindsay Patterson, *The Afro-American in Music and Art* (Cornwallis Heights, Pa.: Publishers Agency, 1978); and Edward Margolies, *Afro-American Fiction, 1853–1976* (Detroit: Gale, 1979).

Earlier works of high quality include Erwin A. Salk, *The Layman's Guide to Negro History* (New York, 1967), useful for its listing of organizations and libraries, etc., that possess collections of material on and by black Americans, as well as sources of visual materials such as films (strips), records, slides, etc. There is also a list of periodicals published on and by black Americans.

Walter Schatz, ed., *The Directory of Afro-American Sources* (New York:

R. R. Bowker Co., 1970) serves a similar function, being a comprehensive compilation of all the major holdings of information on blacks by state and city.

Robert Doty, *Contemporary Black Artists in America* (New York: dist. by Dodd, Mead, 1971), a catalogue to the Whitney Museum show of 1971, contains a bibliography compiled by Libby Seaberg and includes the important published works on black art, each containing extensive bibliographies. See also Marshall W. Fishwick, *Contemporary Black Artists* (New York: Sandak, 1970) with the accompanying Sandak Slide Set #673.

14. Marshall W. Fishwick, *Art and Life in Black America* (Wilmington: American Studies Institute, 1970).

15. Alan Conway, *The History of the Negro in the U.S.A.* (New York: Methuen, 1968), p. 34.

16. Norman Mailer, "The White Negro," in *Dissent*, November 1957, p. 49. Later reprinted by the City Light Books, San Francisco, 1962.

17. The black rhetoric reached its peak with the Black Panthers, especially with Huey P. Newton, Bobby Seale, and Eldridge Cleaver. In addition to their newspaper (*The Black Panther*), see G. Louis Heath, ed., *The Black Panther Leaders Speak* (Metuchen, N.J.: Scarecrow Press, 1976); and Lyman, *Black American*.

18. See Daniel M. Collier, Jr., "The Impact of American Subcultures on the Polity as a Model for Development," in Abdul A. Said, ed., *Protagonists of Change: Subcultures in Development and Revolution* (Englewood Cliffs, N.J.: Prentice-Hall, 1971).

19. Saunders Redding, "The Black Revolution in American Studies," in *American Studies: An International Newsletter*, 9, no. 1, autumn 1970, p. 5.

20. See Charles T. Davis and Daniel Walden, eds., *On Being Black* (New York: Fawcett, 1970); Addison Gayle, Jr., editor, *Black Expression: Essays by and About Black Americans in the Creative Arts* (New York: Weybright & Talley, 1970); and Addison Gayle, Jr., *The Black Situation* (New York: Horizon, 1970).

21. Leslie A. Fiedler, *The Inadvertent Epic* (New York: Simon & Schuster, 1979).

22. Ibid., p. 84.

23. Richard Wright, *Black Boy* (New York: Harper, 1945), p. 67.

24. Albert Murray, *The Omni-Americans: Perspectives on Black Experience and American Culture* (New York: Vintage, 1983). "For all who would deal creatively with who we are," Ralph Ellison wrote in a review, "this book is indispensable."

25. M. Bunch Washington, *The Art of Romare Bearden: The Prevalence of Ritual* (New York: Harry N. Abrams, 1972), p. 9.

HEROS _____ 3

The heroes seen every day on the television screen may be
the gods of our age.

Hidetoshi Kato, *Intercultural Studies*

Demos are the common people, *heros* the uncommmon. History
cannot function without people, and people without leaders.

Heros means superior man, embodiment of composite ideas,
savior of the people. By the process of apotheosis, *heros* was
made into a god since he defied death, danger, and destruc-
tion. History finds its essential meaning in heroes, and popular
culture its unending task in discovering new ones. No Pillar
deserves more careful scrutiny than this Third one.[1]

If the word is Greek, the concept goes back to the dawn of
time. The heroic concept was first framed in myths which were
vehicles of religion and custom. The hero was the answer to
needs and to prayers. Saoshyant, Heracles, Romulus and Remus, Siegfried, Jason, and Jesus all became heroes at least partly
as a result of heavenly meddling.

The hero is archetypal, a paradigm who bears the possibilities of life, courage, love—the commonplace, the indefinable
which define our human lives.[2] Another Greek word involved
is *charisma*—the gift of grace, the endowment with supernatural power. This social force of unmatched power was present
in savage societies; flowed and flowered in antiquity and the
Middle Ages; and has been discredited or discarded in modern
society.[3] For centuries charisma was at the heart of heroics. Heroes, a gift of heaven, a force sent by destiny, became deified
in death. For the people of the Shang dynasty of China (1400
B.C.) the worship of heaven was synonymous with ancestor

worship. In Japan, too, man's worship was tied to service to gods. Kunio Yanagita notes that the verb "matsuru"—to worship—is akin to the verb "matsurau"—to be at the service of.[4] This kinship has persisted over the centuries. When Tokyo emerged as the Japanese capital, it was necessary to establish not only new sacred places but also new gods: the Emperor had to be invented instantaneously.

The search and need for heroes is inherent in human history. Preliterate societies allow men, heroes, and gods to stand on a footing of tolerable equality. "Throughout the inhabited world, in all times and under every circumstance, the myths of man have flourished," writes Joseph Campbell. "It is necessary for men to understand, and be able to see, that through various symbols the same redemption is revealed."[5]

When one attempts a *comparative* study of heroes to see if one monomythic hero has a thousand faces, he quickly realizes the magnitude of the task. How can a Westerner understand the "Middle" or "Far" East? The terms themselves are significant— Occidental subjective inventions implying distance from the West. That distance, Kenneth Scott Latourette points out, is not only geographical but also cultural. "Until the latter part of the 19th century, fewer contacts and less interchange existed between Western European and Far Eastern people than between the Occident and any other of the civilized folk of Asia."[6]

If history has forced Westerners to deal with the great and expansive cultures of Japan, China, and India, it has still slighted the historic and heroic patterns of many other cultures: Tibet, Sinkiang, Mongolia, Korea, Thailand, Burma, Laos, Cambodia, Sri Lanka, and Indonesia, for example. How many Westerners can name "the four Buddhist lands of the White Elephant and the Sacred Sword"?[7]

Yet a surprising number of Westerners know the name of India's Ravi Shankar, a superstar in the global culture of the 1960s. He and other Eastern musicians brought about the "sitar explosion." By 1968 Shankar could write: "I find myself adored like a movie star or singer. I love young people very much, and since they know I love them, they listen to me and are very receptive."[8] This appeal is a tribute both to his art and to the new global culture.

The heroic vision still centers on the "Lost Cause" of the Confederacy in such places as New Castle, Virginia; but the idea expressed stretches back thousands of wars and years: THE GREATEST GIFT A HERO LEAVES HIS RACE, IS TO HAVE BEEN A HERO. *Photo by the author.*

In classic times, heroes were god-men; in the Middle Ages, God's men; in the Renaissance, universal men; in the eighteenth century, gentlemen; in the nineteenth, self-made men. Our century has seen the common man and the outsider become heroic. In keeping with the times they have reacted to our social and scientific revolutions. Some of them now go where once only gods could dwell—in outer space. Heroes must act their ages.

Like a stream, history moves in one direction for a time, then veers off in another. Gaining momentum it washes away old banks and gouges out new channels. Those who perceive and justify this, altering with the flow of events, are heroes.

Some men flash into prominence—one-issue politicians, matinee idols, rock singers, sports champions—only to disappear like a flash flood. The maxim is "Winner take all." We quote and misquote these men with equal ease. At this juncture no one knows if they are true culture heroes or faddish meteors.

Halfway around the world, in Calcutta, India, the words, faces, and circumstances are different; but the hero is still "The Great Gift." *Photo by the author.*

Every age has thousands of aspiring heroes. Some carry through to the second generation, which feels the hero's power in stories told by their fathers. By the third generation his exploits take on a certain remoteness. Always susceptible to legend, a hero becomes superhistorical in myth.

Not that they have identical appeal. Each hero is emphatically him or herself.[9] Yet patterns persist. Time and again one runs into variants of Cinderella and the antithetical Sly Fox. The Persevering Tortoise is the antithesis of the Futile Searcher; the Escapist, of the Returning Prodigal; the Golden Fly, of the Ugly Duckling; and Patient Griselda, of the Inconstant Lover. Heroic fairy tales are universal and primary stirrings of the human soul, and all heroic reputations swing between two poles—the saint (Buddha, Paul, Malcolm X) and the conqueror (Alexander, Napoleon, Eisenhower). The former stresses meekness and renunciation, and the latter aggressiveness and affirmation. Both groups require missions, martyrs, and disciples.[10]

A full-fledged culture hero must develop his own mystique and empower a whole array of hero-makers to propound it. Napoleon's empire has crumbled, his code is outmoded, but his legend flourishes. He did not hesitate to order the Pope to Paris for his coronation as Emperor or to substitute his name for the divinity in the school catechism. His appearance on battlefields, which he methodically documented, was a masterpiece of image-making. French poets, patriots, and dramatists helped create and spread the Napoleonic legend. Nor can we blame this on the gullibility of nineteenth-century man. There has probably never been a more effective hero-making device in history than the propaganda machine perfected by Hitler and his associates during the days of the Third Reich. We must update Emerson's contention in *Representative Men* that "Reputations of the nineteenth century will one day be quoted to prove its barbarism."

To master the macrocosm one must first overcome the microcosm. The source of true heroic power is internal. When he tackles the outer world, the hero faces the inertia of his fellow man; upsetting the social equilibrium brings conflict. Either his triumph or defeat restores the social equilibrium. His importance stems from perceiving the enduring significance of daily flux. Creative leaders are a leaven in the lump of ordinary humanity. They run out threads of relation through everything, fluid and solid, material and elemental.

Julius Caesar symbolized the power of Rome, Kubla Khan the cruelty of Asian hordes, Saint Thomas Aquinas the wisdom of Christianity, René Descartes the method of science. Scholars have long sought patterns and typologies in the heroic story. That there are similarities in birth, youth, and death have long been recognized. Johann Georg von Hahn advanced his "Aryan Expulsion and Return Theory" in 1864, expanded later by Alfred Nutt and Otto Rank. Antti Aarne proposed a tale-type system in 1910, and Vladimir Propp his *Morphology of the Folktale* in 1928. This paved the way for FitzRoy Richard Somerset Raglan's book *The Hero: A Study in Tradition, Myth, and Drama* (1936). Lord Raglan named twenty-two elements in the heroic saga—covering origin, early struggles, marriage, reign, death, and burial—opening the door to comparative study of content and internal structure. The stories of Oedipus, Theseus, Moses, Christ, and King Arthur have marked similarities; all are rooted more in myth than in history. Raglan's formula can be applied with interesting results to the leading American hero of my generation, John F. Kennedy. Kennedy's father was called to a royal court (as Ambassador to the Court of Saint James) and the son was educated by (presumably) wise men (at Harvard). Then he went off to fight an evil dragon (the Japanese navy) and after a bloody fracas (PT 109), triumphed and returned to marry the beautiful princess (Jackie). Having inherited his father's kingdom (politics), he fought and defeated a second contender (Nixon) before taking over as ruler (president). For a time he reigned smoothly, prescribing laws. Then he suddenly lost favor (the Bay of Pigs crisis), tried to rally his people, and died a sudden and mysterious death (did Oswald really shoot Kennedy?). Amidst great mourning (the first worldwide television funeral), he was buried on a sacred hillside (Arlington). Now he has many shrines (a cultural center, airport, library, highway, and a space-launching site).

Yet with all this, and despite his brief cultic worship, Kennedy is not *the* American hero. That honor belongs (as it long has) to George Washington. He is still first in everything, including the hearts of his countrymen; *Pater Patriae*—father of the country. By dissecting the popular images of Washington, we begin to see the hopes and fears of the whole Republic. "America has furnished the world the character of Washington," Daniel Webster said. "If we had done nothing else, that alone would have entitled us to the respect of the world." A century later

William Carlos Williams added, "Know the intimate character of Washington himself, and you will know practically all there is to understand about the beginnings of the American Republic." One of the ablest English scholars—writing from the nation against which Washington had rebelled—concluded, "The man *is* the monument; the monument *is* America."[11]

Washington somehow brings *logos* and *mythos* together. Ezra Stiles stressed this in a 1738 sermon at Yale and thanked God for creating and forming in Washington the great ornament of humankind. Washington fascinates us because he presents the mystery of no mystery. Like Yahweh, that ultimate *patri*, he is what he is. Washington reminds us of patriarchs unearthed by archeologists, who reigned majestically until killed ritually.

In using Washington and his giant obelisk as a case study of our Third Pillar, we shall not attempt to give a full account of either his life or his apotheosis. Both have been attempted—again and again. There is almost nothing new one can hope or expect to say about George Washington. What I might do, in the framework of this book, is to show how quickly he became our prime *heros*, how well the known Washington matched the needed Washington, and how the consensus on his key role has been spontaneous, continuous, and accumulative.

Even during Washington's life, the *demos* knew he was *Pater Patriae*, to be elevated above other *heros*. Of course, they did not use these classical terms. A Pennsylvania farmer of German ancestry wrote a story in 1799, "Washington Ankunft in Elisium," in which *Pater* strolled around heaven (to which he had only recently gone), talking with other *patriarches*. When Paul Svinin visited the new Republic a few years later, he wrote in his diary, "Every American considers it his sacred duty to have a likeness of Washington in his home, just as we have the image of God's saints."[12]

This may have been the Age of Reason, but the adoration of Washington grew ever more irrational and romantic. John Neal could not write or speak the name of Washington "without a contraction and dilation of the heart." For Catherine Maria Sedgwick, Washington's name "conjured up a sentiment resembling the awe of the pious Israelite approaching the ark of the Lord."

This painting on glass, done in China about 1800 for the flourishing "China Trade," depicts the Apotheosis of Washington. Multinational angels (including an American Indian) assist in the elevation. There are so many examples of this theme that in 1981 Smith College mounted a full exhibition called "The Apotheosis of Washington." *Courtesy, The Henry Francis du Pont Winterthur Museum.*

Coca-Cola's popular "American Statesman" series featured Gilbert
Stuart's unfinished portrait of Washington in 1931—the year before the
bicentennial of Washington's birth in 1732. Thus did millions of Americans associate the great man and the great product. *Courtesy of the Archives: The Coca-Cola Company.*

Gilbert Stuart's portrait has been copied, caricatured, and parodied innumerable times. Entering our third century as a nation (1976), *MAD* magazine featured this Washington on the Bicentennial Year cover, along with a note that reads: "Dear Mr. Stuart: I really do not believe this to be a good likeness of me! It would best remain *unfinished!* G. Washington." *Courtesy of* MAD *magazine © 1976 by E. C. Publications, Inc.*

What was George Washington really like? We shall never know. The layers of myth, legend, lore, and fiction are impenetrable. What we can see, however, is the way popular culture operates on various levels. American symbolism is no longer a folk product—revealing as nothing else could before industrialization—the ideas and attitudes of the *demos*.[13] In addition to folk attitudes, the mass sentiment manipulated by media, men, and governments has merely furthered Washington's apotheosis.[14]

On and on Washington's reputation rolled, like a great avalanche. True enough, Hemingway's "Lost Generation" wanted to abandon the "glory words," and debunkers had their inning. William E. Woodward's *George Washington: The Image and the Man* (1926) insisted that Washington was vain and undemocratic, "almost as impersonal at the top of the government as a statue on top of a monument would have been." But Woodward was no match for Sol Bloom (1870–1949), the New York Congressman who spearheaded the bicentennial of Washington's birth in 1932. The son of Polish Jewish immigrants, Bloom began his career in a San Francisco brush factory. Subsequently he became ticket agent, show manager, producer, hootchy-kootchy inventor, music publisher, and backer of the first Ferris wheel. When the Spanish-American War broke out, he demonstrated that he was more than equal to the occasion. The same day that news of the Maine disaster broke, he completed and published a tune called, "The Heroes who Sank with the Maine." If you gave Sol an idea, he could make it go.

Bloom retired in 1923 a millionaire and proceeded to devote himself to public service. Tammany Hall backed him for Congress in the plush Riverside Drive district of Manhattan. He managed to get seated in a contested election and to stay until his death in 1949.

No one in the halls of government was more enthusiastic about the American experiment and the men who had made it than Bloom. He wrote essays and gave radio addresses on America, the Constitution, and George Washington. In 1930 he was named associate director of the George Washington Bicentennial Commission. His coequal on the Commission, Ulysses S. Grant III, grandson of the general who had made a name for himself by sticking it out on a battleline all winter, did not persist like his namesake. He left Bloom in sole control. The new commander not only filled the breach, he spilled all over the wall. Before Congress knew what had happened, he organized a nine month celebration, got an appropriation of $338,000, and hired a staff of 125. During the legislative recess he devoted fifteen hours a day to *Patri* in one way or another. Millions of printed pieces jammed the nation's letter boxes. Tons of Washington badges, buttons, and busts went on sale. Sol even took over—with Washington's help—Mother's Day, Memorial Day, Independence Day, and Goethe's birthday. Finally he set up his own radio station, with an antenna on top of the Washington Monument. Never, but never, has one man said so much about Washington to so many. Will Rogers pointed out that Sol Bloom was the only guy who ever made a party run nine months, and in dry times, too. Bloom made the whole country Washington conscious.

No one can dispute the claim. The printed report of the Bicentennial Commission alone filled five huge volumes averaging seven hundred pages each. Over 16,000 celebrations were staged, featuring 4,760,245 separate programs. That's a lot of Washington.

A newspaper cartoon depicted Sol in a Continental uniform with the caption "First in War, first in Peace, first in Bicentennial publicity." One columnist thought Bloom was getting to look more and more like Washington. A Republican Senator replied there was little cause for alarm just as long as Washington didn't start to look like Sol Bloom.

In the winter of 1983 we turned on the nightly news to witness an incredible sight: an antinuclear protester had backed a truck up against the Washington Monument, allegedly full of explosives; he was prepared to blow it up unless certain conditions were met. We gasped and watched.

"Do you suppose he might possibly *do* it?" my wife asked.

Our small son replied before I could get out a word. "No way, Mom!"

"How do you know, Billy?" she asked.

"Because if the monument came down, America would fail!"

In a way which he may not yet understand, Billy was quite

right. The monument still stands. So does the man: the greatest of great Americans.

The notion of greatness—both as individuals and as a nation—underwent an acid test in the 1960s, when the Youthquake swept the land. For the first time since Washington himself walked the land, the antihero was in command. Ugly became beautiful, queer became normal. Were the pillars of the temple about to crumble?

"What has happened," a Japanese visitor wrote, "is that substantial and structural problems have so shaken American society and politics that the institutions have lost their ability to restore themselves."[15] One corollary was that the heroes had lost their ability to inspire, the generals to lead. "Ours seemed to be an age without heroes."

Certainly there were few heroes modeled on those serenely confident generals, elegant eighteenth-century squires, bold nineteenth-century industrial tycoons. The presidency itself suffered a sea-change under Kennedy: first president born in the twentieth century, first from the political vortex of megalopolis, first Roman Catholic. More important, he was the first who would be neither "official" or "corny." When asked to explain how he bacame a Naval hero in World War II, he replied: "They sank my boat." Out went purple prose and pious platitudes. Kennedy's press conferences were masterpieces of relaxed, popular exposition. Here was the old F.D.R. "Fireside Chat" adapted for television by Prince Charming.

Kennedy's assassination, we now see, was the most crucial event in the heroic history of our generation. Because of the times and technology, Kennedy had a global popularity unlike that of any other president or of any man then alive. That he should be killed senselessly by an ex-Marine, who was in turn killed on television before millions of viewers, formed an unbelievable historic episode—a happening.

This sense of the unexpected, the unbelievable, was flavored with a tang of the grotesque. As in a mixed-up movie in which the film runs backward, we found ourselves in 1964 watching Barry Goldwater campaigning for the presidency on horseback. Old-timers who remembered Buffalo Bill were filled with nostalgia. No so for most Americans. Even a Texas Ranger seemed better than this. Lyndon B. Johnson, presumably the last of the nineteenth-century presidents, took office. Then Ronald Reagan rode out of the West.

The Johnson years mirrored the knotty and perennial American paradoxes: Virgin land *vs.* raped landscape; Arcadia *vs.* Grub City; consensus *vs.* anarchy; citadel *vs.* caravan. Some sat in while others copped out. Consensus disappeared. A single catalytic agent, Vietnam, changed old-style American military heroes into new-style villains. Caught between the corncob and the computer, older Americans didn't know whether to go back to the farm or go forward to the moon. Their children went to Woodstock.

And, of course, their heroes changed. In place of time-honored rural heroes (hunter, scout, cowboy), we had new popular urban heroes—detective, private eye, super spy. Like their earlier country cousins, they were all wanderers, diamonds in the rough, prepared for a violence they could not escape. Women played a much larger role than they had a generation ago. Your urban sophisticate was not a romantic lover, but he had good gonads; he was not seducing but seduced. This produced a new-style temple (i.e., cocktail lounge) prostitute, not so much interested in singing as in swinging.

Certainly the Founding Fathers had a bad inning in the 1960s. Even George Washington himself—the man who became a monument—was attacked. Eldridge Cleaver wrote in his best-selling book *Souls on Ice*: "George Washington and Thomas Jefferson owned hundreds of slaves. Every president since Lincoln connived politically and cynically with the issues affecting the human rights of most people."[16]

Meanwhile, the Chickenshits (given national attention by *Esquire* magazine) wore yellow armbands, carried a yellow flag, and played kazoos: the parody of everything heroic. When approached, they dropped to the floor and crawled away mumbling, "Grovel grovel grovel, who are we to be heroes?"

A whole series of studies reflected the downgrading of heroes.[17] One of them, Harold Lubin's *Heroes and Anti-Heroes*, raised "serious questions about our contemporary culture heroes." Their styles are their fortunes, he complained, and their styles pass like any other fad of the moment—mini skirts, long hair, mod boots, "Today's heroes rise with a dazzling brilliancy, but they are extinguished with all the finality of a shooting star."[18]

Roger R. Rollin published another, *Hero/Anti-Hero* (1973), and made essentially the same points. The "hero" in Society A becomes the "villain" in Society B; you can't tell one from the other without a program. The title of Alice Childress's 1977 book put the idea in groovy slang: *Hero Ain't Nothin' But a Sandwich*.

The rhetoric of the 1980s, which became ever more unified and persistent, reinforced Sarah Grimke's famous 1838 request that the male brethren take their foot from off female necks. But a new relationship between hero and heroine has not yet been widely understood or accepted. In *Cult Heroes of Our Time* (edited by Theodore L. Gross), Jacqueline Onassis is presented as "The Existential Heroine," a queen without court or clout, who insisted on having her cake and eating it too. Whatever charisma she once had has vanished.

In what sense are Janis Joplin, Joan Baez, Jackie Onassis, and Geraldine Ferraro "heroic"? The process by which men and women become heroes, celebrities, or public figures is an enigma of contemporary mass culture. Just how much depends on which media? By studying images of public people in mass media content, we get some clues. A long-term study of popular magazines convinced Leo Lowenthal that "idols of production" (in business, politics, industry) dominated the early twentieth century, but "idols of consumption" (in entertainment, the arts, sports) ruled by World War II. Theodore Green traced magazine biographies from 1787 to 1918, finding a diminished role for individualism in American society over this period. Sociologist Orrin Klapp advanced the idea of social typing, seeing heroes as symbolic leaders who both reflect and influence society. We know that heroic proposition has changed, and is changing. In the 1982 Congressional elections, for example, it was estimated that seventy percent of all votes were determined mainly by television commercials. If this is true, what will be the long-range media impact on the body politic? And on political heroes?

For women and men, the heroic proposition is linked to the new politics of visibility. Both major 1984 conventions demonstrated this. We are dominated by images rather than words.

Instant information cries out for instant action. Faced with instant problems, we want heroes with instant solutions. Yet it does not follow that the heroic process is deteriorating, or the instinct for admiration and acclaim slipping. It may be that a generation which is better educated, more sophisticated, more travelled and media-exposed than any in history, will demand and expect more from heroes and heroines. Because highly publicized figures can no longer hide contradictions, shortcomings, and recorded blunders, the old one-dimensional heroes or paragons are finished. We have to accept the new crop, warts and all or not at all.

What has happened to charisma—that endowment of an individual with supernatural power that has been, for centuries, at the center of heroics? Has our very political survival been reduced to a mixture of image projection, cynical self-seeking, and ruthless ambition? Bryan Wilson summarized the answer given by some American intellectuals in the 1970s:

> We have not produced an alternative language of persuasion with which to manipulate the electronic masses . . . . The basis of confidence that comprises the charismatic relationship is no longer there— and it appears unlikely to be recovered.[19]

While Wilson was worrying about an alternative language, another writer—far less learned and articulate—was settling for the old one which had kept the *Reader's Digest* in American homes and libraries for years. The title he chose sounded little short of regrettable: "Unforgettable John Wayne." Working his way forward, cliché by cliché, and noting how Wayne had stopped "the determined bid of a band of communists to take control of the film industry," the writer concluded that Wayne "gave the whole world the image of what an American should be."[20] Corny? Not everyone thought so. A year later the author of this article, Ronald Reagan, was elected President of the United States.

Surely a celebrity, potentially a hero, Reagan is a master communicator, merging role life and real life, adding a new chapter to American media mythology.[21] Though only six of Reagan's fifty-three movies were Westerns, he was host of

"Death Valley Days" for two years, which certainly helped him become governor of California in 1966.[22] While most politicians spend their lives learning to be actors, here was an actor learning to be a politician. Sarah Russell Hankins thinks we are content to have him play the part. The medium of Ronald Reagan is his message:

Yet it is not the verified message of an Eisenhower, the visionary message of a Kennedy, or the sincere if inept message of a Ford or Carter. It is a xeroxed message, a copy of the original, once removed from reality.[23]

Whether Ronald Reagan will turn out to be a genuine American hero—the political opposite but media-magic twin of Franklin D. Roosevelt—remains to be seen. Those who see "The Cardboard Messiah," starring Ronald Reagan as the Giant Replica of a Statesman,[24] should recall that the hero, like Proteus, takes on many shapes and guises. Observe him starring in the video-game arcade, disguised as Pac Man, Ms. Pac Man, Black Knight, Tron, or Jungle King. The Electronic Revolution has created new environments of invisible power—new patterns, styles, heroes. Electrified, computerized, synchronized, and televised, we approach the twenty-first century with few certainties.

Heroes used to look up to heaven; now they use it as their stage. Astronauts have not only created a new hero-type, but a new area of concern: astropolitics.[25] One of the original space heroes of the 1960s, John Glenn, described by *Life* magazine as "moral and strongly religious,"[26] was pictured before his flight shaping hamburgers for the outdoor grill; twenty years later, he was shaping his candidacy for the White House.

Heroes, like everything else in our society, are getting more complex, more multifaceted. In our "Never Go Out Alone" and "Exact Change After Dark" culture, it is not rapture but rape that characterizes urban living. And how can anyone control nuclear arms, restore the economy, clean up the environment, personalize the machine? We go to the movies to laugh at the bumblers—Peter Sellers and Woody Allen—because we empathize with their plight. We like them because of, rather than in spite of, their incompetency. The same can be said for a line of television favorites, stretching from Wally Cox, Ozzie Nelson, Bob Denver, and Dick Van Dyke to John Ritter. Playing "The Greatest American Hero" in a 1982 television series, Ralph Hinkley (like Superman of old) inherits a magic suit. But he loses the instruction manual and when he finally takes off, runs into a billboard.

This doesn't mean that ancient heroes and gods have disappeared—some have merely changed name and media. Comic books prove the point. Winged Mercury has become the Flash, and Zeus, the super-god, is Superman. Thor has even retained his original name as he battles crime in modern society; so has "The Mighty Isis." Billy Batson understands the heroic power of the word "Shazam," which changes him into Captain Marvel.[27] Wonder Woman is a combination of the goddess Aphrodite and Hippolyta, Queen of the Amazons. Hawkman, reincarnation of an earlier hero, disguises himself as the hawk god he had worshipped in his earlier existence.[28]

The heroic scene is changing too rapidly, and we are too close to it to give final answers to long-range questions. We *can* say that changes in media, lifestyle, priorities, and ideologies are reflected in our heroes. Movies and television confer celebrity, for example, not just on people, but on acts, objects, places, ways of life. Everything is visible with the Big Eye.

To recognize the absence of myth is the first step towards resurrecting it. Today, that recognition is widespread in the Western world. When heroic style is refashioned, remythology thrives. In 1984 neo-conservatism controls key political positions throughout the world; nostalgia is a universal movement; the Hippies and Crazies of the nineteen-sixties are finding Jesus and selling encyclopedias.

The media is changing our views not only of the hero but also of "the great globe itself." Travel, research, translations, documentaries, and satellites are eliminating old barriers and frontiers. Only a few men have been on the moon—tens of millions have watched them once they got there. C. P. Snow's "two cultures" dilemma is outmoded. The sharp line between the arts and sciences is disappearing. Think of words that apply equally well to both: far-out, experimental, interface, turned-on, dynamic, nebular, free-fall, random, fused, amorphous. Traditional disciplines have come tumbling down. Much future research will reflect the change.

Cultural relocations and heroic transformation always go hand in hand. Freed by technology and fed by media, image-makers are engaged in a worldwide scavenger hunt involving Mali masks, Zen fables, raga music, the camp style of Victoria, and the click-clack of computers. By telescoping time, tradition, and geography, the first universal heroic tradition may emerge. Then the Third Pillar of Popular Culture would stretch not just from pole to pole, but from planet to planet.

NOTES

1. My own contributions to the vast literature of heroes include *American Heroes: Myth and Reality* (Washington, D.C.: Public Affairs Press, 1954); *The Hero, American Style* (New York: David McKay, 1969); and *Heroes of Popular Culture* (Bowling Green, Ohio: Popular Press, 1972). Each has an extensive bibliography. Like everyone else interested in this subject, I work under the shadow of four pivotal studies: Sidney Hook, *The Hero in History* (New York: John Day, 1942); Dixon Wecter, *The Hero in America* (New York: Charles Scribner's, 1941; reprint, Ann Arbor, Mich.: University of Michigan Press, 1966); Joseph Campbell, *The Hero with a Thousand Faces* (New York: Pantheon, 1949); and Otto Rank, *The Myth of the Birth of the Hero: A Psychological Interpretation of Mythology* (New York: Robert Brunner, 1957).

2. The theory that the hero is generated by the *demos'* needs, and is the answer to our prayers, is fully developed by Bill Butler, *The Myth of the Hero* (London: Rider, 1979).

3. Bryan R. Wilson, *The Noble Savages: The Primitive Origins of Charisma and Its Contemporary Survival* (Berkeley: University of California Press, 1975).

4. Hidetoshi Kato, "From Pantheon to Presley: Changes in Urban Symbolism," in *Communication and the City: The Changing Environment*, Paper 7 of the East-West Communication Institute, Honolulu, Hawaii, November 1973.

5. Campbell, *Hero with a Thousand Faces*, p. 107.

6. Kenneth Scott Latourette, *A Short History of the Far East*, 4th ed. (New York: Macmillan, 1964), p. v.

7. See John F. Cady, *Thailand, Burma, Laos, and Cambodia* (New York: Prentice-Hall, 1966). Important for intercultural understanding is chapter

6, "The Impact of Colonial Rule." Nor are other non-Western areas given the attention and understanding they deserve. See, for example, James W. Buel, *Heroes of the Dark Continent* (London: Faber, 1890) and Martha B. Banks, *Heroes of the South Seas* (New York: Macmillan, 1896).

8. Ravi Shankar, *My Music, My Life* (New York: Simon & Schuster, 1968), p. 9. Another helpful study in this context is Harold Rosenberg, *Tradition of the New* (New York: Horizon, 1959).

9. Arnold A. Rogow, "The Revolt Against Social Equality," in *Dissent*, 4, Autumn 1957.

10. For a full discussion of these matters see Otto Rank, *The Birth of the Hero and Other Essays* (New York: Vintage Books, 1964); David Malcolmson, *Ten Heroes* (New York: Duell, 1939); and Campbell, *Hero with a Thousand Faces*.

11. Marcus Cunliffe, *George Washington: Man and Monument* (New York: Mentor, 1958), p. 213.

12. Marshall Fishwick, "The Man in the White Marble Toga," in *Saturday Review*, February 20, 1960, p. 12.

13. For more on this, see Ralph H. Gabriel, *The Course of American Democratic Thought* (New York: Ronald Press, 1956), pp. 103ff. For the continuation of folk-produced symbolism, see Merrill Peterson, *The Jefferson Image in the American Mind* (New York: Oxford University Press, 1960) and John Williams Ward, *Andrew Jackson: Symbol for an Age* (New York: Oxford University Press, 1962).

14. Of the many who have tried to describe this process, the three most successful have been Daniel J. Boorstin, Bernard Mayo, and Dixon Wecter. See Boorstin, "The Mythologizing of George Washington," in *The Americans: The National Experience* (New York: Random House, 1967), pp. 337–356; Mayo, "Washington 'Freedom's Myth' and 'More Than Man,' " *Myths and Men* (New York: Harper & Row, 1959), pp. 37–60; and Wecter, "President Washington and Parson Weems," in *Hero in America*, pp. 99–147. For an extended introduction to the most famous legend-maker and his work, see Marcus Cunliffe's edition of Mason L. Weems, *The Life of Washington* (Cambridge: Belknap Press, 1962), pp. ix-xii. All these can be profitably studied against the background of Cunliffe's *George Washington: A Biography in His Own Words* (New York: Harper & Row, 1972).

15. Yonosuke Nagai, "The United States is Disintegrating," in *Psychology Today*, May 1972, p. 26.

16. Eldridge Cleaver, *Souls on Ice* (New York: McGraw-Hill, 1968), p. 49. Cleaver's soul had thawed considerably by 1983, when he toured the country on behalf of a conservative religious group (the Moonies), urging audiences to love America.

17. Harold Lubin, *Heroes and Anti-Heroes* (San Francisco: Chandler

Press, 1968); and Roger R. Rollin, *Hero/Anti-Hero* (New York: n.p., 1973). Both deal with the literature of the period and include bibliographies.

18. Lubin, *Heroes and Anti-Heroes*, p. 21.

19. Wilson, *Noble Savages*, p. 231.

20. Ronald Reagan, "Unforgettable John Wayne," *Reader's Digest*, October 1979, p. 117.

21. Of the many articles written on this subject, three of the most insightful are Allan Fotheringham, "A Lifetime of Rehearsals from Stagecoach to Stage," *Macleans*, July 28, 1890; Walter R. Fisher, "Rhetorical Fiction and the Presidency," *Quarterly Journal of Speech*, 66, April 1980; and Sarah Russell Hankins, "Archetypal Alloy: Reagan's Rhetorical Image," presented at the Western Speech Communication Association Convention, February 21, 1982.

22. Kurt Ritter, "Ronald Reagan and 'The Speech': The Rhetoric of Public Relations," *Western Speech*, Winter 1982.

23. Hankins, "Archetypal Alloy," p. 21.

24. The title is suggested by Pat Oliphant in *Oliphant: An Informal Gathering* (New York: Simon & Schuster, 1978), p. 88.

25. See David S. Bertolloti, "The Astro-Political Hero," in Ray Browne and Marshall Fishwick, eds., *The Hero in Transition* (Bowling Green, Ohio: Popular Press, 1983). Tom Wolfe explores the matter fully in *The Right Stuff* (New York: Simon & Schuster, 1979).

26. *Life*, March 3, 1961, pp. 24–31. Already spacemen "possessed a prestige that makes them front page news."

27. The Greeks could be sure their heroic past was not unforgotten knowing the derivation of SHAZAM: S—Solomon, H—Hercules, A—Atlas, Z—Zeus, A—Achilles, M—Mercury.

28. For details of these and many other heroic transformations, see Jules Feiffer, *The Great Comic Book Heroes* (New York: Basic Books, 1965); Tristram P. Coffin and Henning Cohen, eds., *The Parade of Heroes: Legendary Figures in American Lore* (New York: Dutton, 1978); Hubert H. Crawford, *Crawford's Encyclopedia of Comic Books* (Middle Village, N.Y.: Village Press, 1978); and *Thor*, vol. 1, no. 319, May 1982.

THEOS _____ 4

Our government makes no sense unless it is founded in a
deeply felt religious faith—and I don't care what it is.

Dwight D. Eisenhower,
Peace With Justice: Selected Addresses

Theos in Greek means God. Combined with *legein*—to speak—
we get theology: the critical, historical, and psychological study
of *theos*. Wherever *demos* is, there will *theos* be too—often looking down from a high mountain (Sinai, Olympus, Kilimanjaro,
Fujiyama) in judgment. *Theos* is the Fourth Pillar of Popular
Culture.

Early Greek philosophers distinguished three kinds of theologia—mythical, natural (rational), and civil, the last dealing with
popular public rites and ceremonies. Tertullian, St. Augustine,
and many Church Fathers used the division. Another patristic
Greek use was "the account of God, or the record of God's
ways." With Peter Abelard (1120–1140), *Theologia* was conceived as a department of academic study centering on the Bible; hence the earliest English use.[1] This "science of things divine" was long the Queen of the Sciences. Theology took on
various categories: dogmatic beliefs (endorsed by the Church);
natural (theology based upon natural facts apart from revelation); and pastoral (religious truth in relation to the spiritual
needs of man). Because the questions involved are eternal, they
are also perennial.

In his recent book on *Popular Religion in America*, Peter W.
Williams agrees that we have only to scratch slightly our modern secularized skin to find the *theos* of old; but he insists on
defining "popular religion" as various phenomena (revivals,

reading, religious literature, electronic religious programming) that exist outside the organized structure of the churches.[2] I opt for the broader view and interpretation: *theos* is popular in and out of church, century after century, culture after culture. God need not spend his time on a mountain top. He can—and does—fit in where He can.

Let me give you an example: "Our Lady of Exxon," a squat gray-brick building, snuggled in between two white-and-blue Exxon signs in the busy Washington suburb of Rosslyn, Virginia. While attendants pump gas on one level, the preacher pumps God on another.[3] "I told them if they can pump as much downstairs as we're pumping upstairs, they're doing good!" the Preacher told me. I had found both the metaphor and the title I was seeking: *The God Pumpers: Theos in America*.

There are, admittedly, embarrassing moments for "Our Lady." Recently when a wedding service reached the "Speak now or forever hold your peace" stage, an Exxon mechanic revved up a 3,000 horsepower race car; only a quick trip downstairs quieted the work long enough to finish the service. Both the couple and the car got off to a good start.

Why not a combination double-filling station (gas and God) in the 1980s? Are these not, after all, two American essentials? And has not God always chosen His own way of entering our lives and cultures?

America is saturated with pollution, persuasion, and popular religion. Much of the pollution is of recent origin; persuasion (as now practiced) has taken to new media and messages; but popular religion has been with us for centuries. This great land was, in fact, explored and conquered by zealous God-Pumpers. Long before they arrived, the native Americans were profoundly dedicated to the Great Spirit. Their approaches to the landscape were essentially religious; that of the European invaders, economic. The Indians knew this land was strong medicine; only after we had destroyed much of their culture and religion did we find out how right they were.

With all the changes of cultures and technologies and lifestyles, God has always been popular in America. Americanism has, in itself, become a kind of popular religion. Twenty years after the "God is dead" movement (an elitist idea that only caused the fundamentalists and evangelists to pump harder) the "official" statistics of the *Yearbook of American and Canadian Churches* indicated that in 1982, church membership was growing twice as fast as the population.[4] The 1984 Republican Convention in Dallas took on the guise of an evangelical revival service. Somebody sure must be pumping.

Most of the growth (however measured) is occuring with the theologically conservative churches and the Roman Catholics. The so-called mainline Protestant churches, such as Baptist, Methodist, Episcopal, and Presbyterian, are still losing members, although at a slower rate than in recent years. The move is to the right—in politics, religion, economics, and education.

Geography and sociology still matter. No matter how mobile we claim to be, there is still a strong correlation between map and church. The Solid South remains solidly Baptist, the "border states" from Maryland to Kansas have strong Methodist leanings, while the upper Midwest abounds with Lutherans. Utah is a Mormon empire, while the Northeast and the Great Lakes are predominantly Roman Catholic. Protestants dig in deep in suburbia, and are all but unassailable.[5] One recalls the old Bantu proverb: "He who never visits thinks his mother is the only cook." We are not nearly as mobile and media-saturated as some claim. We deal with cocoons of meaning, webs of belonging, emotional loyalties. Such things give meaning to the term "popular religion."

But the regions themselves are changing, along with attitudes of churches and their members. In no area of American life is the changeover from traditional rural society to electronic urban society more dramatically revealed than in religion. Literally millions of people have made the switch in their own lifetime, or grown up with parents who made the transition. We are only beginning to understand what this means. Tradition—however defined or understood—has long been assigned to preindustrial societies and folklore. When we substituted *mechanical* solidarity for *organic* solidarity, the very foundations on which we had built crumbled. It was, Max Weber noted, the ascendance of the mechanistic over the traditional that determined the trend of development—and religion—in modern societies.[6]

In the bleak hills of East Tennessee, the symbol, words, and people all agree that *theos* is a central part of their lives. *Photo by the author.*

For untold centuries, traditional societies were ruled by elites who had the mandate of Heaven. Then a series of revolutions—in America, France, Russia—insisted on widespread participation by the people, using secular values of justice, freedom, and efficiency. The churches (which had held the keys to Heaven) were not only separated from, but in some instances suppressed by, the state. In no place was the change more dramatic than in the British colonies that became the United States. It is on them that we shall focus.[7]

We must study not only cultural change but also cultural resonance—events or images that evoke deep emotional response (positive or negative) from large numbers of people. Think of the "resonance" of Christmas, Fourth of July, Super Bowl, state fairs, presidential campaigns, Miss America contests, the World Series, Mickey Mouse, Michael Jackson, John Paul II, Billy Graham, Bob Hope, and Jane Fonda. Such items, rich in symbolic content, touch both our sense of the past and our anticipation of the future. They are ultimately *serious*—which is what Paul Tillich says is the best definition of "religion."

Such resonance and reputation is continually contested and changing in our dynamic pluralistic society. Cultural resonance is what makes "news," day after day; it is also the clue to the dissolution of consensus—the breakup. We shall have to keep it constantly in mind when examiing *theos*, American style.[8]

The Judeo-Christian tradition, introduced by the first American settlers, reinforced by nearly all who came later, and perpetuated by conscious constant effort, was the chief stone on which American life rested. No other intellectual interest, Merle Curti points out, has served so effectively to unify the different classes, regions, and ethnic groups.[9] There was a common core of beliefs and values, a common Judeo-Christian conception of human nature, social relationships, and the nature of knowledge and beauty. The fact that Christianity sprang from Judaism, greatly emphasized in Puritan thought, made the lot of the Jewish minority in America much better than in much of Europe. "In God We Trust" seemed to hit a strong central note for both religions. It still does.

What is "characteristically American," Ralph Barton Perry points out, is the general Hebraic-Christian-Biblical tradition,

transmitted from generation to generation, continuously af-
firmed by our churches, sects, and cults, nourished by reading
and rereading a standard body of literature whose metaphors,
parables, and forms of thought saturate our culture.[10] All this
embraces ideas so familiar that, like the air, they are inhaled
without effort or attention. The most fundamental of these is
the idea of one personal God, the Creator of nature and the ruler
of mankind, flanking human life on all sides—above, below, at
the beginning and end of time. This God is invested with *pa-
rental* attributes: like a father he both loves and chastens his human children who, having erred, are restored to favor and af-
firmed in their innate attributes by a way of salvation
exemplified, if not mediated, by Jesus of Nazareth. Within this
broad framework there is room for countless differences of detail in matters of dogma and worship, for differences of pious
fervor, and for differences of strictness.

From the first, American community and cohesion rested on
two factors: Biblical religion and unlimited individualism. To
name the factors is simple enough; to analyze them takes a lifetime. Certain thinkers, like Thomas Hobbes and John Locke,
certainly played key roles. Locke crossed the ocean with the help
of American thinkers like Thomas Jefferson, who managed, after
a long colonial struggle, to shape a free, independent republic,
in which both church and state flourished separately.

Whoever came to America had to have a reason for coming;
at one time or another, he had to declare the intention (at
whatever level of consciousness) of exchanging an existing set
of conditions for another in a new land. The American was
purposeful from the outset; each of the first generation, as he
decided to emigrate, did so with a sense of resolution. Even the
transported thief or the indentured servant must have asked how
he happened to be where he was, and must have sought some
kind of answer. Everyone who made up the first waves of migration felt that his presence in America had some purpose. They
all arrived in the New World with an expectation, whether dimly
or precisely formed.

Some found these expectations met by churches; others by
sects; others by cults. Still others rejected the whole religious
framework: agnosticism and atheism have deep roots too. As

used here, "church" shall mean a well-ordered body or community, rooted in the past, emphasizing an official creed or
confession of faith. The Lutherans have their Augsburg
Confession, the Dutch Church their Confession of the Synod of
Dort, the Presbyterians their Westminister Confession, the
Church of England their Thirty-Nine Articles. Classical Protestantism accepted and practiced the state church principle rather
than those of the sects. What the church affirms, the sect de-
nies: state churches, creeds, and confessions of faith. The Bible
is seen as the only rule of faith and practice—one thinks of such
groups as the Church of God, Assemblies of God, Pilgrim Holiness, and Seventh-Day Adventists.[11] Being simple and easy to
form, the sect has had great appeal to ordinary Americans—
and has made tremendous contributions in the area of freedom
of conscience and its corollaries.

A cult is a religious group seeking special authority outside
the traditional Christian tradition. Additional "scriptures" or
inspired leaders carry them beyond the general Christian claims.
The largest and most important American cult is Mormonism—
which in the late twentieth century is one of the fastest-grow-
ing religious groups in the world. *The Book of Mormon* is considered of divine authenticity, of equal authority with the Bible. Another major American cult, Christian Science, considers
Mary Baker Eddy's *Science and Health* an absolute necessity for
a correct understanding of the Bible. Theosophy and New
Thought are other cults affecting popular American religion.[12]
Even in this brief survey of our religious roots, we must note
the power of sects and cults. The common denominator, which
holds not only diverse groups but also peoples and ideologies
together, is the Myth of the Chosen People.

Once God had launched the new Israel in the New World,
the "chosen people" idea gained credibility and importance.
Preservation of this conviction of God-elected uniqueness was
part of the country's survival apparatus. The kind of government we established was different from any that had ever preceded it—violating, as a matter of fact, almost all traditionally
accepted European rules for successful governments. If it *were*
to succeed, the Founding Fathers realized that they had to preserve their conviction of God's guidance.

They considered their society irreconcilably different from Europe's; to survive they must continue to emphasize the differences. Hector St. John Crèvecoeur put it this way in *Letters of an American Farmer*: "The American is a new man, and acts upon new principles; he must therefore entertain new ideas and form new opinions." There was no other way for Americans to think and act if they were to accomplish their divine mission.

Thus when Tom Paine remarked that "My country is the world; my countrymen are all mankind," he succinctly expressed how American revolutionaries meant to give their principles universal application. So too Jefferson, in his belief that his generation "acted not for ourselves alone, but for the whole human race," implied that those ideals which motivated the colonies were ultimately exportable.

Americans have pumped God because they were the chosen of God: their first and continual assignment smacked of Mission Impossible. They were sent into the untamed wilderness in order to found a society in which the individual would possess all that liberty to which God had entitled him, far from the interferences of Europe, free from the burden of the prejudiced past, to become an inspiration and a model to the world.

Since its beginnings, this conviction of mission and of special providence has provided the core of America's religions. Edward Johnson, who came to Massachusetts in 1630, saw the new country as "the place where the Lord will create a new Heaven, and a new Earth, new Churches, and a new Common-wealth together." Johnson and his fellow settlers were convinced that God had brought them to New England for providential purposes—just as He had once directed Moses and the children of Israel.

To Americans, caught in the serpentine twists of late twentieth-century power politics, the literature of our seventeenth- and eighteenth-century forefathers is almost too idealistic, naive, and optimistic to be believed. John Winthrop, writing in his *Journal*, expressed the hope that this new society would be so constructed that "men shall say of succeeding planations: the Lord makes it like that of New England. For we must consider that we shall be as a city on a hill, the eyes of all people upon us." The Revolutionary generation, too, was conscious of the responsibility which rested upon the new nation to provide a paradigm for the world. The Declaration of Independence embodied the notion that its framers had an overpowering sense of the importance of the document, that they believed they were doing something of great import to the future of mankind. Issues of far greater importance than taxes or parliamentary authority led them to ask the judgment of "the Supreme Judge of the World" and the protection of "Divine Providence." The Reverend Timothy Dwight believed the United States to be "by Heaven designed, the example bright, to renovate mankind." Philip Freneau had a vision of America as "a new Jerusalem sent down from Heaven" to serve "a pattern for the world beside." His fellow-poet Joel Barlow hailed the founding of the Republic as "the mild morning, where the dawn begins, the full fruition of the hopes of man."

Dramatic stories, dating back to the early settlements, illustrate the claim. On a bitter cold night in February, 1675, Indians ravaged the little town of Lancaster, Massachusetts. The details never faded from the mind of the minister's wife, Mary Rowlandson. "We had six stout dogs belonging to our garrison," she later recorded, "but none of them would stir. So another time, if any Indian had come to the door, they were ready to fly upon him and tear him down. The Lord hereby would make us the more to acknowledge His hand, and to see that our help is always in Him." [13]

Everything that happened in early America was related to divine providence. God's hand was everywhere. Pilgrims risked all to find a new Haven, a new Canaan, a new England. We wrong our colonial ancestors if we think of them merely as a bigoted, stiff-necked people. There were plenty of taverns, celebrations, and merriment in the early settlements. And there was abundant faith in a righteous, just God who still thundered. Their faith was realistic and intolerant of evil. In time of prosperity it filled their hearts with joy; in time of scarcity, with fortitude. They understood well that they were strangers in this cruel land, destined to go to a better one. Justice, repentence, and the pursuit of happiness were indivisible. For centuries after Atlantic settlement, the main thrust of American religion stemmed from the Reformation. Even when the Puritan ethic is derided, it is secretly admired. Over three centuries have passed since the little town of Lancaster was overrun, but the Puritan spirit still stalks the land. No wonder this was a favorite Bible verse of both Cotton Mather and Ben Franklin: "Seest thou a man diligent in his work? He shall stand before kings!"

Colonial America's most impressive theologian was Jonathan Edwards (1703–1758). To study him is to see the old system switching to the new, the head give way to the heart, logic to emotions. Long before America was ready to assert her complete political independence, Edwards saw that a leader could no longer satisfy his congregation merely with logically impregnable postulates. This might work in the seventeenth century, or in Europe, but not in eighteenth-century America. By 1740, preachers had to stress participation in an experience that was not for the privileged few but for all men. Religion must be popular.

Edwards insisted that emotions, not intellect, were central in life. We crave emotional connection with something greater than ourselves. This, religion must supply. God uses emotions as channels for entering the individual and reforming him. God must enter, since passions untransformed are bad; the original sin is selfishness. Virtue is unselfishness. No man can achieve this virtue by himself; grace can and will save him. If we will let God enter our lives, He will. Jonathan Edwards was a forerunner of American evangelical Protestantism.

The movement paved the way for the separation of church and state, broke down denominational barriers, produced widespread ferment among the lower classes, and put an emphasis on activism and lay leadership that American popular religion has never lost. Yet this first Great Awakening was cooled off by Deism—a mild, reasonable faith which had widespread appeal to the educated and strong European precedents.

Deism, which conceives of a god beyond the range of human experience, offers no chance whatever for fiery, emotional preaching: it shifts the emphasis from theological doctrine to ethics. Many of our Founding Fathers, including Thomas Jefferson and Benjamin Franklin, were "mild deists"; even Thomas Paine could exhibit religious piety. Deism is, as the name implies, a form of theism, whose essential point is not the denial of deity, but the affirmation of God on strictly rational grounds. Like mathematics and natural science, deism was thought to need no support beyond that of man's free and natural intelligence; it has continued down through the years, under the broader name "liberal religion."

A second Great Awakening started in the early and mid–1800s; only then did "soul-winning" and "preacher celebrities" come into their own. In the earlier Great Awakening, under Jonathan Edwards, people *waited* for revival. In the new one, people were *baited* and *provoked* into "making the decision." A new form of popular religion was created.

The opening gun was sounded at Yale University where, starting in 1802, President Timothy Dwight was so effective that one-third of the student body professed conversion.[14] But it was not in this cloistered atmosphere that the real effect was felt. It was on the frontier (especially in Kentucky and Tennessee) that the movement took off.

Suddenly the American woods were alive—not so much with the sound of music as the sound of preaching. A whole band of itinerant God-pumpers, like so many new Savonarolas, preached down-home, shirtsleeves, sulphur-smelling religion to huge crowds, lonely in soul and starved for companionship. Tense nerves and repressed spirits broke loose in the name of God: shrieking, groaning, speaking in tongues. Old-timers allowed that it was enough to make a hound-dog break his chain; and guessed that with all the new enthusiasm there would be new pregnancies in the valleys.[15]

Nor was revivalism confined to the backwoods. Sunday schools were opened, missionary societies were organized, colleges were built. Even Dr. Benjamin Rush, a leading American scientist, led the movement for renewed emphasis on Christian faith, writing a vigorous *Defense of the Use of the Bible as a Schoolbook* (1791). All told, historian Dixon Ryan Fox has concluded that this period should be called the "Protestant Counter-Reformation."[16]

No one is sure, but most scholars think the first "camp meeting" (so named because people camped out three or four days, generally around a clearing with log benches and a rude preaching platform) was held by the Presbyterian revivalist James

McGready in the spring of 1799 in Logan County, Kentucky. Other ministers followed suit (William and John McGee, Barton Stone, and William McKendree among them) and the form spread as fast as the boll weevil.[17] Crowds of up to 200,000 assembled; prayer meetings, hymn singings, baptisms, and weddings abounded. Camp meetings became so spirited the Presbyterian Church refused to sponsor them after 1805; but that didn't stop the Methodists, Baptists, Shakers, Disciples, and Cumberland-Presbyterians from singing and shouting their way westward. Alleluia!

Indeed the Methodists, profiting from this popularity, gradually institutionalized camp meetings into their systems; by 1811 Methodist Bishop Francis Asbury reported in his *Journal* that over four hundred camp meetings were being held annually along the cutting edge of the frontier, all the way from Michigan to Georgia.[18] Praise the Lord!

Powerful preachers (and spirits) inhabited the back-woods, no doubt; but it would not be there that Princes of the Pulpits would find their proper milieu—they would flourish in the teeming new cities after the Civil War. Richard Quebedeaux explains:

Within the rapidly growing population of the cities, the spoken word was the primary means of education and entertainment. Anyone who could speak well at the popular level was assured of an audience. A marked feature of the preaching was its awareness of the popular mind.[19]

Pulpit thunder gave way to humor; dead theological arguments to "living" urban problems. People sought not liturgy but celebrity; the focus moved from damnation to drama. The city mouse took over where the country mouse left off.

More than any other person, Charles G. Finney (1792–1875) deserves credit for this. Finney brought the revival techniques he learned in isolated upstate New York hamlets to New York City—the frontier revival meeting to the expanded metropolis, thus serving as the transitional figure and archetype for one figure in our religious history.

Born in Warren, Connecticut, Finney grew up in Oneida County, New York, and became a lawyer in 1818. References to Mosaic matters in his law studies impelled him to study the Bible. At the age of twenty-nine he was converted, convinced he had been "given a retainer from the Lord Jesus Christ to plead His cause." Adopting features found in frontier revivals—especially the "anxious seat"—and pleading with congregations as he would with a jury, he fomented wild revivals in nearby villages.[20] His great gift was popularizing complex doctrines for Everyman, without oversimplifying them. Finney, one observer noted, spoke precisely, logically, with wit, verve, and informality. But he used tricks of the trial lawyer. The congregation was "on trial," and those "convicted of sin" were escorted to the "anxious bench"—the equivalent of the witness stand. Finney used "you," not "they," when speaking to spellbound audiences. *You* were on trial—and the matter wasn't over once you left church. You were pursued. Groups of volunteers swooped down on neighborhoods; prayer meetings were held at any and every hour. There were "inquiry sessions" after formal meetings—often hours in length. Thus did Finney marshal the kind of group pressure which came easy in frontier camp meetings, but was almost impossible in sprawling cities. Instead of taking the people to the frontier, he brought the frontier to the city.

City after city fell under his spell; by 1830, according to the minister of Philadelphia's First Presbyterian Church, every major city had been touched. Finney and his associates had made the urban revival part of American popular culture.

The pattern they set was closely attuned to the Jacksonian sentiments of their day: an ardent faith in progress, the benevolence of God, and the dignity and worth of the common man. Popular religion, in short, was made an adjunct of popular culture—and it has been ever since.

Finney's mission, as he saw it, was to create a universal church based upon the fundamentals of the Gospel. The millennial age was about to dawn—right here in the United States of America. Finney was convinced that democracy was the form of government most approved by God. Combining legal training and religious leaning, he invented devices to get this message across to millions of Americans.

Such devices were soon known as "New Measures" and got

ever wider attention. In 1832 Finney began an almost continuous revival in New York City, as Minister of the Second Free
Presbyterian Church. When he outgrew this—and angered some
of the conservative Presbyterians—Finney's followers built the
Broadway Tabernacle for him in 1834. We can say he was the
first God-Pumper to play Broadway. Thus had he leaped from
raw frontier villages to burgeoning urban centers of financial and
social power. Even before the Civil War and the emerging Robber Barons, he had lived out the rags-to-riches success story,
putting aside emotional outbursts for sermons and lectures which
resembled the lawyer's brief. Finney stressed common sense and
common needs, making the test of truth the number of converts. This played havoc with traditional standards of doctrine
and polity in the churches; in his latter years he chose to leave
the teeming cities for Oberlin College, where from 1851 to 1866
he held several posts including the presidency. He was undoubtedly a Prince of the Pulpit.

His equally effective and more flamboyant successor was
Henry Ward Beecher (1813–1887), the eighth child of the Reverend Lyman Beecher of Litchfield, Connecticut. The father was
competent, but the son grew up to be spectacular, "the greatest preacher the world has seen"—in the oft-quoted overkill of
John Hay—"since St. Paul preached on Mars Hill."

Such genius was not immediately apparent.[21] Indeed Henry
had to overcome a congenital distaste for study even to grad-
uate from Lane Theological School, where his father was president. But he soon tuned in to the needs of his time and wrote
Seven Lectures to Young Men (1844). No one knows how many
young men these lectures helped. But they did help young
Beecher, who subsequently received a call to the posh Plymouth Presbyterian Church in Brooklyn, New York. He accepted. Once there, he removed the pulpit and installed a
preacher's platform which some wag said was as large as Plymouth Rock. Beecher wanted to be near to the congregation. He
also wanted to do and say things that would bring him national notoriety. And he did. Pushing aside his father's Calvinistic theology, he quickly built a radical reputation by denounc-
ing slavery, supporting the transportation of armed settlers into
"Bleeding Kansas," supporting women's rights, auctioning slaves
to freedom from his pulpit, and insisting on giving freedmen

the right to vote. He accepted evolution and the higher criticism of the Bible, yet never faltered in his open admiration for
successful businessmen and chauvinistic nationalism. As Henry
Clay, John C. Calhoun, and Daniel Webster began to fade from
the scene, Henry Ward Beecher emerged as the most popular
orator in America—and held that position for over thirty years.[22]

"This Brooklyn church," James Parton wrote in *Famous Americans of Recent Times* (1867), 'is simply the most characteristic thing
of America. This is the United States, the New Testament,
Plymouth Rock, and the Fourth of July, all in one."

How Beecher got to that exalted place, fell from grace following a notorious adultery scandal, and became known as "a neglected hero of American history,"[23] is a fascinating, complex
story. What seemed damnable to the 1880s seems admirable to
the 1980s; here was a man willing to "do his own thing."

Accounts of the period give conflicting views on how and why
Beecher achieved such popular acclaim.[24] Certainly it was not
based on any systematic theology. Beecher was no theologian
and never wrote anything which attempted to be academic. In
fact, he attacked theological systems and the factionalism that
had split Protestant America into over one hundred and fifty
different sects by 1850. Probably his clearest statement came in
a novel, *Norwood*, published in 1867—the first fully developed
statement of Liberal Protestantism to appear in popular fictional form.[25]

William McLoughlin offers a convincing explanation. Newly-
rich Americans were hounds for culture, mad for self-improve-
ment. For them, Beecher became a model, an intellectual sponge,
sopping up all that was new and popular in art, architecture,
or literature. Through the popular press, magazines, and conversations, Beecher picked up the hopes, fads, and desires of
those whom he felt an obligation to instruct and uplift. How
could he not appear to such a congregation as a Prince of the
Pulpit?

The once Puritanical nay-sayer became a yea-sayer. He left
behind the bleak fears of Calvinism and began to preach "the
ritual of a higher life, the highway upon which our thoughts
are to travel toward immortality, and toward the realm of just
men made perfect that they inherit it."[26]

What Beecher was beginning to perceive, and preach, was the

relationship between industrial progress, culture, self-improve-
ment, natural law, and God's spiritual laws of human development. By 1866 he felt that "we cannot come to the conviction
of the divinity of Christ so well by the intellectual and philosophical method as we can by the spiritual and experimental
method."[27] But even more astonishing—considering his stern
Calvinistic upbringing— "You can afford, when you have done
your best, to take things easy and enjoy yourself."[28]

Unfortunately, evidence strongly suggested that he himself
began to enjoy himself with a married lady named Mrs. Elizabeth Tilton. While the case itself was moot, and the jury split,
Beecher became in due time the classic example of a pompous
ass who got caught off base. The fact that for the last twelve
years of his life, following the 1875 trial, he went on to even
greater heights of popularity, was conveniently forgotten.

The next reigning Prince, once Beecher got entangled in the
snares of Satan (or at least clever prosecuting lawyers) was
Dwight L. Moody (1837–1899). Twenty-four years younger than
Beecher, coming from the same Yankee atmosphere (he was born
in Northfield, Massachusetts), he left his mother's farm at seventeen, went to Boston, and was converted from Unitarianism
to orthodox evangelicalism. Moving to Chicago, Dwight pros-
pered in the boot and shoe business, but decided in 1860 to
dedicate his life to Christ. For twelve years Moody worked with
the Young Men's Christian Association, served as president of
the Chicago Y.M.C.A., and founded the Moody Church. He was
not a prince yet, but he had royal leanings.

In 1870 he joined ranks with Ira D. Sankey, a gospel hymn
writer; the pair made extended evangelical tours of Great Brit-
ain (1873–1875 and 1881–1883), and with a colorful dramatic style
swept all before them. Lo and behold, Moody had to go to the
land of ancient kings to become himself a Prince of the Pulpit.

Full of confidence and well funded, he founded the Chicago
(now Moody) Bible Institute in Chicago and taught the "retail-
ing techniques" which would help set the style and tone of
twentieth-century evangelism. He favored "whirlwind campaigns," counted converts as he had once counted shoes, and
kept records with "decision cards." He planned his campaigns
as carefully as the best Civil War generals, moving from prayer

to Bible study to home visitation. Each city was divided into "districts," to be visited by "squads" of specially trained recruiters. In this sense, he anticipated the massification of religion that would take place when radio, television, and computers came on the scene.[29]

This is not meant to impugn either his tactics or motives. Moody had no formal theological training, deplored "higher criticism" and evolution, and preached the literal Bible, the Second Coming, and "old fashioned gospel."

While he strongly favored various charitable works (no one has done more for the Y.M.C.A.), he did not think this assured salvation, nor a better life. Social problems could only be solved by the regeneration of human beings, one by one. Practically speaking, that meant that the poor should be honest, sober, pious, hard-working, and obedient—a formula that so pleased employers that big money flowed into Moody's coffers. Could one conclude that Moody was not unlike the famous Pennsylvania politician, Senator Matt Quay, who admitted "I work for the people that the people work for"? One has to make up one's own mind, on this and other questions of motive and profit where evangelicism is concerned.[30]

The key point is that each major Prince of the Pulpit made his peace with rampant laissez-faire capitalism, at a time when Robber Barons roamed the land. They preached Christ *and* Culture . . . and threw in a little chauvinism for spice. If Christianity was their religion, Success was their cult, and they took no pains to conceal it. Instead, they linked the two together. *Logos*—the word—and *mythos*—the myth—became a monomyth. They were themselves "Self-Made Men" and believed they spoke for the Lord. The question that we must ask is this: Did their God ever fly higher than the American eagle?[31]

People live by the theology of their times: *theos* is a sturdy pillar. What people confront is not theories *about* God, but God. Theology depends on, and helps create, tradition. Traditions (long established customs or practices that have the effect of unwritten law) have themselves undergone drastic changes, as we substitute robots for laborers, computers for craftsmen. This ascendancy of the rational over the traditional, Max Weber believed, was the primary determining factor in modern life—and hence modern theology. Whereas traditional societies are ruled by elites who have the mandate of heaven, modern technological societies have the mandate of machines. They tend to use secular values of justice, freedom, and efficiency. In a traditional society, the cultural horizons are static. In a machine society, horizons are dynamic—oriented to change and innovation.[32]

This does not mean that old modes and methods are abandoned; indeed, one of the remarkable facets of contemporary theology is its return to primordial or long-discarded roots. In Iran, for example, a "revolution" in the 1970s overthrew a machine-minded Western-oriented nation, and tended to take it back to ninth-century Islam. Even as America sent a man to the moon, thousands were turning to faith-healing and fundamentalism. One out of every four American adults is an Evangelical.[33]

Pray TV has become a growth industry; prime-time religious broadcasting increased 30 percent in 1983. "Supersavers" like Robert Schuller, Pat Robertson, Jim Bakker, Jerry Falwell, and Oral Roberts thought in terms of megabucks. No tattered tents for them; they built crystal palaces, universities, medical schools, and television networks. In the reign of Reagan, America is absorbing electronic religion at an incredible rate—and with unclear results. The notion that "God is dead" seems laughable. You can tune Him in, on not one but scores of stations, twenty-four hours a day. Just *what* God is another question; but then, it always has been. That is the enduring power of *theos*.

NOTES

1. *The Compact Edition of the Oxford English Dictionary* (New York: Oxford University Press, 1971), 11, p. 3283.

2. Peter W. Williams, *Popular Religion in America: Symbolic Change and the Modernization Process in Historical Perspective* (Englewood Cliffs, N.J.: Prentice-Hall, 1980, chapter 1.

3. See Patricia B. Bauer, "A Place Upstairs," Los Angeles Times-Washington Post Service, nationally syndicated article, May 31, 1983. The quotation is by the Reverend James L. Robertson, founding minister of the Arlington Temple United Methodist Church, to use the more formal name.

4. Official—but reliable? Even Constant H. Jacquet, veteran editor of the *Yearbook of American and Canadian Churches* (Nashville: Abingdon Press), warned that the overall figures were "somewhat inflated" as the result of statistical reporting in various denominations. For example, the Church of God in Christ updated its figures for the first time in sixteen years, from 425,000 to 3.3 million. The Church of Jesus Christ of Latter-day Saints changed its reporting practices to include 650,000 unbaptized youths. The growth-rates of several Pentacostal and Holiness churches—in the 5 percent range—raised questions of credibility. In any case, the official figure showed a .9 percent increase in population and a 2.69 percent annual increase in church membership.

5. See Douglas W. Johnson, Paul R. Piacard, and Bernard Quinn, *Churches and Church Membership in the United States* (Washington, D.C.: Glenmary Research Center, 1974).

6. Max Weber, *The Theory of Social and Economic Organization* (New York: Free Press, 1964), chapter 2.

7. See S. N. Eisenstad, *Tradition, Change, and Modernity* (New York: John Wiley, 1973), pp. 10ff.

8. Bennett M. Berger, *Looking for America: Essays on Youth, Suburbia, and Other American Obsessions* (Englewood Cliffs, N.J.: Prentice-Hall, 1971), p. 4.

9. See Ralph H. Gabriel, *The Course of American Democratic Thought*, (New York: Ronald, 1940) chapter 3, and Merle Curti, *The Growth of American Thought* (New York: Harper & Bros., 1943), p. 21. Chapter 3 on "The Christian Heritage" is still one of the best summaries available.

10. Ralph Barton Perry, *Characteristically American* (New York: Knopf, 1971).

11. Here I am drawing from the basic definitions and examples used by William W. Sweet, *American Culture and Religion* (New York: Cooper Square Publishers, 1972).

12. Ibid., p. 95.

13. *The Narrative of the Captivity and Restoration of Mrs. Mary Rowlandson* was first printed in 1682. Here I am using the 1903 reprint, edited by Henry A. Nourse and John E. Thayer, and published by J. Wilson and Son, Lancaster, Mass., 1903. The quotation is on page 15. A good overview of the literature we are discussing is found in Russel B. Nye, *The Almost Chosen People* (East Lansing: Michigan State University Press, 1966).

14. Richard Quebedeaux, *By What Authority: The Rise of Personality Cults in American Christianity* (New York: Harper & Row, 1982), p. 21.

15. The standard account is still Catherine C. Cleveland, *The Great Awakening in the West* (Chicago: University of Chicago Press, 1916). See

also Timothy L. Smith, *Revivalism and Social Reform in Mid-Nineteenth Century America* (1957).

16. Dixon Ryan Fox, "The Protestant Counter-Reformation," in *New York History*, 16, January 1935.

17. See Charles A. Johnson, *The Frontier Camp Meeting*, (1955).

18. Francis Asbury, *Journal*, 3 vols. (New York: Bangs and Mason, 1821).

19. Quebedeaux, *By What Authority*, p. 20.

20. Charles Finney's techniques are clearly set forth in *Lectures on Revivals* (1835) and *Lectures on Systematic Theology* (1847), republished by the Harvard University Press in 1960. Finney's own *Memoirs* (1876) are in effect an autobiography.

21. The standard biography, by Lyman Abbott, appeared in 1903. See also Lionel G. Crocker, *Henry Ward Beecher's Art of Preaching* (Springfield, Ill.: Thomas, 1934).

22. William C. McLoughlin, *The Meaning of Henry Ward Beecher: An Essay in the Shifting Values of Mid-Victorian America, 1840–1870* (New York: Knopf, 1970), p. 125. A number of other studies are cited in this well-annotated book.

23. Ibid., p. 12.

24. See, for example, Walter E. Houghton, *The Victorian Frame of Mind, 1830–1870* (New Haven, Conn.: Yale University Press, 1957); George Frederickson, *The Inner Civil War* (New York: Doubleday, 1965); and John Higham, *From Boundlessness to Consolidation* (Ann Arbor, Mich.: William L. Clements Library, 1969).

25. Beecher's statements can also be found in the more traditional essay format by studying the files of *The Independent*, a Congregational journal which he edited for eight years.

26. Henry Ward Beecher, *Star Papers: or, Experiences of Art & Nature* (New York: Arno, 1955), p. 310.

27. Henry Ward Beecher, *Royal Truths* (Boston: n.p., 1866), p. 214. Reprinted in London by Strahan in 1873.

28. Ibid., pp. 20–21.

29. An early insightful bibliography was by Gamaliel Bradford, *D. L. Moody: A Worker in Souls* (1927), followed by the more traditional story by William R. Moody, *D. L. Moody* (1930). See also W. G. McLoughlin, Jr., *Modern Revivalism: Charles Grandison Finney to Billy Graham* (1959) and James F. Findley, Jr., *Dwight L. Moody, American Evangelist: 1837–1899* (1969).

30. The most comprehensive account of the Moody-Sankey merger is in Irvin G. Wyllie, *The Self-Made Man in America: The Myth of Rags to Riches* (New York: Free Press, 1954).

31. See Robert Jewett and John Shelton Lawrence, *The American Monomyth* (New York: Doubleday, 1977).

32. See the reprint of Max Weber's classic *Theory of Social and Economic Organization*; and Eisenstad, *Tradition, Change, and Modernity.*

33. The best source of such statistics is Jacquet, *Yearbook of American and Canadian Churches*, but religious figures are often inaccurate, and must be used with caution.

LOGOS _____ 5

In the beginning was the Word.
                    Gospel According to Saint John, I, 1.

What would popular—or any other—culture be without words? Spoken, written, recorded; taped and faked, shouted and spouted; words, words, words. *Logos*—Greek for the word or form that expresses a thought; also, the thought. *Demos, ethnos, heros, patri* thrive on *logos*. That is our Fifth Pillar of Popular Culture.[1]

One of our chief ways of communication is with words (as we are doing now, on this page); it is communication that makes us human. The quintessential tradition of humanism is verbal. When we deal with *logos*, we do indeed go back to some place of beginning, some wellspring of our humanity.[2]

Today the word *communication* conjures up images of satellites, computers, new electronic gadgetry; but a look at the root meanings shows how much deeper it goes: *comm*—with—and *uni*—one—& *catus*—past participle of *care*, which means to share or relate. Communication, then, is to share or relate with one another; to impart, transmit, interchange. Think of it as the tool that makes societies possible; the mechanism through which human relations exist and develop. Involved are not only all the symbols of the mind, but also the means of conveying them through space and preserving them in time.[3]

Communication refers to a social process—the flow of information, the circulation of knowledge, the external and internal flow of thoughts—not just to linguistics and media.[4] *Logos* is far more than a static word: it is word, thought, and consequence, all moving at the speed of sound and light. In this basic sense, communication is the root of our civilization, our very humanity.

There can be no philosophy without communication, and vice versa. To be morally and intellectually informed about the world around us is the basis on which communication takes place. Society is a sum of humane relationships in which information is exchanged.

Humane—marked by compassion, sympathy, consideration for other human beings; the branch of learning tending to refine. Education has always had this great goal: to understand, teach, and broaden the horizons of humane communication.

The task is difficult, if not impossible. History was still blind when man began communicating. Scholars suggest possible origins: (1) the "bow-wow" theory—words came into being through the imitation of natural sounds; (2) the "poo-poo" theory—speech grows out of involuntary expression of emotions; (3) the "yuk-yuk" theory—words arose from chance sounds that happened to be associated with events of special importance or excitement; (4) the "sing-song" theory—words grew out of primitive and wordless chants, celebrating special events; (5) the "yo-heave-ho" theory—words develop from grunts and sounds of physical exertion.[5]

Who knows which one (if any) is closest to the truth—the facts are buried too deep in the past. Somehow, language *did* grow; we got *logos*. Today there are more than three thousand spoken languages extant, and no one can even estimate how many words. If language is a miracle and mystery, so is writing. Only man has been known to draw unaided a picture of his environment, using petroglyphs, hieroglyphs, alphabets.

Communication, like all Gaul, can be divided into three parts: beginning, middle, end (sender, message, receiver). Messages exist in three distinct realms: intrapersonal (inside the sender—dreams, for example); interpersonal (between two or more people, within eyeshot and earshot); and mass (largely dispersed by electronic devices to an anonymous audience).

English—the words we are using here—form a mass medium, as does every language. That point is clear when we deal with *logos*. What is less obvious is that the new mass media (film, radio, television) are new languages, with new *logos*. Each codifies reality differently—each conceals a unique metaphysics.[6]

No two media work the same way—so no *logos* means the same in different media. Writing didn't just record oral sounds; it was a new language which the spoken word came to imitate. Oral languages tend to be polysynthetic, in which images are fused and forced like tight knots; written languages tend to be linear, using little words in chronological order. Subject became distinct from verb, actor from action, essence from form. Spoken words are temporary, on the tip of the tongue; printed words are permanent, truth embalmed for posterity.

How the newer languages (film, radio, television) create new syntax and meaning we are still finding out.[7] Evidence so far indicates that all old languages (including print) have profited enormously from the development of new media and languages. "The more the arts develop," E. M. Forster writes, "the more they depend on each other for definition."[8] This much seems certain: Popular culture is popular communication.

Popular culture is also humane communication. Why not look to the findings in the area of communication (as well as in literature, history, art, or sociology, which is usually the case) for new answers? Why try to see words only as products when they are in fact also processes? *Logos* is multi-faceted. No word, no meaning, no culture (popular or otherwise) exists in a vacuum. Communication is circular, irreversible, and unrepeatable. *Logos*—a word, a sound that has meaning. We hope for precise meanings, written down in a word-book (dictionary). But as early as the eighth century, an unknown Chinese poet noted that art is best which to the soul's range gives no bound.

Words have no exact meaning—in fact, they never mean the same thing twice. The time, place, context, stress, inflection cannot be duplicated. The meaning of the *logos* is what the speaker intends to be understood by the listener. Words not only channel, but also form and program thought.

When we think of *word*, we usually think of print and records. The word's original home—and still its native habitat—is sound. *Logos* grew in an oral-aural culture, where there is no history in our modern sense of the term. "The past is indeed present," Walter Ong points out, "but in the speech and social institutions of the people, not in the more abstract forms in which modern history deals."[9] The human voice has been the great transmitter, the human ear the great receiver, for most of man's history. Following this lead, we could go now to an examination of voice, hearing, and perception; language and meaning; verbal behavior; language and culture; and linguistic propriety. We could become even more technical and analyze phones, phone-types, phonemes, morphemes, and syntactical structure.[10] Where does all this confront the *demos*, and popular culture? On the stage, in church, at home, in the town square, at elections: as *rhetoric*.

The Greek root of *rhetoric* is *eiro*—"I say"—and *rhetor* means orator. For many centuries what we now call history, poetry, and drama were all *heard* as oral discourse, and shaped by the rhetorical theory of the time. Invention, arrangement, style, delivery, and memory were all involved—and still are.[11]

Aristotle defined rhetoric as "the faculty of finding in any given case the available means of persuasion." The Greeks recognized the latent power in an advocate who, through logical and emotional appeals and the manipulation of language and symbols, could influence decisions and public opinion. In the fifth century B.C., Gorgias asked, "What is there greater than the word which persuades?" There can be no doubt that H. I. Marrou is correct when he says "Hellenistic culture was above all things a rhetorical culture";[12] for over two thousand years rhetoric held a central place in humanistic education.

Early Roman education emphasized rhetoric. Rhetoric formed one of the seven liberal arts in medieval European universities. The *trivium* consisted of grammar (to teach a man to speak correctly), logic (to teach a man to speak consistently), and rhetoric (to teach a man to speak effectively).

Over the years rhetoric lost its central position, and by the end of the nineteenth century generally meant oratory or elocution. A "rhetorical question" was not meant to elicit an answer but to cause an effect. Then new movements and theories revitalized rhetorical interest; today rhetoric is concerned with all the ways in which we influence thinking and behaving through the strategic use of symbols.[13]

Modern rhetorical studies also involve the description and analysis of public discourse. Akin to literary criticism, rhetorical criticism concerns itself with the values, assumptions, and language style in oral communication events. Most important, it looks at the *effects* of messages on audiences, to discover why and how messages persuade or fail to persuade. Similar to much historical investigation, rhetorical studies are by their very nature essentially descriptive and analytical, attempting to explain the causes and effects of speech acts in human affairs rather than to generate "new knowledge" or theoretical insights.

One possible way to pursue the *logos* in our day would be to trace contributions by such rhetorical scholars as I. A. Richards, Chaim Perelman, Wayne Booth, and Kenneth Burke. This task, already well done, is not central to our needs.[14] We shall choose another route—the printed word—and single out for close examination two popular and influential links between print and popular culture.

Man spoke long before he wrote; but for many centuries—certainly since the printing press—print has been our Supreme Court, keeper of records, laws, and literature. From the printed birth announcement to the printed obituary, print daily dictates our fortunes and failures. Print is our medium of continuity. Phonetic writing translated man from the tribal to the civilized sphere. *Civilized* and *literate* are generally held to be synonymous.

To trace that process, matching *logos* and communication would take us back to clay, the stylus, and cuneiform script from the beginnings of civilization to Mesopotamia; papyrus, hieroglyphics, and hieratic to the Greco-Roman period; reed pen and alphabet to the forming and failing of the Roman Empire; on up through parchment, paper, brush, celluloid, plastics, and laser in our own century. There would be chapters on the Egyptians (who with abundant papyrus and skilled labor worked out an elaborate system of writing), the Babylonians (whose dependence on clay and the stylus developed an economical system of writing), the Phoenicians (who improved the alphabet so that separate consonants were isolated in relation to sounds), and the Greeks (who took over the alphabet and adapted it to the demands of a flexible oral tradition by the creation of words). We would stress the adoption of the Ionian alphabet in Athens (404–403 B.C.), and the emergence of Athens as the center of the city-state federation in 454 B.C. By 430, a reading public had emerged in Athens and Herodotus had turned his recitations into book form.[15]

Yet it was not a Greek, but a Roman, who did the most to make *logos* a pillar of Western Civilization. If ever a man's fame grew from words, and combinations of them, it was Marcus Tullius Cicero (106 B.C.–43 B.C.)[16] So great was his influence, so pervasive his *logos*, that we shall single him out for special attention. In the long-range scheme of things, he comes closest to being "Founding Father of Popular Culture."

Over two thousand years ago Marcus Tullius Cicero's severed head was nailed to the rostrum in the Roman Forum. But neither his voice nor his influence was silenced. This great writer and orator turned out to be the major transmitter of Greek culture to and through Rome, the shaper of civilized speech, a unifying force in the Western world. Cicero has so infiltrated our literature and lore that we have no way of measuring his impact. He has influenced people who never heard his name or read his works. Since little is written in oral cultures, and most people throughout history have been illiterate, we know next to nothing about those whom Cicero passed en route to the Forum; and little about most people in most streets from his day to ours. As a writer and critic, Cicero had measurable influence on the academy; what about on the *demos*, then and now? How does he relate to our Seven Pillars, and contribute to them? Most would point directly to *logos*, specifically to rhetoric. In ancient times, the role of rhetoric could hardly be overestimated; for two thousand years, it was central to Western education. For centuries history, poetry, and drama were all *heard* as oral discourse—but who can say now how Cicero sounded? How he affected those who heard him?

We shall never know. What we *do* know is that he spent years paraphrasing, selecting, translating—always adding direction and emphasis. Depending finally on his own option and discretion, he adapted great works from other cultures to Rome's environment, needs, and tastes. In this sense, he was one of history's greatest popularizers, whose essential insight was comprehending that what could not be digested and passed on to Rome would soon be buried and fragmented. He knew (as does anyone who studies popular culture) that being simple was never simple; that being widely understood was the highest achievement; that whatever people may remember, who said or wrote something is of secondary importance.

What sort of craftsman was Cicero? Did he extemporize? How close were his spoken words to the written ones? The tantalizing thing is that we do not have very good answers to these questions and we never shall. "All the king's horses and all the king's men couldn't put Humpty together again." We can never hear the voice, see the original text, watch the performance itself. All we can do—and have done—is examine every clue, test every theory, string together every hint, and make an educated guess.

Some Ciceronian devices and patterns are plain enough. They helped create expressive, compact prose with its own special harmony and counterpoint. Cicero's genius at subordinating clauses and ideas resulted in an intricacy and delicacy which had never existed before. With him, the question mark and exclamation point came to be powerful weapons. He was a genius with the hexameter, giving literature a new degree of self-revelation and self-analysis.

Style and craft were critical for Cicero. He thought prose should be metrical in character, though not so controlled as poetry. He knew that the ears of his well-educated, contemporary Romans were very sensitive to rhythm and cadence. Once, when he used a double trochee, an assembly was "stirred to wild applause." Cicero never forgot that.

Cicero advised would-be orators that if the order is changed, the effect is lost. The same rhythm must be found in the chief clauses of the sentence. "Read your words aloud. Your ears tell you if they are good or bad."

Cicero's own style ideas changed over the years. In early life he stressed ornament, antithesis, alliteration, and assonance: words were inserted merely to achieve rhythmical effect, the flamboyant Asian style. But Molo of Rhodes convinced him that this florid "Asiatic" style was ineffective. So Cicero lowered his voice, condensed his sentences, and depended more on content than embellishment.

He worked endlessly on a single passage, generally cutting

rather than adding words. His oratory took on the same unity, proportion, and harmony that prevailed in Roman architecture, sculpture, and mosaics. All these could be identified as *classical*. Others come and go, but the return to harmony, symmetry, and proportion seems inescapable. In a real sense, what we now call popular culture began in republican Rome. The individual achievement of Cicero, who brought the Greek ideas over for Roman reading and consumption, was a key factor.

As for *logos*, Latin was Cicero's vehicle. For centuries, Latin had been only a minor branch of the Indo-European family of languages, confined to a small coastal plain of western Italy. About 400 B.C. it spread across the peninsula, beginning an evolution from a crude dialect to a powerful instrument—eventually becoming the glue that held civilization together. Latin, which drew heavily from Greek, had by Cicero's time become a formidable force, capable of producing *classics*—from Classicus, of the highest rank or authority. Cicero, with poets like Lucretius and Catullus, nurtured and shaped Latin into a sensitive means of expression, reflecting not only meanings but also values. To them, speaking and writing were not isolated acts but part of a whole social process . . . the basis of community.

Cicero's greatest gift was his incomparable use of Latin. He helped to distill and transmit Greek learning into Latin, making new use of emphasis, contrast, repetition, word order, questions, exclamations. He learned how to work and rework, making a harmony that was almost musical. While much of his writing (and all his oratory) is gone forever, we still have his early work, *On Invention* (written when he was twenty-six), as well as *On Friendship* and *On Duties* completed the year before his death.

He left us translations, dialogues, discussions. Rhetorical works centered on oratory, technique, and case studies of famous orators. When it came to murder trials, he had no equals. His *Phillipics Against Marcus Antonious* was so effective that he was killed for delivering the words.

Cicero was one of the greatest letter writers of all times. Over eight hundred examples are left, most not intended for publication. In them he expressed every shade of sense and feeling, with a spontaneity seldom, if ever, equalled. Consequently we know Cicero better than anyone else in ancient times—better than almost any historical figure until recent centuries. In this sense, we can say he established Latinity—for Latin is still *the* language of churchmen, scientists, physicians, academics, bureaucrats, and historians. Latin became—and remained—a language of general ideas, capable of serving as a clear voice to human thought.

As every student of *logos* discovers, Cicero laid the foundations of what became European and American prose and prosody. Nor do his distinctions stop here; there are many more. Unlike most Latin writers and speakers, Cicero wasn't overawed by Greek. He was convinced that Latin was the better vehicle for philosophy. That's debatable, but it is clear that Cicero was our fullest source for many Greek thinkers.

Cicero was more than merely Rome; part and product of a vital mix, going back to the Etruscans and Greeks and beyond to the Egyptians, nomad-barbarians . . . a world of art and astrology, circus and senate, sand and sun, dedication and decadence. He was shaped by, and helped to shape, the greatest structure of imperial government and empire the world has ever known. His goal was related to that mix and that empire. From it he extracted universal laws, goals, and formulas that would serve not only his time, but *any* time, any empire. That is why he is our Founding Father.

Part of Cicero's distinction was his common sense, his pragmatism. He knew, as had many Greeks before him, that *logos* is not *phusis*—nature; language cannot be a true substitute for experience. Nature as such has no meaning; men and women must learn to "read" or interpret what is "out there," using what is "in here." What is our best way of transmitting discoveries to neighbors and offspring? *Logos.* Yet there is something dangerous in this. How can we avoid the subconscious belief (since words are so clever at conveying information and arousing emotions) that language *is* a substitute for experience?

To put it differently, objects (the sources for most of our sensations) have properties that have no exact verbal equivalent. Samuel Johnson understood this well, pointing out in the

"Preface" to his *Dictionary of the English Language* (1755), "I am not yet so lost in lexicography as to forget that *words are the daughters of earth, and that things are the son of heaven.*"

Logos—those daughters of earth—charm but deceive us; Things—those sons of earth—remain unchanged by what we say or believe about them. How does this affect human understanding and popular culture?

Few people have thought so deeply about this as Alexander Bryan Johnson, a banker in Utica, New York, who in 1828 published a book called *The Philosophy of Human Knowledge; or, A Treatise on Language.*[17] He pointed out that words have a radical and inherent defect—they are general names or terms, but the things they refer to are always individual and particular. So even though we know that no two trees are alike, the word *tree* suggests a clear entity. This encourages us to overlook or disregard the infinite variety of trees—to take a word that is an approximation as a specific.

Consider the long-range consequence. Since words have this generalizing characteristic it is inevitable, Johnson argues, that if we contemplate the created universe through the medium of words, we will impute to it a generalized unity that our senses cannot discover in it. In our writing, thinking, and speaking, we habitually, "disregard the individuality of nature, and substitute for it a generality which belongs to language."[18]

One result of the delusive generality of verbal symbols is that two people can be in verbal agreement without meaning the same thing. You can say to me that television commercials are sometimes revolting, and I may reply, "Yes, they certainly are revolting sometimes." We are in complete verbal agreement. But the particular commercials you had in mind may not be the ones I was thinking of. Perhaps I have never seen commercials like those you were referring to; perhaps if I had seen them, I would not have thought them disgusting. I might have enjoyed them. The less our direct, firsthand experience of television commercials coincides, the less chance there is that any verbal agreement—or disagreement—in our discussion will have reached any significance.

Verbal symbols, then, are inherently "defective." They are at best a sort of generalized, averaged-out substitute for a com-

plex reality comprising an infinite number of individual particularities. We can say that a pane of glass is square, oblong,
round, or a half-dozen other shapes, and that when it is shat-
tered the pieces are fragments or slivers. But for the infinite variety of forms which those slivers in reality assume, we have
no words. The multiple reality we generalize as "slivers of glass"
can never be known through words. We can know that reality
only through our senses, the way we experience blades of grass
in lawns or commercials on television.

A century later, under very different circumstances, the Sur-
realists were coming to the same conclusions. Rene Magritte
(1898–1967), for example, painted *The Treason of Images*. One inscription ("Ceci n'est pas une pipe"—this is not a pipe) became
one of the catch-words of modern art: a brief manifesto about
logos and the way meaning is conveyed (or blocked) by symbols. What was an avant-garde idea in the 1920s had become a
popular cliché by the 1960s. In our own time, we have seen how
logos, *ethnos*, and *mythos* intertwine. *Culture and Language: The
Black American Experience* is a good example. William S. Hall and
Roy O. Freedle use sociolinguistics as a basis for analyzing intellectual functioning, ethnocentrism, and black identity transformation. They give us a model for probing one of the world's
most serious problems, noting:

> The fleshing out of such a model can lead to a greater understand-
> ing of those salient cultural institutions that will make effective use of
> existing subcultural behaviors so as to make the melting pot a reality,
> not a myth, through cultural pluralism.[19]

This generalizing characteristic of language is its great value.
It is what makes human communication possible. A language
consisting of separate words for each of the particularities in the
created universe would be bulky beyond reckoning. No one
could ever master its vocabulary. We can be thankful for the
ingenious symbol system that averages out reality into the mere
ten thousand words that are necessary for ordering dinner,
writing poems, and composing essays on popular culture. And
no harm would come of it if we did not fall into the habit of
assuming that reality corresponds to the words we have invented to represent it.

Yet harm does come, as we all know, from the use and abuse of words. One of the major aspects of popular culture—modern advertising—is built on the art of confusing illusion and reality, not only consciously but also subliminally.[20] Nor can we make Madison Avenue the villain and sit smugly by. All of us are part of the plot. We are constantly committing crimes not only against society but also against words. C. S. Lewis, the superb English stylist, calls it *verbicide*.[21] We murder words by inflation, misdirection, overenthusiasm, salesmanship. From an American perspective, Benjamin DeMott calls ours the Age of Overkill.[22] Overkill is a dense, polluting wave, penetrating the very marrow of the culture. Speech and song, poem and proclamation, are all affected. Little by little, things get worse, leading to episodes of uncommon vulgarity and tastelessness. Overkill is essentially the loss of belief in a substantive outer reality—the same thing Dr. Johnson warned us about in 1755, and Alexander Johnson in 1828. Looking back on the sixties, when overkill ran riot, DeMott asks if verbal dementia is not the other side of the coin of physical violence—a sobering and serious question which anyone concerned with popular culture must ponder.[23] If the Pillar we have called *logos* goes, what else can stand?

This does not mean that we can set words in concrete and deny the fluidity and adaptability which is their greatest asset. Even the most common and crucial words can never be more than approximations. Words change with circumstances; *logos* is wedded to *ethos*. No meaning (and no popular culture) exists outside the *demos*. The pillars we are describing are intertwined and interlocking. The complexity and intricacy overwhelms us. We resort to jargon (specialized technical language that is fundamentally impersonal and serious) and to slang (basically friendly and humorous).[24] We rub one cliché against another until finally we have an archetype.[25] No wonder then that both popular and academic vocabularies are hagridden with ambiguity. Words and phrases melt into each other with a lack of coherence more suggestive of Franz Kafka or Archie Bunker than of Aristotle. Argument becomes so confused with the ease with which terms avoid meaning that there is no argument at all. Bombarded with words, we are sometimes shell-shocked, more often confused. Some of this, Richard Hoggart points out, is caused by the communicators themselves, posing as Messianic fixers equipped with elaborate jargon.[26]

If languages, words, and messages have increased almost beyond belief (more communication research has been published in this generation than in the whole prior history of communication studies), the results are not entirely gratifying. David Cohn asserts that we are living in a night of total crisis, in which great Truths are denied or distorted, or what Eric Fromm calls our "syndrome of decay": love of death, malignant narcissism, self-centeredness.[27]

Only simpletons have simple answers. That we should improve the scope, quality, and impact of communication—on all levels—is indisputable. How should we proceed?

All these dilemmas and crises involving the printed word would have been inconceivable to Johann Gutenberg (1400–1468), Father of Print Culture and (some say) of the first mass-produced media. By any standards, he has an heroic role in our study of the Seven Pillars: like Hercules, he seems almost strong enough to serve as a pillar himself.

His achievement, simply stated, was this: he made the printed word available to almost everyone, and this founded mass culture.[28] For generations the publishing business was the tool of church and state; but now, five hundred years later, printed words literally circle the globe and cover the earth.[29]

As more and more of those words were heard, not read, writers in the 1960s (led by their mischievous guru, Marshall McLuhan) predicted the demise of the Age of Print. Time has proved them quite wrong. Not only are printers printing more; we have all become our own printer, so to speak, thanks to the automatic copying machine. (Pity the poor copyright lawyers!) True enough, many major newspapers and magazines have disappeared; the mix between sound and sight, ear and eye, is undergoing radical changes which we still don't understand. The most impressive thing, to me, is the adaptability of old printed forms to new challenges and needs. To name a single example: magazines.

Derived from the old French word *makazin*—meaning warehouse or storehouse—magazines have played a continuous and unique function in American culture. I should like to sketch briefly their history, their current strategy and role, and comment on the way the "magazine format" is spilling over into other media. In this way I hope to show how our Fifth Pillar, *logos*, is finding new uses and strengths in the Age of Information.

Benjamin Franklin and Andrew Bradford issued the first full-blown American magazines in 1741, and another dozen sprang up to aid and abet the American Revolution.[30] These "easy vehicles of knowledge" (to quote General George Washington) helped to explain and enhance the birth of our nation. They have been explaining and enhancing ever since.

"The whole tendency of the age is magazineward," wrote an enthusiastic Edgar Allan Poe in 1824 in the *Southern Literary Messenger*. Himself a magazine editor from 1835 to 1837, Poe set a standard for quality and influence which has seldom been equalled. So did Emerson, Thoreau, and Margaret Fuller as editors of *The Dial* (1840–1844). Other effective publications were *The United States Magazine and Democratic Review*, *The Youth's Companion*, and *The North American Review*, one of the longest-lived and most influential American magazines, whose contributors included writers from Lord Byron and Henry Wadsworth Longfellow to Mark Twain. From 1815 to 1939 the *Review* was one of the leading intellectual forces in the country.

The Knickerbocker in New York and both *The Saturday Evening Post* and *Graham's* in Philadelphia were addressed to the entire literate public. Francis Parkman's *The Oregon Trail* ran serially in *The Knickerbocker*. *The Saturday Evening Post*, starting in 1821 in an office once occupied by Benjamin Franklin, featured a department called "The Ladies' Friend," shipping news, editorials, and an "Almanack." In the 1830s, a banner underneath its logotype set the tone: "A Family Magazine, Devoted to Literature, Morality, Science, News, Agriculture, and Amusement." Before the Civil War its circulation had passed the 90,000 mark.

Graham's Magazine, an offshoot of *The Saturday Evening Post*, appeared in 1840 and published the works of Mrs. Seba Smith, Mrs. Frances Osgood, and Mrs. Lydia Sigourney. It also made pictorial illustration a distinctive feature of American magazines.

Godey's Lady's Book was founded in 1830 by the fat and joking Louis Godey, who hired the lean and serious feminist, Sarah Josepha Hale, as editor. *Godey's* became an institution in middle-class America, affecting manners, morals, fashions, fancies, and diets of generations of readers. Unconcerned with political or economic matters, it concentrated on telling American women how to act, dress, and cope in a male-dominated society. There were also "embellishments" (beauty hints, embroidery patterns, and elaborate illustrations). A combination of good taste, good sense, and feminine intuition made *Godey's* second to none in popular acceptance and influence. Sarah Hale, editor from 1837 to 1877, also had time to write a classic nursery rhyme:

Mary had a little lamb;
Its fleece was white as snow;
And everywhere that Mary went
The lamb was sure to go.

Godey's, Sartain's, and *Graham's* helped maintain Philadelphia as the hub of popular magazine publishing in the mid-nineteenth century. The city's reputation for sophistication, urbanity, and fashion served it well. Sarah Hale championed causes that would be popular a century later: women's equality, physical fitness, and wider educational rights. She not only introduced new writers (like Harriet Beecher Stowe), but she also insisted that they use their own names rather than initials or masculine pseudonyms. Mrs. Hale resigned in 1877; Godey died in 1878; and the magazine hung on until 1898. Then New York became the magazine capital.

From 1870 to 1900 the "modern American magazine" was born. These included *McCalls's* (1870), *Popular Science* (1872), *Woman's Home Companion* (1873), *Farm Journal* (1877), *Good Housekeeping* (1885), *Cosmopolitan* (1886), *Collier's* (1886), *National Geographic* (1888), and *Vogue* (1892).

The "modern" magazine began, then, when nineteenth-century technology and capitalism intersected. Now the real target was the consumer rather than the reader—and that has been the popular culture formula ever since. Consumers were reached by advertisement—the subscription rates hardly ever paid all the bills. Once this was clear, magazines could and did start to fall into categories: juveniles, women's, literary, trade, and general reader, for instance.[31]

American business found a happy home in extending into magazines—early advertisers like Royal Baking Powder, Ivory Soap, Baker's Chocolate, and Eastman Kodak have not changed their minds over the decades. By 1900 over fifty magazines had wide national distribution with a million magazine-reading families. Of all agencies of popular information, nine enjoyed a greater success in this era. And were these not the years that saw America move to the forefront as a major world power?

Cyrus H. K. Curtis's *Ladies' Home Journal* was the first American magazine to reach the one million circulation figure. Frank Munsey and S. S. McClure were almost as successful as Curtis, making advertisements, not subscriptions, pay the bills. Then came syndicates. In 1902 Joseph Knapp arranged for thirteen leading Sunday newspapers to carry an identical "magazine supplement." Some syndicate writers were hacks, but others (Stephen Crane, Frank Norris, Jack London, and Lincoln Steffens) were not. With them came a powerful new movement: Muckraking. Rakers of "muck" appeared in Bunyan's *Pilgrim's Progress*, but the term Muckrakers for investigative journalists and artists derives from a 1905 speech by Theodore Roosevelt. The movement itself cropped up in the January 1903 issue of *McClure's Magazine*. Also heavily involved were *Munsey's, Collier's, The Outlook, World's Work, Cosmopolitan*, and *Frank Leslie's Popular Magazine*. There had been earlier exposures—such as the Tweed Ring in New York City. What was remarkable now was the concentration of magazines that muckraked, either because of a crusading zeal or financial interest. Few earlier journalists had gone deeply into issues. Now editors paid writers for research rather than for the amount of copy they turned in.

Ida Tarbell's fifteen articles on the Standard Oil Company were written for *McClure's* over a five-year period beginning in 1902. Thorough and complete, the articles were concerned with bribery, fraud, violence, corruption of public officials, and wrecking of competitors. Tarbell's *History of the Standard Oil Company* provided the model which would become newsworthy again in the 1970s, when windfall profits from oil shortages again made national news, and a Rockefeller was Vice President of the United States.

In fact, the whole meaning of investigative reporting and the "New Journalism" has given magazines an impetus and importance they seemed to be losing in the placid 1950s.[32] Journalism school enrollments are skyrocketing as reporters and magazinists become heroes in their own right: Bob Woodward and Carl Bernstein of the *Post*, Jack Anderson, Seymour Hersch, Tom Wicker; and nonfiction essayists like Tom Wolfe, Truman Capote, Gail Sheehy, and Norman Mailer. Some say the trendy New Journalism is old hat—that personal, subjective reporting began at least as early as *Robinson Crusoe*. Perhaps so; but we are confronted with a new consciousness, a more complex sense of the contemporary situation. James H. Dygert has gone so far as to call the new breed "Folk Heroes of a new Era."[33] Instead of being seen as a hard-drinking bully or an amoral lout, the reporter has become a serious, persevering searcher for truth in the public service; a person pursuing the factors, not a juicy angle. The superb portrayals of such reporters by Robert Redford and Dustin Hoffman in *All the President's Men* helped the new image immensely.

If some of the startling findings of New Journalism appeared in newspapers, the movement's roots were in *Esquire*. What started in magazines quickly spilled over into other media, as Roger Rappaport noted:

> The elements of New Journalism—basically fictional techniques used by Wolfe, Breslin, Talese, and others at *Esquire*, have been consumed by other media. Irreverence, for example, is a staple of *Rolling Stone* features. Now *New York*, *New Times*, and many others are regularly ripping people to shreds. New Journalism keeps turning up in the city magazines, like *Philadelphia*, *Chicagoan*, or *Washingtonian*.[34]

There are important and evocative similarities between popular culture and the New Journalism:

1. Both are subversive, reacting against the Establishment, whether it be in the university, media, government, or society.
2. Both like the "puts"; both put-downs and put-ons abound. One has to see into, under, and around the material being presented—in the words of Gilbert and Sullivan, "Things are seldom what they seem."

3. In the bull's-eye of both targets is a single word: *Entertainment*. The success of the archer can be measured by scanning a single document: his bank account.

4. The operative word is *now*, the focus is the *immediate*. Old reporters wanted a "scoop"; new journalists want an "inside story." Popular culture is terrifying in its transience. "When you're hot you're hot/When you're not, you're not."

5. Transience breeds tension, irony, and despair. Hence the Cult of the Young Dead—James Dean, Marilyn Monroe, Janis Joplin, Jimi Hendrix, Mama Cass, John Belushi. These died in the flesh. Others die in the memory. "I'll never forget Ol' What's-His-Name . . . ."

6. The tangible and specific is crucial. We want something different, something new: no matter how small or trivial it might be. This might be the key to a "theology." "God," said Paul Tillich, "is in the details."

7. Style is supreme. "It ain't Whatcha Do, it's the Way that you Do It." If an entertainer or writer has "real style," almost anything else can be overlooked or forgiven. "I would like to do a book," Gustave Flaubert once wrote, "about absolutely nothing."[35]

The overall impact of "New Journalism" seems on the decline, but the debate over its significance continues. Who can challenge the statement that Henry Luce, using as his vehicle *Time*, *Fortune*, and *Life* magazines, built a global empire of sorts, which still makes itself felt all over the world? Newsstands of the world are not only covered with *Time* itself, but with successful imitators: *L'Express* in France, *Der Speigel* in Germany, *Elseviers* in Holland, *Tiempo* in Mexico, and *The Link* in India. These words are from a March 1961 issue of *Der Spiegel*, the leading German weekly:

No man has more incisively shaped the image of America as seen by the rest of the world, and the Americans' image of the world, than Henry R. Luce. Every third U.S. family buys every week a Luce product; 94% of all Americans over 12 know *Time*. Luceforic printed products are the intellectual supplement of Coca-Cola, Marilyn Monroe, and dollar diplomacy.[36]

And who can deny the power of that very different magazine empire which Hugh Hefner built on *Playboy*? The "Playboy Philosophy" shaped a whole generation of thinking about sex, hedonism, and "the good life." The so-called underground magazines have flourished for more than three decades—*I. F. Stone's Weekly* appeared in 1953, followed shortly by the *Village Voice*—highly articulate, abrasive, and antiestablishment. Their impact, at home and abroad, was far greater than their circulation figures or advertising revenue suggested. How can we measure the impact of the journals which "rejected the sterile old mythology" and almost turned our society upside down—*Berkeley Barb, East Village Other, Rolling Stone, Avatar, Free Press*, and many others?

Obviously magazines affect our economy and life-styles by stimulating our desire for products and services, as simulations and models on all levels. But they do much more than this. Life is not as ephemeral as the daily headlines, or as simplistic as the stereotypes we get unceasingly on television and radio. The solid values held by millions of Americans are reported by the national magazine, unsensationally but vividly and accurately, in articles, fiction, pictures, and illustrations. The magazine provokes results and reactions. Much magazine material goes into reprints, books, and motion pictures. The "ripple effect" is enormous. Directly or indirectly, our entire population (including those who cannot read) is affected by magazines in ways which no one can accurately measure. So it has always been with *logos*.

Through the first eight decades of the twentieth century, advertisements have become almost as interesting as, and more artistic than, the regular content. (Is this also becoming true of television?) How we live, think, and smell, our purchase of everything from toothpaste to Toronadoes, depends on what we read and see. Has some of the free-swinging, sassy aggressiveness of earlier editors given way to the need for such ads? In *The Mind Managers* (1973), Herbert Schillar says just this: the advertising dollar calls the tricks. Yet magazines continue to lead the fight against big labor, big government, big business, and big medicine.[37]

Several trends are clear, such as the move toward smaller,

more specialized publications.[38] Whether you're a snake han-
dler, skin diver, diamond cutter, or sheep raiser, somewhere
there is a specialty magazine with you in mind. An exact number is hard to come by—but it must exceed 10,000.[39]

Every major cause spawns scores of magazines: the Black
Revolution, Sexual Liberation, and Feminism are cases in point.
In *Sex, Sisterhood, and Self-Delusion: What's Happened to Women's
Magazines* (1980), Mary L. Coakley tried to follow through in one
major genre. Recent scholarship shows how the delicate balance of reader, word, and world is always changing: a new
magazine is always just on the horizon. Like everything else in
the Age of Reaganomics, such printed ventures are risky and
tricky. Many magazines die; but since 1980, for every one that
expired, two new ones were born. Who says "The Age of Print"
is over?

The "magazine mentality"—the well-stocked storehouse that
has something for everyone, with graphics and pictures to
strengthen the words—is affecting other media. Most newspapers (especially the elephantine Sunday editions) are what we
used to call magazines. C.B.S.'s "60 Minutes," for many seasons among the top-rated programs on any network, is a "television magazine," as are its many imitators (like "20/20" or
"Nightline") on other networks. Those who can't afford major
magazines might enjoy the so-called "mini-magazines"—there
are fifteen different ones for aviation enthusiasts alone. Then
there is *Wet* for bathing buffs, *Games* for puzzle fans, *Blue Boy*
for homosexuals, and *Inspiration* for the born-agains. If you
happen to get sick, requiring that you stay in bed in the after-
noon and watch television, you can pick up a copy of *Soap Op-
era Digest*.

"Radio magazines" are emerging in that media, pioneered by
KMPX and KSAN in San Francisco. How about the new technology? Such innovations as photo-and-sound activated com-
position, electro-chemical printing, and facsimile transmission
by satellite might soon allow us to order our *own* magazines,
computerized for our individual tastes, available in our living
rooms. *Logos* from outer space!

Yet this "Buck Rogers optimism" about future communications and understanding has been challenged by some thoughtful

critics. Thus has it always been. We should recall that Plato was opposed to writing things down in 520 B.C.—it would destroy memory. Prophetic Walter Benjamin, who died in 1940, surveyed the tentative beginnings of mass culture as we have it today, and suggested that it would soon be hard (if not impossible) for any child raised in the electronic jungle to find his way back into the "exacting silence" of a book.[40] What he feared from radio, movies, and advertising became a thousand-fold truer with television, some of whose cultural effects are intrinsic in form rather than content. The result, Robert Hughes believes, is to insulate and estrange us from reality itself, "turning everything into disposable spectacle: catastrophe, love, war, soap. Ours is the cult of the electronic fragment."[41]

If this be true, *techne*—the Greek word from which technique, technical, and technology come—is fast becoming the enemy of *logos*. The language itself, so the argument might run, is being "bombarded" by oversound and overkill—polluted by media fallout. Many who teach language and literature would agree. Our schools have struggled to teach the written language, producing semiliterates, whose measured ability to read and write declines year after year. Millions of dollars and thousands of remedial programs have hardly dented the problem. How can this be, with our wonderful new media methods and *techniques*?

Ortega Y. Gasset gave one possible answer over thirty years ago. "It has become impossible to do more than instruct the masses in the *technique* of modern life," he wrote in 1951. "It has been found impossible to educate them. They have been given tools for an intenser form of existence, but no feelings for their great historic duties."[42] T. S. Eliot agreed, pointing out that a technological society creates media and masses detached from tradition, alienated from religion, and susceptible to suggestions; in other words, a mob.[43] And it will be no less of a mob, filled with fast foods and driving fast cars. An even more threatening thought is set forth in a 1981 report from the Foundation for National Progress: an homogenized culture is developing. Prefigured in Nazi Germany and, less clearly and effectively, by Soviet Russia, its outlines are most perceptible in the United States. It is dominated and pervaded by technology.[44]

"In progressive, scientific societies," Joseph Campbell writes, "every last vestige of the ancient human heritage of ritual, morality, and art is in full decay . . . . The conscious-unconscious zones of the human psyche have been cut: we have been split in two."[45]

But have we not *always* been split in two? Is the dilemma any worse today than when it confronted Thales, Plato, Marcus Aurelius, Augustine, Descartes, Freud, and Einstein? Is the "fallout" any worse in today's Washington than it was in Socrates's Athens, where the babbling Sophists drove him to drink? And is the prospect for Europeans facing Communism at the Berlin wall in 1985 A.D. any grimmer than it was when they faced Islam at Tours in 732 A.D.? *Plus ça change, c'est plus la même chose.*

Perhaps it is part of the human predicament to say with one of the major philosophers of our day, Woody Allen, that my only regret is that I am not someone else. But we are who and where we are: the media will be no better and no worse than we make them. Because Woody Allen has moved so easily from media to media and role to role—and because he is a genius whose appeal crosses "brow" lines and oceans with ease—let's give the last *logos* to him. A joke writer in the 1950s, a comedian in the 1960s, a film director in the 1970s, he has become a living embodiment of the best American talent in the 1980s. Starting with *What's New Pussycat?* and *Casino Royale* in 1965, he has given us some of the acknowledged film classics of our generation: *What's Up Tiger Lilly?*, *Take the Money and Run*, *Bananas*, *Everything You Always Wanted to Know About Sex But Were Afraid to Ask*, *Play It Again Sam*, *Sleeper*, *Love and Death*, *The Front*, *Annie Hall*, *Interiors*, and *Manhatten*.[46] His imagination and wit seem to have no boundaries: we find him impersonating tuxedoed robots, talking to Bogart, being attacked by hair dryers, and ordering wheelbarrows full of coleslaw. He prefers fantasy to reportage, but he never flinches from the most agonizing prospect: "Not only is God dead, but try getting a plumber on the week-end."[47] Writer, musician, director, ascetic, he is first and foremost a survivor. "I don't think my parents liked me," he confided to one of his biographers. "They put a live teddy bear in my crib."[48] Ever since then, he has tackled his terrors head on. "Love is the answer," he concludes. "But while you're waiting for the answer, sex raises some pretty good questions." [49]

Woody Allen has not only made us laugh more consistently than any other popular actor—he has also kept good talk on the screen. His continuing success is already a phenomenon of the popular arts; and one hopes he still has a long way to go.

Not only "he" but "we." This is not to minimize our difficulties and dilemmas. The Pillars on which our culture rest seem to be shaking. Even if we contain the nuclear bomb, we are already caught up in a "communications explosion"—and have been, ever since 3300 B.C. when the Egyptian genius Menes consolidated power and knowledge by changing oral *logos* into hieroglyphics. Stone, clay, tablets, parchment, paper, film—explosion after explosion; yet we carry on. "In the beginning was the Word." If and when we reach Armageddon, someone might close the book of human history with these six words: "At the end was the Word."

NOTES

1. In theology, *logos* has come to have a different and more specific meaning: the actively expressed, creative, and revelatory thought and will of God; the second part of the Trinity, identified with Christ in the Fourth Gospel (John I, 1–18). See Walter J. Ong, *The Presence of the Word* (New Haven, Conn.: Yale University Press, 1967) and Bruce B. Wavell, *The Living Logos: A Philosophico-Religious Essay* (Washington, D.C.: University Press of America, 1978). Wavell believes that language contains a natural wisdom of the greatest human significance. Martin Heiddeger has attempted to make the Christian conception of logos central in metaphysics. See his *Introduction to Metaphysics* (New Haven, Conn.: Yale University Press, 1959).

2. Marshall W. Fishwick, "Humane Communication," in *Virginia Tech Magazine*, Fall 1977, pp. 15ff.

3. Wilbur Schramm, *Men, Messages, and Media* (New York: Harper & Row, 1973), chapter 1. In short, human communication is something people do. Of course, animals communicate—and did so for millions of years before any of them developed the ability to generalize on signals they had learned to give. This required *logos*. How did it start? Many different forms of both verbal and nonverbal communication, including kinesics (body and eye language), paralanguage (such as laughs, yawns, grunts), proxemics (human use and percep-

tion of space), smell, touch, etc. How did all this result in *logos*? We are only beginning to get some hints at answers.

4. This idea is further explored by Y. V. Laskhmana Rao, *The Development of Communication* (Minneapolis: University of Minnesota Press, 1966). Looking at the subject from the viewpoint of his own "traditional" culture (India), he points out that communication in a "progressive" (Western) culture includes urbanization, industrialization, division of labor, mobility, literacy, media consumption—in short, widespread participation in nation-building activities.

5. These particular designations are made by Schramm, *Men, Messages, and Media*. Other labels abound in various studies.

6. Edmund Carpenter, "The New Languages," in *Explorations in Communication* (Boston: Beacon Press, 1960).

7. For T. S. Eliot's comments on differences in realism when a play becomes a film, see George Hoellering and T. S. Eliot, *Film of Murder in the Cathedral* (New York: Harcourt, Brace & World, 1952); Bela Balázs, *Theory of Film* (London: Dennis Dobson, 1952); and Alan Casty, *Mass Media and Mass Man* (New York: Holt, Rinehart & Winston, 1968).

8. Casty, *Mass Media*, p. 46.

9. Ong, *Presence of the Word*, p. 23. This brilliant book has been most helpful in sorting out my own thoughts on *logos*, as has been his *Rhetoric, Romance, and Technology: Studies in Interaction of Expression and Culture* (Ithaca, N.Y.: Cornell University Press, 1971).

10. An excellent source would be H. A. Gleason's *An Interpretation to Descriptive Linguistics* (New York: Holt, Rinehart & Winston, 1961). See also Theodore Clevenger, Jr., and Jack Matthews, *The Speech Communication Process* (Glenview, Ill.: Scott, Foresman, 1971).

11. James L. Golden, Goodwin F. Berquist, and William E. Coleman, *The Rhetoric of Western Thought* (Dubuque, Iowa: Kendall/Hunt, 1968). I am also indebted to an unpublished essay by my colleague Professor Elizabeth Fine, called "Introduction to Communication" (1982).

12. H. I. Marrou, *A History of Education in Antiquity*, trans. by George Lamb (New York: New American Library, 1964), p. 269.

13. Douglas Ehninger, *Contemporary Rhetoric* (Glenview, Ill.: Scott, Foresman, 1972), p. 3; and Wayne C. Booth, *Modern Dogmas and the Rhetoric of Assent* (Notre Dame, Ind.: University of Notre Dame Press, 1966).

14. Excellent points of beginning are Kenneth Burke, "Rhetoric—Old and New," in *Journal of General Education*, 5, April 1951; and I. A. Richards, *The Philosophy of Rhetoric* (New York: Oxford University Press, 1965).

15. Here I paraphrase the opening chronology of Harold A. Innes,

whose study *The Bias of Communication* (Toronto: University of Toronto Press, 1964) is indispensable to an understanding of the subject. See also J. R. Pierce, *Symbols, Signals and Noise: The Nature and Process of Communication* (New York: Harper, 1965).

16. To read and study Cicero is a lifelong job. Among the standard biographies in English, those by J. S. Reid, H. J. Hackell, B. F. Harris, and D.R.S. Bailey have much to offer. For the general reader, six recent books in the "Penguin Classics" series, published in England, are a delight. Each has a long interpretative essay, as well as the best modern scholarship. Three—*Cicero, On the Good Life; Cicero, Selected Works*; and *Cicero, Selected Political Speeches*—were edited by Michael Grant. Two others—*Cicero's Letter to Atticus* and *Cicero's Letters to Friends*—were edited by D. R. Shackelton Bailey, and the sixth—*Cicero, The Nature of the Gods*—by Horace C. P. McGregor.

17. Alexander Bryan Johnson, *The Philosophy of Human Knowledge; or, A Treatise on Language* (Utica, N.Y.: n.p., 1928). Johnson's contribution is analyzed by John A. Kouwenhoven, *American Studies: Words or Things?* (Wilmington, Del.: Wemyss Foundation, 1963). He argues that we depend too heavily on verbal evidence. "We tend to forget that a novel about life in the slums of Chicago is not life in the slums of Chicago."

18. Johnson, *Human Knowledge*, p. 139.

19. Robert Hughes, *The Shock of the New* (New York: Random House, 1981); and William S. Hall and Roy O. Freedle, *Culture and Language: The Black American Experience* (New York: John Wiley & Sons, 1975), p. 174.

20. The literature here is voluminous. See, for example, Rosser Reeves, *Reality in Advertising* (New York: Knopf, 1960); Robin Wight, *The Day the Pigs Refused to be Driven to Market: Advertising and the Consumer Revolution* (New York: Random House, 1972); and (for the Marxist viewpoint) John Berger, *Ways of Seeing* (Baltimore: Penguin, 1980).

21. C. S. Lewis, *Studies in Words* (Cambridge: Cambridge University Press, 1967). In book after book, no author treated words more tenderly than did he.

22. Benjamin DeMott, *Supergrow*, (New York: Dutton, 1969). The book turns around "a single simple idea, namely, that people ought to use their imaginations more." and should not tolerate "dumbness before the wonder of language." Bravo!

23. Ibid., p. 243.

24. Kenneth Hudson, *The Jargon of the Professions* (London: Macmillan, 1978), p. 2. Jargon, Hudson believes, "is the natural weapon of highly paid people with very little of any value to say." He then goes on to show how it works in The Learned Professions, Politics, Litera-

ture and the Arts, the Near-Professions, and the Would-be Professions—a splendid and helpful exercise. See also Mario Pei, *Double Speak in America* (New York: Hawthorn Books, 1973).

25. Marshall McLuhan, *From Cliche to Archetype* (New York: Viking, 1970). Any extension of man's sensory life, McLuhan argues, imprints numerous clichés in any language.

26. Richard Hoggart, *The Uses of Literacy* (London: Chatto and Windus, 1967), p. 10.

27. For more on Cohn, Fromm, and the "Doom Boom," see Marshall W. Fishwick, *Zebras of the World, Disunite* (Wilmington, Del.: Wemyss Foundation, 1968).

28. The most comprehensive single volume is Elizabeth Geck, *Johannes Gutenberg: From Lead Letter to the Computer* (Bad Godesberg, F.R.G.: Inter Natione Books, 1968). See also Frank E. X. Dance, "The 'Concept' of Communication," in *Journal of Communication*, June 1970, pp. 201–10. See also McLuhan, *The Gutenberg Galaxy*.

29. S. H. Steinberg, *Five Hundred Years of Printing* (New York: Criterion Books, 1974); and Charles A. Madison, *Book Publishing in American Culture* (New York: McGraw-Hill, 1966).

30. The outstanding work on U.S. magazines is Frank Luther Mott's five volume *History of American Magazines* (Cambridge: Harvard University Press, 1930–68). The fifth volume, edited by Mott's daughter, includes a 250-page index of all five and an extensive bibliography. Other standard sources are John Tebbel, *The American Magazine: A Compact History* (New York: Hawthorn, 1969); Theodore Peterson, *Magazines in the Twentieth Century* (Urbana: University of Illinois Press, 1964); Edwin Emery, *The Press and America* (Englewood Cliffs, N.J.: Prentice-Hall, 1972); and Roland E. Wolseley, *The Changing Magazine: Trends in Readership and Management* (New York: Hastings House, 1973). But of course the best source about magazines is magazines. Their name and number is legion.

31. The process is analyzed by Rowena Ferguson in *Editing the Small Magazine* (New York: Columbia University Press, 1976).

32. Theodore P. Greene, *America's Heroes: The Changing Models of Success in American Magazines* (New York: Dutton, 1970).

33. James H. Dygert, *The Investigative Journalist: Folk Heroes of a New Era* (Englewood Cliffs, N.J.: Prentice-Hall, 1976). Chapter 14, "Pretenders and Heroes," is particularly interesting from our point of view. As for the origins of the term "New Journalism," see Michael Johnson, *The New Journalism* (Lawrence: University of Kansas Press, 1971), p. 152. There had been some early warning signals several years earlier—for example, Nat Hentoff's piece called "Behold the New Journalism—It's Coming After You!" in the July 1968 issue of *Evergreen Re-*

view. See Everette E. Dennis's *The Magic Writing Machine; Student Probes of the New Journalism* (Lawrence: University of Kansas Press, 1971) and Curtis D. MacDougall's *Interpretative Reporting* (London: Macmillan, 1972). The pros and cons are summed up by Ronald Weber, *The Reporter as Artist: A Look at the New Journalism Controversy* (New York: Hastings House, 1974), and Charles E. Flippen, *Liberating the Media: The New Journalism* (Washington, D.C.: Acropolis Press, 1974). Students in my seminar at Virginia Tech assembled a full annotated bibliography in 1983.

34. Rappaport is quoted in Marshall Fishwick, *New Journalism* (Bowling Green, Ohio: Popular Press, 1975), p. 235.

35. Ibid., p. 25.

36. Quoted by W. A. Swanberg, *Luce and His Empire* (New York: Charles Scribner's, 1972), p. 473. Few books tie together *logos* and popular culture as well as does this one.

37. Dorothy Schmidt, "Magazines," in M. Thomas Inge, ed., *Concise Histories of Popular Culture* (Westport, Conn.: Greenwood Press, 1982), pp. 195ff.

38. James L. C. Ford, *Magazines for Millions* (Carbondale: Southern Illinois Press, 1969); and John W. Tebbel, *The American Magazine: A Compact History* (New York: Hawthorn, 1969).

39. *Magazine Industry Market Place*. Annual. (New York: R. R. Bowker, 1980–).

40. Quoted by Robert Hughes, *The Shock of the New* (New York: Random House, 1981). His own duality on these issues makes Hughes's work fascinating. He derides the "Myth of Pop," insisting that even in a culture split as disastrously and in so many ways as ours, the problems of choice, taste, and moral responsibility for images still remain. See also Malcolm Bradbury and James McFarlane, eds., *Modernism 1890–1930* (London: Penguin Books, 1978).

41. Hughes, *Shock of the New*, p. 345.

42. Ortega Y. Gasset, *The Revolt of the Masses* (London: Allen & Unwin, 1951), p. 65. His ideas are further expounded in *The Modern Theme* (New York: Harper Brothers, 1961).

43. T. S. Eliot, "Religion and Literature" in *Essays Ancient and Modern by T. S. Eliot*, (New York: Harper, 1936). Duncan Williams uses and explores the ideas of both Ortega and Eliot in *To Be or Not To Be: A Question of Survival* (Oxford, U.K.: Pergamon Press, 1974).

44. Joel Garreau, *The Nine Nations of North America* (Boston: Houghton Mifflin, 1981).

45. Campbell, *Hero with a Thousand Faces*, p. 388.

46. For complete details, consult the "Filmography" in Myles Palmer, *Woody Allen: An Illustrated Biography* (London: Proteus, 1980). See

also Eric Lax, *On Being Funny: Woody Allen and Comedy* (New York: Charter House, 1975); Lee Guthrie, *Woody Allen: A Biography* (New York: Drake Publishers, 1978); and Maurice Yacowar, *Loser Take All: The Comic Art of Woody Allen* (New York: Frederick Ungar, 1979). The last of these includes an extensive discography and bibliography.

47. Guthrie, *Woody Allen*, p. 8.

48. Ibid., p. 26.

49. Ibid., p. 121.

EIKONS _____ 6

The war of the icons has long been under way.
> Marshall McLuhan,
> *Understanding Media*

Watch a child fondle a doll or a toy gun; observe his parents rouge their face or wax their car. These simple acts are *iconic*. The *demos* and *ethnos* need not only *heros*, *patri*, and *logos*, but *eikons*—tangible symbols of intangible beliefs. They need to touch the truth. *Eikons* are the Sixth Pillar of Popular Culture.

The word is once again Greek—meaning image, picture, or representations that are external expressions of internal convictions. Icons (to use the English spelling) objectify deep mythic structures of reality, expressing the eternal in terms of the temporary—everyday things that make every day meaningful. This Pillar can be described, in simplest terms, as tangible mythology.

Let us note at once what icons are *not*. They are not messages for thought but reasons for rejoicing. They are not to be debated but applauded. They are not for the learned but the illiterate. What they say is: "Lift up your hearts!"

Embodying crucial values and even some residue of the sacred, icons are constantly recreating power, in accordance with some independent principle. They have good energy, lasting from generation to generation, age to age, media to media—even though the outer form may go from stone to wood to metal to cardboard to plastic to neon. Their power is invisible.

Every age and culture is iconic. History is transformed into *mythos*, mythos into *logos*, logos into *eikons*. We see the process at work in Plato's Ideas, Christ's Parables, Kant's Categories,

Jung's Archetypes, and McLuhan's Media. Iconic form might survive (the cross, eagle, swastika) even when the meaning changes.[1] How, Denis Williams asks, might some future historian assess the meaning and force of the cross?[2] Its cruciform shape has survived many style changes and a bewildering number of regional interpretations. Still the iconic power of the cross is clear, without reference to aesthetics or the vagaries of idiomatic expression.

Icons accumulate and alter meanings; they also lose them. The iconic Virgin Mary does not speak to the twentieth century as she did to the thirteenth. The swastika does not motivate European youth of the 1980s as it did those of the 1940s. Man carries meanings, not merely objects invested with meanings. The image precedes the idea in the development of human consciousness; the idea drives the image on to glory or oblivion.

In *Icon and Idea* Herbert Read observes that "thinking in pictures" is the first stage of icon-making. The ensuing steps leading to the construction of icons were taken in the prehistoric period. All cultures invent icons. Freud spoke of "optical memory-residues—things as opposed to words." The mind is not so much a debating society as a picture gallery. We look with our eyes, see with our minds, make with our hands. Form and formula fuse. The word becomes flesh and dwells among us.

There is a long record of sacred meaning-bearing objects going back to the dawn of time. To the sophisticated eye, the small crude figures of prehistoric time hardly seem like human images at all. Discoveries made by Heinrich Schliemann when he excavated the ancient strata of Troy permit us to follow the development from the formless stone to the human figure.[3] Findings have allowed scholars to date early figures in the period from 30,000 to 50,000 years ago, the best-known example being the so-called Willendorf Venus, coming from the Aurignacian culture. Female obesity, which exaggerates the lower part of the body, dominated these statues for centuries, diffused through the whole of Europe in the relics of primitive statuary.[4]

Vitality is the prime attribute of early icons, including those found in ancient tombs and on walls, showing the isolation in time and space of painted animals. Here we have visualizations of awesome natural animated power. Eventually, Herbert Read notes, such symbolic imagery tends to be "conventionalized, systematized, and commercialized."[5]

Studies in classical Greece and Rome confirm this. Ancient Pompeiians made their domestic house shrines a gathering place for traditional memory, tutelary powers, and gods, using conventional canons and rigid postures.[6] Yet color, detail, portrait quality, and execution made each one different. What David Pye calls "the workmanship of risk" helped to attain a vital, if irregular, ritual group of icons.[7] Similarly, as we shall see, the pop icons of today are constantly being evoked and evolved, redesigned and reshaped, as our high-tech society seeks to revitalize our icons.[8]

Images as well as icons fascinated the early Greek philosophers, especially the Stoics. Images have always been central in the Judeo-Christian tradition. In Genesis, the Bible begins with God's saying: "Let us make man in our image, after our likeness" (1:26). And a bit later it adds: "When God created man, he made him in the likeness of God" (5:1–3).[9] Arguments over how God could or could not be depicted rocked the church for centuries; and what about sculpted and painted images of the saints? How could the Eastern religious concepts of spirit meld with Western ideas of material culture? "We do not say to the Cross or the Icons, 'You are God,' " wrote Bishop Leontius. "For they are not gods but opened books to remind us of God and to His honor set in our churches and adored."[10]

Eusebius, Bishop of Caesarea in Cappadocia (265–340), claimed to have seen a great many portraits of the Savior and of Peter and Paul. The catacombs were iconic centers, both for the *demos* and the *ecclesias*. But the battle over icons raged, especially after Islam prohibited them.[11] Leo III (717–740) tried to abolish the image of Christ in the church. The resulting schism brought a major crisis, partially resolved in the Council of Nicaea (787), which ruled that "the honor which is paid to the image passes on to that which the image represents, and he who shows reverence to the image shows reverence to the subject contained in it."[12] Ever since, the word *icon* has been banded with ringlets of magic; key words have been *legend, belief, sacred object,* and *veneration.*

Icons are associated with age and class groups. They demand a cult, a lore, a spot of veneration. "All sacred things must have their place," Claude Levi-Strauss notes in *The Savage Mind.* "Being in their place is what makes them sacred. If taken out of their place, even in thought, the entire order of the universe would be destroyed." [13] As the old order has changed, yielding place to the ever-new, the sacred spots for icons are no longer churches and monasteries but, in the new statements of man's beliefs and aspirations, on superhighways, television screens, and in discotheques. Wherever they are placed, the icons objectify something near man's essence.

This is why, in the late Roman Empire, the emperor became god on earth, the apex of order and stability, master of a symmetrically structured state hierarchy. The emperor image (icon) became a devotional focus. He became a "holy type," and his form and function changed little from one ruler to the next. So it was that Ammainus Marcellinus could say of Constantius II, "The emperor was not a living person but an image." [14] Can we not say the same thing centuries later of Babe Ruth, Ronald MacDonald, Superman, and the Cowboy?

We can, I think, because icons are symbols and mindmarks. They tie in with myth, legend, values, idols, and aspirations. Because of the great stress placed on icons by religion, some would limit icons to conventional religious images typically painted on a wooden panel. I reject this idea, and seek instead to revitalize the word and relate it to popular culture. Icons still move men, even when they are not recognized as such in supermarkets, super bowls, used car lots, and funeral parlors. They pop up on billboards, magazine covers, and television commercials. Manna may still come from heaven, but much daily information flows through the Big Tube, which constantly flashes images and cools outer reality.

Icons traditionally connote stability and permanence, but pop icons deal with the flux and impermanence of contemporary Protean Man. A style of self-process and simultaneity is emerging; icons, like everything else, adapt accordingly. Objects are the stuff of life, ideas the cement holding them together. Modern man is starved for ideas and objects that give coherence to electric-age culture. What he finds most acceptable, Robert Jay Lifton notes, are "images of a more fragmentary nature than those of past ideologies. These images, though often limited and fleeting, have great influence upon his psychological life."[15]

This is not to deny that religious icons persist, even flourish, in the late twentieth century. A flood of fundamentalism has driven liberal Christians from center stage and reestablished long-abandoned ideas and icons. On the other extreme, the "God is Dead" movement, proclaimed by the martyred German theologian Diedrich Bonhoeffer, had profound long-range effect. Many who are resigned to endure a world without God cannot exist without icons. Those who opt for the Secular City busy themselves creating secular icons.[16]

Communist Russia is a case in point. Confronting well-defined religious iconic styles dating back a thousand years, Marxists tried somehow to humanize divine authority. No matter how they scorned religion, they could not dismiss icons. So as James H. Billington points out in *The Icon and the Axe* (1968), they replaced the old "prayer row" with Lenin and his henchmen—the axe with the crane. After all, the Tzar had been known as "The Living Icon of God." Anyone visiting contemporary Russia knows how desperately the new leaders have tried to do the same with Lenin. Once again, the radical has become the orthodox, the concept the creed. In our own day, reputations of Mao Tse-tung, Albert Einstein, and Lenin confirm it. Heroes and icons survive because they function: when warm for devotion, when cool for companionship. They are indispensable in what Jacob Bronowski has chronicled so brilliantly in *The Ascent of Man* (1973).

Science "went iconic" with Werner Heisenberg and Niels Bohr—some would say with Plato. Since then scientists have thought more like poets than technicians. "Thinking in pictures" is the very essence of icon making. A new generation gets them not from crypts or cathedrals, but from the media and markets of popular culture. Icons reflect the change.

A cluster of compatible words emerges—fetish, symbol, artifact, emblem, amulet, totem, allegory, charm, idol, image. Erwin Panofsky's pioneering *Studies in Iconology* begins by defining iconography as "the branch of art history which concerns itself with the subject matter of meaning of works of art, as opposed to their form."[17] Then follows an involved dis-

cussion on the distinction between meaning and form. Later
we learn that the act of interpretation requires not only "pre-
iconographical description (and pseudo-formal analysis) but
iconographical analysis in the narrower sense of the word
and iconographical interpretation in a deeper sense (iconographical synthesis)."[18]

Profiting from Erwin Panofsky's work, we should apply the
same serious analysis that was used for the Italian and French
period to the current American Renaissance. This would involve not only surface data (identification, description, authen-
tication), but also interior qualities (evaluation, interpretation,
significance).

Most of all, it would involve an intensive reappraisal of the
thingness of things (for our purposes, the iconness of icons).
Filling the space-time continuum, haunting our dreams, things
determine not only our lives but also our fantasies. Primitive
man wrestles with life's raw stuff, stone and wood, until he develops a technology. And as cultures have a technology, so do
they have a history.

In the complexity of present-day icons, can we find bases for
new definitions and implications? Today, as always in the past,
men want to make sense out of the universe. That "sense" must
be made in the context of present time, place, and belief. Even
"natural" facts such as birth, growth, and death are reacted to
in a "cultural" fashion.[19] Every style that develops is complete
in itself and *sui generis*—of its own order. Former styles are no
longer viable because they are not ours. Iconologically, the consequences are profound and traumatic.

The mainstream of iconology in our time—because of its dis-
semination through the mass media—is the popular stratum.
Because of its position, it has received severe criticism. Elitist
critics have long preached that those elements in our lives that
are aesthetically satisfying are aristocratic and for the minority.
Other elements—those catering to and acceptable to the majority—are aesthetically deficient and therefore contemptible.
Though this condescending attitude is still popular among some
aesthetes, it is being powerfully roughed up by such sensitive
critics as Susan Sontag:

What we are getting is not the demise of art, but a transformation of the function of art. Art, which arose in human society as magical-religious operation, and passed over into a technique for depicting and commenting on secular reality, has in our own time arrogated to itself a new function—neither religious, nor serving a secularized religious function, nor merely secular or profane . . . . Art today is a new kind of instrument, an instrument for modifying consciousness and organizing new modes of sensibility.[20]

Many today agree with philosopher Abraham Kaplan: popular art, although not yet arrived at aesthetically great accomplishment, has great potential and is working toward considerable success.

Aesthetically great or small, satisfying or terrifying, the most irrefutable statement about popular art—and icons—could be a paraphrase of Samuel Johnson's contradiction of the philosopher George Berkeley's belief of the Ideal. Johnson merely kicked a rock. All we need do is hold up an icon.

Objects in general, icons in particular, are the building blocks of reality. They are sensitive indicators of who we are, where we come from, where we intend to go. Long after an individual has died, and even his language and culture have disappeared, artifacts remain. By digging into the earth, archeologists uncover the story of the past. Things form the solid basis of our understanding, and concern for millions of human beings who preceded us. Archeology plus imagination equals historical insight.[21]

Dynamos, telephones, cameras, computers, film, printing presses, plastic discs, picture tubes: are these icons not the essence of popular culture? Have they not shaped the mass media and our sense of the holy? Are they not what "really matters"?

The thingness of things has fascinated the liveliest intellects since Aristotle's time. A conscious interest in what Lewis Mumford calls (in *Art and Technics*) "the go of things" has been such an obvious major factor in history that one posits and predicates it in every period, event, and sequence. Yet how few people in the academy know how to deal with—even to describe or classify—the artifacts that make things go. Having defined artifact as "a thing made by man purposefully, so that he transforms materials already existing," the academician goes back to his notes and his lecture.

There is ample evidence to support Professor Harold Skramstad's article "American Things: A Neglected Material Culture." Some readers were surprised to find him singling out
"New Journalist" Tom Wolfe for special praise, since Wolfe
"demonstrates how insights from a study of new artifact forms
are able to increase our understanding of present day American civilization."[22]

More frequently praised is Professor James Harvey Robinson, whose "New History" (now over fifty years old) insisted
that we study not only the written records, but the remains of
buildings, pictures, clothing, tools, and ornaments.[23] A promising start was made in the mid-twenties in the twelve-volume
History of American Life series edited by Arthur M. Schlesinger
and Dixon Ryan Fox in which some attention was paid to "non-
literary remains and physical survivals." T. J. Wertenbaker's
volumes on *The Middle Colonies* and *The Puritan Oligarchy* made
use of material culture. But when Caroline F. Ware edited *The
Cultural Approach to History* for the American Historical Association in 1940, neither her introduction nor the thirty-six essays
describing the so-called new tools of the cultural historian had
a word to say about the historic artifact. Since then, only occa-
sional efforts have been made to look at some of the most significant and enduring items in the culture.

Toys, for example—are perhaps the most important products
of popular art, since they impinge on a completely receptive
being. Archetypal and omnipresent, they are the oldest and most
widespread icons. We have never discovered a culture, living
or dead, which did not have some form of dolls, balls, and tools;
and there has been no fundamental change in them over the
millenia.[24]

We develop relationships with things in general, toys in particular. They affect our sense of continuity or discontinuity.[25]
Toys are delightful objects that give us affirmation and pleasure; we become so attached to them that they smack of the
iconic. But then they are abandoned and destroyed—should they
merit our serious study? Indeed they should. Toys help us to
accept the limitations of the world and to control behavior. It is
with and through them that we pass from the dream world into
the real world. The symbolic value of balls, fires, motors, lights,

animals, and mud stays with us the rest of our life. Toys are delightful objects that give pleasure—and they are tools for survival. Toys of infancy are of a fundamental and universal nature. Their universality may be compared to the mysterious way in which folk myths or religious traditions appear and disappear around the world, showing an identity of pattern, but no provable connection with each other.[26] Nothing is more natural than that a toy should reflect the life of its period and become an icon.

We think toys are "ours" only because we know so little of their history. The yo-yo, for example, has been used in the Far East since ancient times and in the Philippines as a weapon (the user hides in a tree and strikes his victim in the head with it). A form of the yo-yo was brought home from China by Europeans and swept France during the 1790s. America's turn came later. Having one in my grade school in the 1930s was as necessary as having paper and pencil.

Toy making is only one of the understudied and underestimated popular arts, so dear to the people. If few have dealt with the imagery of today's popular icons, many have examined those of the earlier elite arts. Emily Male's monumental study, *The Gothic Image: Religious Art in France of the Thirteenth Century*, has been a standard reference for eighty years.[27] Erwin Panofsky's studies have also been vastly influential.[28] Scores of books dealing with literary imagery have appeared in this century, and continue to come out in a steady flow. Shakespeare's work remains a central source for such scholarship.[29] In fact, the literature is vast enough to allow some confusion of terminology, and hence thought. What some call "stage imagery" others insist is "presentational" imagery; one man's "illustration" is another's "icon." Where does the "mimetic mode" stop, and the "emblematic mode" begin? How does the iconic staging of civic pageantry differ from that of the historic staging? Just what are "verbal images"? Are they mimetic, symbolic, iconic, or a combination?

Further work may reveal answers to these and other long-unexplored questions; it may be that so far as the popular arts are concerned, the branch of study called "iconic imagery" is the bridge between artist and audience . . . the storehouse from which the creative mind can draw, with which the receptive mind is always familiar. Hence they are an integral part not only of popular culture but of common culture, reaching back beyond the "now" to primordial, primitive "then." All icons are, by definition, conventions. The true popular aesthetic, as Michael Marsden has observed, lies in the artist's ability to use conventions in a new way, both entertaining and enlightening a large audience "with a work which becomes part of the shared cultural traditions in a way that is paradoxically old and new."[30]

The Pop Artists of the 1960s certainly tried to use conventions in a new way. They turned from the forests and the fields to the juke boxes and junk yards. "I am for 7-Up Art," said Claes Oldenberg, one of the school's leaders, "Pepsi Art, Sunkist Art . . . the art of tambourines and plastic phonographs and abandoned boxes tied like pharaohs."[31] Along with people like Andy Warhol, Roy Lichtenstein, and Robert Indiana, Oldenberg tried to make art out of the retail emotions, gadgetry, and packaging of plastic America. Yet twenty years later, their work was in the very museums they scorned: they had become, in their turn, part of the Establishment.[32]

Critics must seek a point of significant beginning. This involves not only comparative study between arts but also configurational or structural analysis of the total *gestalt*. The mechanized, trivialized, standardized world of which elitists complain provides the raw material for a new lifestyle. That pop artists have singled out objects for extensive use is an iconic clue. Ever since Robert Rauschenberg's 1958 "Coca-Cola Plan," that famous container has been featured. The history of soup cans was altered by Andy Warhol; hamburgers will never be the same after Claes Oldenberg.

Coke bottles and soup cans are apt motifs not because they are unique, but because they are omnipresent. In the old traditional sense, they are anti-icons. The nature of icons has changed between the Age of Faith and the Age of Atoms. Not the unique, but the omnipresent, triumphs.

Perhaps our significant beginning is actually a return—to the iconic objects themselves. One such object is surely the Coca-Cola bottle, quite possibly the best known artifact in the world. The "pause that refreshes" has become the most popular international soft drink in history. Every day over 150 million people in 150 nations have a coke. The Coke Break cuts across nations, classes, races, and sexes. The company has its own archives and a curator who has spent all his working life collecting and preserving the history and memorabilia of Coca-Cola.[33] Craig Gilborn has undertaken a detailed study of the coke bottle, and has shown how the latest anthropological techniques can be applied.[34] This study is important not only in itself but also as a model for many others we must have if we are to quantify and organize the study of popular icons.

How the Coca-Cola Company itself has expanded and exploited this phenomenon is an elaborate and intricate story not yet fully told. The amount spent on advertising, and the items involved, is staggering. Beginning with calendars and outdoor signs, the company has become involved with trays, change receivers, dishes, coasters, mirrors, clocks, periodicals, posters, cardboard cutouts, signs, blotters, bookmarks, bottle caps, stationary, emblems, coupons, menus, games, toys, openers, ice picks, thermometers, pocket knives, pens, pencils, pencil sharpeners, music boxes, paperweights, radios, smoking paraphernalia, jewelry, etc.—like the Sorcerer's Apprentice, there seems to be no way of stopping the iconic flow. Nor has the company hesitated to purchase the endorsement of athletes, movie stars, writers, politicians, and war heroes. Legendary figures are cultivated too. "The Coca-Cola Company," Cecil Munsey writes in his official history, "has made one of the largest contributions to the legend of Santa Claus." He then documents how this was done, stressing that every year since 1930, Santa Claus has appeared on posters, cardboard cutouts, blotters, Christmas cards, billboards, and magazines promoting Coca-Cola.[35] All this, plus the multi-million dollar campaign on television.

The Coca-Cola Company started the same year the Statue of Liberty was unveiled—1886—showing how two very different icons can serve the needs of an expanding culture. The "Lady with the Lamp," standing at the entrance of New York harbor, has become one of the best-known and revered objects in the world. The statue itself, by Frederic August Bartholdi, resembles the output of dozens of other sculptors and monument-makers of the period. Bartholdi's conventional art was meant

On the Ides of March, 44 BC, Julius Caesar, standing on the steps of the Senate, saw Brutus approaching. Assuming his friend would like a refreshing drink of ice-cold Coca-Cola, Caesar called out, "Et tu Brute?" meaning, "You want some, too, Kiddo?" Unfortunately, Brutus had flunked Latin, and, thinking he'd been insulted, immediately slew Caesar, speaking the immortal words, "Res melius evinissent cum Coke," a translation of which appears below.

"Things would have gone better with Coke."

Because it has moved beyond conventional time and space, Coca-Cola turns up in ads like this one. Here is yet another interpretation of the death of Julius Caesar—and an amusing use of the *eikons* of *Seven Pillars of Popular Culture*. *Courtesy of the Archives: The Coca-Cola Company.*

CALENDAR 1919

This is how World War I looked in the mirror of Coca-Cola advertising. The soldier in the center does not seem to have suffered greatly from trench warfare. *Courtesy of the Archives: The Coca-Cola Company.*

Between wars, America went fishing—and Coca-Cola commissioned Norman Rockwell to paint "The Fishing Boy" in 1935. It is one of the best-loved ads ever to appear. *Courtesy of the Archives: The Coca-Cola Company.*

By World War II, women were not only knitting but serving in our forces—and still drinking Cokes. Chic and fresh in her army nurse's uniform, this young woman enjoys "The Pause that Refreshes." *Courtesy of the Archives: The Coca-Cola Company.*

"Coke is it!" Neighborhood 2/82

Coca-Cola adapts to all climes, all media. Its brilliant television commercials in the 1980s have won numerous awards and countless customers. In "Neighborhood," the bottle itself is fondled in a way that would give Freudians grounds for comment. Notice the number of teeth in these two stop-frame images. Ours is a happy, happy land—in myth, if not in reality. *Courtesy of the Archives: The Coca-Cola Company.*

to turn our attention to myths, not museums. In fact the statue partakes of a Pop Art gimmick or toy, since visitors look out from its row of windows as through the eyes of a giant, thus *becoming* the colossus. Marvin Trachtenberg has done a full-length book on this icon which has aroused more intense emotion than any other work of art in the New World. He points to the symbolism of the torch, the history of female figures of liberty (including the central personage in Delacroix's celebrated "Liberty Leading the People"), and the placement of the statue just when the floodgates of immigration were opened.

Taken together, he suggests, the symbols of Liberty were reshuffled into a new icon, "If the significance of the Statue of Liberty has in our day again been altered, it remains constant in the memory through its association with America's grandeur as Mother of exiles."[36] Restoring it for its centennial in 1986 has become itself a popular crusade.

How does the new Space Age environment affect icons? Profoundly, of course, dunking entire populations in the two great electronic themes of "remember when" (nostalgia) and "anticipate when" (utopianism); so in addition to the new icons, we are shown the old ones in the rear-view mirror. To live with both sets of icons at the same time is the peculiar drama of the twentieth century, recalling the words Shakespeare put into the mouth of the protagonist in *Julius Caesar*:

> Between the acting of a dreadful thing,
> And the first motion, all the interim is
> Like a phantasma, or a hideous Dream:
> The genius and the mortal instruments
> Are then in council; and the state of man,
> Like to a little Kingdom, suffers then
> The nature of an insurrection.

Was it a phantasma or a hideous dream when the world learned on October 5, 1957, that Russia had made a quantum leap forward, launching a space satellite called "Sputnik"? Twenty-three inches in diameter, the 184-pound device was orbiting the globe every 96 minutes at an altitude of 560 miles. The Space Age had begun.[37]

The reverberations of Sputnik, and the "beep beep beep" signal it sent, were immeasurable in social, political, and cultural terms. Questions of the utmost importance were raised— and are still unanswered. Has outer space become the future iconic museum of earthlings? Will these newest icons not only survey but also destroy our civilization? What is the ultimate meaning of Sputnik, of the rocks from the moon which American astronauts brought back—one of which is now featured in a stained-glass window at Washington's National Cathedral? And when the great globe itself is seen through the lens of astronauts' cameras as a cosmic green baseball spinning in endless space, does it become an art object? The ultimate icon?

The real problem is not outer but inner space. We must return to the human center—retrieve for the *demos* the authority that belongs to the human personality. And the visual proof of that authority, century after century, is iconic.

Whether the material comes from reality, or dreams, or both, is impossible to say. Certainly the idea of worship and veneration has always been central. Hence we should ponder the words of the contemporary Greek art critic, Nicholas Calas, "What relics are to worshippers of icons, Dada and Surrealistic objects are to the devotees of modern icons, i.e., things that possess an element of magic, of having been made without hands."[38]

If icons are old, ways of using them are constantly changing. A new field of iconic communication has developed since 1965, when a group at the Johns Hopkins University began research with computer-generated films. Iconic communication deals with nonverbal communication through visual signs and representations that stand for an idea by virtue of a resemblance or analogy. How do films, for example, communicate visual messages to human beings? No one approach or discipline can answer that question. Relevant information from psychology, perception, anthropology, education, popular culture, computer graphics, and other fields must be considered. We are only on the threshold of this new frontier.[39]

Consider this: now we can generate moving pictorial images by computers. The ability to convey concepts by moving images and symbols is a radically new genre. Instead of expressing concepts in the traditional static symbolic forms of natural languages or mathematics, we can contrive modes of expression, using dynamic visual imagery.[40] Soon there will be a science of iconics. How will it affect the humanities?

Icons are pictorial, and everyone "understands" pictures. "Iconic" implies a mode of communication using primitive visual imagery, relying on the ability of people to perceive natural form, shape, and motion, rather than relying on alphabetic symbols defined in terms of arbitrary conventions.

Language must be taught. Iconic images, and structural information about the three-dimensional world, are acquired merely by maturing. Will that be the hope or the despair of the world?

Icons come in all shapes, sizes, and substances. They may be as small as the pill, as large as the skyscraper, as lethal as the H-bomb. They can be outmoded (like the six-shooter), untried (like the MX missile), or unearthed (like King Tut). We have looked briefly at some of the most pervasive—icons which are so common as to be seldom examined. Taken together, they may help to explain the iconic process and our Sixth Pillar.

As iconologists, we must seek points of entry—not just to single objects, but to the *gestalt* in which they function. Scholarship and criticism must catch up with life-as-lived, and with performance. What are our categories, our criteria? What do we have, as we prepare to enter the twenty-first century?

Not much, many traditionalists and elitists moan. Instead of dismissing objects of our increasingly mechanized, trivialized, and standardized world as contemptuous, I argue that they must be treated as seriously as the stuff from which a new iconology has evolved. Either we stand on *these* Pillars, or we fall.

Does it offend you to think that a coke bottle, Pac Man, or a plastic Jesus is in a grand tradition? The Greeks had their mythological metaphors, the Romans their biographical archetypes, the early Christians their hagiography. They fade into history. Like the snows of yesteryear, they had their season and fulfilled their purposes. Today our fetishes and icons are standing in place and serving a purpose. They are *us*. Can we find sanity and salvation in them? In the 1380s all experience found visual form in a single metaphorical system. Will this be true in the 1980s?

NOTES

1. The literature of icons is enormous, much of it centering on religious icons in general, and Russia's in particular. Three classics are Erwin Panofsky, *Studies in Iconology* (New York: Oxford University Press, 1939); Leonid Oupensky and Vladimir Lossky, *The Meaning of Icons* (Basel: Otto Walter, 1952); and Victor Lasareff, *Russian Icons* (New York: UNESCO, 1962). See also Otto Demus, *Byzantine Mosaic Decoration: Aspects of Monumental Art in Byzantium* (Boston: Boston Books, 1955) and Ernst Benz, *The Eastern Orthodox Church* (New York: Anchor Books, 1963). "Through the icons," Benz points out, "the heavenly beings manifested themselves to the congregation and united with it." (p. 6)

2. Denis Williams, *Icon and Image* (New York: New York University Press, 1974); and Franz Boas, *Primitive Art* (New York: Dover, 1955).

3. Max von Boehn, "Prehistoric Idols," *Dolls*, trans. by Josephine Nicoll (New York: Dover, 1972).

4. Ibid., p. 28.

5. Herbert Read, *Icon and Idea* (Cambridge: Harvard University Press, 1955), p. 17.

6. George K. Boyce, *Corpus of the Lararia of Pompeii* (Rome: American Academy, 1968); and Joseph J. Deiss, *Herculaneum: A City Returns to the Sun* (New York: Crowell, 1966).

7. David Pye, *The Nature and Art of Workmanship* (Cambridge: Cambridge University Press, 1968). I am grateful to David Gerald Orr, who has helped develop these ideas in our conversations.

8. Ray Browne and Marshall Fishwick, *Icons of Popular Culture* (Bowling Green, Ohio: Popular Press, 1970).

9. David Cairns, *The Image of God in Man* (London: SCM Press, 1953).

10. J. M. Hussey, *The Byzantine World* (New York: Harper & Brothers, 1961), pp. 30–31.

11. H. P. Gerhard, *The World of Icons* (New York: Harper & Row, 1971); and David Talbot Rice, *Byzantine Art* (Harmondsworth, U.K.: Penguin, 1968).

12. Williston Walker, *A History of the Christian Church* (New York: Charles Scribner's, 1959). See also Thomas H. Bindy, *The Oecumenical Documents of the Faith* (New York: Methuen, 1950).

13. Claude Levi-Strauss, *The Savage Mind* (Chicago: University of Chicago Press, 1967), p. 72.

14. Ranuccio Bianchi Bandinelli, *Rome: The Late Empire* (New York: George Braziller, 1971), p. 41.

15. Robert Jay Lifton, "Protean Man," in *Partisan Review*, Winter 1968, p. 47. Two other books pursuing the same theme are William Zinsser, *Pop Goes America* (New York: Harper & Row, 1966) and Ray Browne and Marshall Fishwick, eds., *Icons of America* (Bowling Green, Ohio: Popular Press, 1978).

16. In his best selling book on *The Secular City* (New York: Anchor, 1965), Harvey Cox argued that Biblical faith desacralizes the cosmos, and takes meaning from icons. The sacred always goes bad unless it is working with the secular. Similar explorations take place in Gibson Winter, *The New Creation as Metropolis* (New York: Knopf, 1963) and Larry Shiner, *The Secularization of History* (New York: Basic Books, 1966). All agree that the secular world requires life-giving icons.

17. Panofsky, *Studies in Iconology*, p. 59.

18. Ibid., p. 241.

19. Myron Bloy, *The Crisis of Cultural Change* (Cambridge: MIT Press, 1965). He defines technology as the "mind-set" which has become the "objective spirit" of the Western world. But he is quite aware that this has not altered the iconic process.

20. Susan Sontag, *Against Interpretation* (New York: Farrar, Straus, & Giroux, 1969), p. 123.

21. Pioneering work in this field was done by John Kouwenhoven, whose classic *Made in America* was reprinted as *The Arts in Modern American Civilization* (New York: Dutton, 1960).

22. Harold Skramstad, "American Things: A Neglected Material Culture," in *American Quarterly*, Spring 1973, p. 141. This article contains a long helpful bibliography.

23. This and many other points about material culture were brought to my attention by Dr. E. McClung Fleming, another pioneer in the field.

24. The best single volume is Antonia Fraser, *A History of Toys* (London: Delacorte, 1966). For the psychological connection, see Susan Isaacs, *Intellectual Growth in Young Children* (London: Routledge & Kegan Paul, 1930) and M. Rabecq-Maillard, *Histoire du Jouet* (Paris: Hachette, 1962).

25. Bernard Barenholtz and Inez McClintock, *American Antique Toys, 1830–1900* (New York: Harry N. Abrams, 1980). Chapter 1, "Historical Background," is important for the case I am trying to make here. Nineteenth-century America was a world leader in manufacturing and distributing toys.

26. Fraser, *History of Toys*, p. 25.

27. Dora Nussey translated Male's classic into English in 1913. A more

recent reprint was issued by the Fontana Library, London, in 1961.

28. Panofsky's approach was set forth in 1930, with the publication of *Hercules am Scheidewege und andere antike Bildstoffe in der neuron Kunst* (Leipzig, G.D.E.: B. G. Teubner), and his masterpiece appeared as *Studies in Iconology: Humanistic Themes in the Art of the Renaissance* (1939; reprint, New York: Harper & Row, 1962).

29. Examples of such work include Rosemond Tuve, *Elizabethan and Metaphysical Imagery: Renaissance Poetic and Twentieth Century Critics* (Chicago: University of Chicago Press, 1947); Wolfgang Clemon, *The Development of Shakespeare's Imagery* (Cambridge: Harvard University Press, 1950—first published in German in 1936); and Kenneth Muir, "Shakespeare's Imagery, Then and Now," in *Shakespeare Studies*, 18 (1965), pp. 46–57.

30. Michael Marsden, "Iconology of the Western Romance," in Browne and Fishwick, *Icons of America*, p. 291.

31. Christopher Finch, *Pop Art* (New York: Vista, 1968), p. 67; and John Russell and Suzi Gablik, *Pop Art Redefined* (New York: Praeger, 1964).

32. For the fluctuations in the New York art world, see Dore Ashton, *The New York School: A Cultural Reckoning* (New York: Viking Press, 1972); Tom Wolfe, *The Painted Word* (New York: Farrar, Straus, & Giroux, 1975); and Robert Hughes, *The Shock of the New* (New York: Random House, 1981).

33. The man is Wilbur G. Kurtz, Jr., and his indispensable work is summarized by Cecil Munsey in *The Illustrated Guide to the Collectibles of Coca-Cola* (New York: Hawthorn Books, 1972). See also Lawrence Dietz, *Soda Pop: The History, Advertising, Art, and Memorabilia of Soft Drinks in America* (New York: Chelsea House, 1973); and E. J. Kahn, *The Big Drink* (New York: Random House, 1960).

34. Craig Gilborn, "Pop Iconology: Looking for the Coke Bottle," in Ray Browne and Marshall Fishwick, *Icons of Popular Culture* (Bowling Green, Ohio: Popular Press, 1970), pp. 13ff. See also Irving Rouse, "The Strategy of Culture History," in *Anthropology Today* (Chicago: University of Chicago Press, 1958).

35. Munsey, *Coca-Cola*, p. 119. Recently Coca-Cola has embarked on a major expansion and diversification program, moving into such areas as movies, cable television, frozen foods, and video games. What will all this do to the iconic image of Coke?

36. Marvin Trachtenberg, *The Statue of Liberty* (New York: Viking, 1976), p. 156.

37. Two good volumes for putting the icon in the framework of its launching are Eunice Holsaert, *Outer Space* (New York: Holt, 1959) and

Sergei Gouschev, *Russian Science in the 21st Century* (New York: Mc-Graw-Hill, 1961).

38. Nicolas Calas, "Pop Icons," in Browne and Fishwick, *Icons of America*, pp. 39ff.

39. W. H. Huggins and Doris R. Entwisle, *Iconic Communication: An Annotated Bibliography* (Baltimore: Johns Hopkins University Press, 1974).

40. K. C. Knowlton's *Computer-Produced Movies* (New York: Science, 150, 1965) gives an excellent summary of potential capabilities of computer-controlled displays. See also Gyorgy Kepes, ed., *Sign, Image, Symbol* (New York: George Braziller, 1966).

MYTHOS ———————— 7

The way for a technological society to take a step into the future is to shift the weight of its emphasis from machines to myth.

William I. Thompson,
Darkness and Scattered Light:
Four Talks on the Future

The essence of every culture is *mythos*—brave and bold stories that explain how things came to be, and why we are as we are. *Mythos* is the Seventh Pillar of Popular Culture.

Mythos is a Greek word. Greek myths have magnetized the minds of men through twenty-five centuries. Originally received as gifts from the gods, they have successively been regarded as supreme models of heroism and courage; pithy and enchanting stories; childish fables not worth serious attention; enigmas to be explained by speculative theory; pagan superstitions to be refuted and denounced; and stories to be interpreted in ancient ways. Enlightened eighteenth-century *savants* like Bernard le Bovier de Fontanelle and Pierre Bayle ridiculed and disdained not only pagan but also Christian myths. A century later Giovanni Battista Vico, Johann Gottfried von Herder, and others celebrated myths as central and creative products of the "people" or *Urvolk*—the formative agent of its special character.

Certainly myths were central in forming Greece and Rome: gods, goddesses, centaurs, cyclops, lovers, raiders, and rapists. The art, architecture, and literature of the classical world is full of mythology, much of which still persists (with varying degrees of credibility). How much the ancient philosophers and poets believed in them is debatable; Cicero, for example, thought the myths of Rome were for the masses, but not for him. That the *demos* lived out their lives within this mythic framework there can be no doubt.

Christians had to dispose of all this paganism when their day came. Sometimes they merely adapted. The Saturnalia, long sacred to Saturn, became Christmas. Various female fertility myths went into the concept of the Virgin Mary and what scholars now call Maryolotry. Myths transformed are myths still.

Not only Christ but also various of his followers became mythic as saints' tales, fableaux, and miracle tales sprung up. The cycle which the Greeks had used so successfully—*agon*, *pathos*, and *theophany*—continued. To the old lists of heroes and kings were added martyrs and miracle-makers. Now authority was centered not in Caesar but in Christ; the popes took over where the emperors left off. Style and tradition merged in Rome, where old basilicas were transformed into cathedrals. Most Christian churches still reflect basic architectural elements used in Roman law courts and villas.

Not all *mythos* is religious. The same people who knew about Saint Sebastian's arrows and Saint George's dragons also knew about Patient Griselda and the Ugly Duckling. Myth found a happy home in the medieval festival. There were family festivals, community festivals (honoring patron saints or local heroes), and annual festivals (not only Christmas and Easter but also May Day, Midsummer, and New Year). People lived in remembrance of one festival and in expectation of the next.

For most peasants the great festival was carnival, when the "world was turned upside down." Carnival was a holiday, a game, a myth: a time of ecstasy and of liberation; of food, sex, and violence.[1] Contemporaries didn't bother to record what carnival meant to them—it must have seemed obvious. The same European scholars and romantics who "discovered" the people in the eighteenth and nineteenth centuries also "discovered" carnival, secular myths, and traditional man.

Traditional Man, heir of the *demos*, expressed the acquired wisdom of the race, through the "collective unconscious." He inherited not centuries but millenia of experience and lore. Myths lived on, in, and through him.

Believing in the dust-to-dust cycle and mysteries which he could never hope to fathom, Traditional Man saw purpose woven into every aspect of daily life. Nature redefined but did not alter this purpose; heroes understood and defended it. There was no dividing line between the sacred and profane. Repetition of stories, seasons, and events had profound meaning. When it was dry, one must pray to God (or the gods) for rain. When sickness came, local people with special power could help, but only God could cure. Death was a part of life—in the crops that bloomed then withered, in the animals raised then slaughtered. These animals talked in legends and fairy tales. Traditional Man believed in enchantment, witches, spirits, and the devil.

Life had its lighter moments. Traditional Man enjoyed carnivals and roared at the antics of clowns nad charlatans. Mythic characters portrayed in songs, stories, and plays were as real to him as the people in his own family or village; timeless, tender, part of a transcendent reality.

This thinking was prescientific, but nonetheless both sensitive and poetic. Words were symbolic. Common sense and uncommon events were all of a piece. Authority was clearly defined, depending on revelation, which centered in a continuously inspired church. All roads led to Rome, all thoughts to God. Sacraments were the means to grace. Christendom was another name for community as well as salvation. Suffering was inevitable but not final. Good Friday was but a prelude to Easter; death was overcome by resurrection.[2]

Man drew substance from nature, not media; there was a healthy tension between mind and feeling, percept and concept. Reason and revelations were friends, not foes. Traditional people knew what they knew. They believed.

Looking back five centuries, the Romantics called this "The Age of Faith," and minimized the lack of faith, the heresy, and the bloodshed that also existed. Yet this view can be defended: for centuries the Western world shared a monomyth. Reason and revelation, mind and matter, did not seem incompatible. Oral myths—history transmuted into poetry—flourished. Songs, dances, legends, and tales were more than entertainment, they were channels into which creativity could and did flow. No social or economic lines cut men off from tradition, ritual, and ceremony. Tyrants abounded—but not the tyranny of facts.[3]

Gradually, and for reasons not fully understood, a new kind of man emerged in the West.[4] At first he was viewed as a curiosity; as his power grew he was treated as a heretic; finally, staging his magnificent Renaissance and Reformation, he came into power.[5] His premises, attitudes, and goals quickly separated him from his predecessors. Believing that the proper study of mankind is man, he changed the intellectual center of gravity from heaven to earth. For myths he substituted experiments; for poetry, prose. We might call him Fact-Finding Man.

Fact-Finding Man was determined to throw out the cyclical theory of history and substitute the doctrine of progress. History, he asserted, didn't repeat itself; it climbed onward and upward. Life should be seen not as a call to prayer but a supreme challenge. We could be the masters of all things. Fact-Finding Man must acquire methods and formulas by which to comprehend and control nature; depend not on myths but theories. The difference is significant: myths are meant to be believed, theories are meant to be challenged. Consequently the world of *might-have-been* has been overridden by the world that *is*.

The scientific revolution was based on three devastating (from the standpoint of Myth-Making Man), glorious (from the standpoint of Fact-Finding Man) premises: data can be gathered, experiments can be repeated, predictable physical laws can be derived. Figuratively speaking, a whole epoch began when Alexander Pope wrote in his *Essay on Man*:

> Nature and nature's laws lay hid in night,
> God said, 'Let Newton be,' and all was light.

As the fear of the unknown subsided, materialism and determinism increased. Scientists applied their knowledge to daily problems with startling results. Priests in white coats replaced priests in black robes. Myth-Makers had striven for the poetic and vague; Fact-Finders favored the prosaic and precise. They could explain this in two words: it worked.

Myths and "superstitions" were identified with the worst

features of the Old Regime—a tyrannical church, the divine rights of kings, feudal stagnation. There was only one thing to do: *écraser l'infame*—get rid of superstition.

At this point in history the United States made their formal entry onto the stage of history. Though France provided much of the intellectual leadership for the eighteenth century, the American colonies put the revolutionary ideas to work. They fired the shot heard round the world. That ideology and Revolution set the intellectual pattern of what became the United States of America. Columbia, the Gem of the Ocean!

The rapid growth and expansion of the Republic glorified science, with applied science (technology) as a new godhead. What happened to the old myths, the old understandings? John Crowe Ransom answered in *God Without Thunder*: "Myths are construed simply by the hard Occidental mind. They are lies. They are not nearly good enough for men brought up in the climatic blessedness of the scientific world."[6]

To think we have no myths is part of the mythology of our time. Mythology, like nature, abhors a vacuum. True enough, we don't speak much of centaurs (though Mark Twain's riverboat men were half-man–half-alligator) or giants (though we invented Paul Bunyan).[7] We no longer venerate the motifs and materials of ancient Greece or medieval Christendom. Instead, we have invented our own mythology, which is as much a part of our environment as is water for the goldfish. We never ask why we are swimming in it.

We deny the power of myth and the subconscious at great risk. As Carl G. Jung warns, if one is not conscious of his internal contradictions, he will project them outward and inflict them upon himself in the form of his fate. We kick the devil out of the front door only to make it easy for him to return through an open window in the back.

Anyone studying myths knows their recounting changes with time, place, and person.[8] That they are part of a tradition does not mean they are standardized; texts and contexts change, and myths take on a highly personalized meaning.[9] The tradition is externalized—the myth exists in people's minds. Behind it, as the constant backdrop, are shared beliefs and assumptions which put personal experience in a larger framework.

With any myth or ritual, each person has his or her special angle of vision; each one regards as primary and axiomatic his ideals, values, and norms. Victor Turner has demonstrated this with the Ndembu, but it applies equally well to us in our contemporary world.[10] I shall try to describe some myths in the United States, using the insights of two leading scholars and theorists.

The first, a Polish anthropologist, spent his last years in America—Bronislaw Malinowski (1884–1942). In defining and defending the theory of functionalism, he insisted that myths must include not only what reality looks like, but also what it does. Our myths are not only in our books but also in the market place. Myths thrive because they function.[11]

To put it differently, myths serve basic needs which alter little from century to century. Culture is essentially an apparatus by which we are put in a better position to cope with concrete, specific problems that face us in our environment. Culture is a system of objects, activities, and attitudes in which every part exists as a means to an end; an integral in which various elements are interdependent.[12] Artifacts, organized groups, and symbolism are three closely related dimensions of the cultural process.

For Malinowski, human institutions are related to both cultural and biological needs. Hence, *function* always means the satisfaction of a need. Man needs myths—they function in a way which is indispensable to the whole belief-structure. Myths are not mere adornments on the culture house—they are part of the very foundation on which it stands.

Myths are tied to essences; they illuminate God, men, and society. Herman Melville called them "luminous scenes grasped in flashes of intuition." *Mythic* implies an instant vision of an enduring truth. They are part of our survival kit.

Malinowski's work is marked not only by common sense but also by compassion. He insists that the study of human thought, belief, and action be inspired not merely by the artistic touch, but "by full human sympathy extending even to the humblest, simplest, and most defenseless manifestations of mankind."[13] By insisting that *demos* and *mythos* are organically joined, he strengthened both Pillars of Popular Culture.

So did Carl G. Jung (1865–1961), who believed there is no theology without sociology and no mythology without archetypes—original patterns on which subsequent things of the same type are modeled.[14] *Archetype* is by no means a new idea, having for centuries been synonymous with *idea* in the Platonic scheme of things; but with Jung it became a hypothetical model—something like the "pattern of behavior" in biology. He and others began analyzing such archetypes as the Shadow, the Trickster, the Mother, the Temptress, the Wise Old Man, the Helpful Animal, and the Holy Fool. All could be found not only in myths and fairy tales, but also in modern stories, songs, and comic books. In *Patterns in Popular Culture*, Harold Schechter and Jonna Gormely Semeiks showed how comic books, comic strips, and underground comics, rock, soul, and country western songs, spy, detective, and western stories all perpetuate the ancient myths, confirm the role of archetypes.[15] Beowulf and Batman are connected.

They spring from the realm of the unconscious—a repository of memories, impulses, and fantasies which relate to childhood. But myths go back further than this, to a deeper level of the mind which Jung called "the collective unconsciousness." Ideas here are inborn and universal variations, so do we possess a basic psychic structure which gives us typically human perceptions, responses, and insights. This collective unconsciousness is the seedbed of popular culture.

What we think and dream on this level is common and meaningful to us as a special force. These dreams contain universal human truths—in other words, *mythos*.[16] Myths are common property of the *demos*. Joseph Campbell explains:

> Dream is the personalized myth, myth the depersonalized dream; both dream and myth are symbolic in the same general way of the dynamics of the psyche. But in the dream the forms are guided by the particular troubles of the dreamer, whereas in myth the problems and solutions shown are directly valid for all mankind.[17]

These mythic symbols and archetypes crop up in all epochs and cultures, sometimes in ways and forms which we cannot or will not recognize. Mythology is only dead with those who refuse to study the living.

Jung was convinced, moreover, that "the posture of the unconscious is compensatory to consciousness."[18] If our conscious beliefs move too far from normalcy or health, the unconscious will then communicate a symbol to the conscious, stressing what is being overlooked or ignored. When in our waking world a pathological state of imbalance ensues, or neurosis or psychosis, Jung writes, a compensating symbol will appear in fantasies or dreams.[19] No wonder so much popular culture springs from, or leads to, Disney World, the Land of Oz, prime time television, or Never Never Land.

Not only individuals face this imbalance. Whole cultures, from time to time, veer off, and activate the corrective mechanism:

Every period has its bias, its particular prejudice, and its psychic malaise. An epoch is like an individual, with its own limitations of conscious outlook, and therefore requires a compensatory adjustment.[20]

Where are "the dreams of a culture" to be found? In its popular culture and popular arts. Are not the magico-religious functions once served by priests now met by athletes and entertainers—by people we watch just to "kill time"? "A myth itself never disappears," writes Mircia Eliade. "It only changes its aspects and disguises its operation."[21]

What forms the mythic core in contemporary America? Is there a central myth-tree, with many branches? How deep are the roots, how strong the pillar?

These questions cannot be fully answered in a single chapter, a single book, or indeed a whole series. We can only suggest beginning points for further investigation. That is what I would like to try.

The mythic core in our culture is *mobility*. Movement as conceived here is physical, psychological, spiritual, and institutional. *Outward* mobility is key to the physical myth called Manifest Destiny. *Upward* mobility gives us, in economic terms, the Success Myth, and in spiritual terms, the Salvation Myth. These are central trunks, with many branches and twigs.

Central to the mythic core is the notion that we are a Chosen

People, a seed sifted out of the world's people; a community of saints destined to create a newer, better society. Like the Israelites of old, we sailed at God's command, as a favorite old hymn made explicit: "O God, beneath Thy guiding hand our exiled fathers crossed the sea!"

This religious mission was quickly linked to an economic one: to get rich quick, in this land of the second chance, this asylum for the poor. So we began with three national myths: America was the land of goodness, of liberty, and of plenty. As time went on, they tended to merge into a single item: the "M-factor"— movement, migration, mobility. The restless temper—*inquiétude du caractére*—which Alexis de Tocqueville had observed a century and a half ago proved to be the dynamo of our mythology.[22]

This restlessness, this passion to succeed, did not originate in America. Who was more restless and successful than Alexander the Great? The people who propelled the commercial, scientific, and religious revolutions of modern times were restless and daring. Characterized at various times as Protean, Faustian, and Dionysian, modern man is a complex creature. We imported not only people, but also doctrines to the New World: progress, capitalism, Calvinism, Darwinism, and ethnocentrism. The first European settlers had hardly disembarked before being told that God favored the diligent and frugal. There were no positive assurances that such traits belonged to the elect, but there were powerful hints. While material prosperity did not necessarily assure God's favor, it appeared as such to the mortal eye. If the workers weren't worthy of salvation, who was? Pick up thine ax and swing.

Because he embodied the quintessence of orthodox Puritanism in America, Cotton Mather spoke effectively about the self-made man. Precocious, ambitious, and pontifical, Mather (1663–1728) tended to associate the will of God with success; to think it was not honest, nor Christian, that a Christian should have no business to do. His eyes glowed with satisfaction when they fell upon Proverbs 22:29: "Seest thou a man diligent in his business? He shall stand before kings." The implication was plain enough. Thou shalt find a fitting work, and in this work thou shalt succeed. Religion and activism were partners.

Mather's most imposing book was *Magnalia Christi Americana*. For pious hero-worship it is unexcelled in American biography. The longest character sketch dealt with Sir William Phips, a self-made man. He took the road Horatio Alger heroes later travelled, from rags to riches and fame. Never mind if he erred slightly and indulged in a little piracy. Boys will be boys. At the end Phips succeeded, "defying pale Envy to fly-blow the Hero." For the New Englander seeking a moral sanction for money-making, here was a book to ponder.

Other works demonstrate how Mather wedded Puritanism to ambition in early America. His *Two Brief Discourses* bluntly asserted that man must serve Christ and achieve success in a personal calling. *The Essays To Do Good* held it was every man's privilege and duty to help the Lord, but wealthy people could do the most. They were stewards, whose special ability gave them special opportunities. "Honor the Lord with thy substance; so shall thy barns be filled with plenty." One detects the suggestion that charity itself can be a profitable business venture.

Benjamin Franklin is the best colonial example of the mythic man in America. There is a direct relationship between the thoughts of Mather and Franklin. The Philadelphia sage adopted, rather than imitated, Mather's outlook, writing like a Puritan and living like a pragmatist. Franklin's own *Autobiography* and *Poor Richard's Almanack* (issued from 1733 to 1758, and subsequently as *Poor Richard Improved*) had a great impact on America. His homely maxims influenced the colonies more than all the combined formal philosophies of the time. The debt in both instances to Protestant mores, and particularly to Cotton Mather, is plain. Mather's *Essays To Do Good*, Franklin admits in the *Autobiography*, "had an influence on some of the principal future events of my life." Yet Mather's God is unlike Franklin's God-without-thunder. The thunderbolt which was the stern voice of Jehovah to Mather, trickled harmlessly off a kite string into Ben's Leyden Jar.

Franklin knew better than to turn openly against the American Puritanical household morality. Instead he substituted a political and economic base for the religious one of Mather. Writing from the commercial capital of the New World, as a diplomat who had distinguished himself at Versailles, he emphasized things about the self-made man that belonged to his age and temperament. Never immodest, he listed his own achievements in a best-seller autobiography because he thought his life "fit to be imitated." He extolled the "incontestable virtues of frugality, industry, cleanliness, resolution, and chastity." "Lose no time. Be always employed in something useful; cut off all unnecessary actions." Even more familiar are the aphorisms popularized in almanacs which (like the Bible) were read everywhere in America. God helps those that help themselves. He that would catch Fish, must venture his Bait. Idleness is the Dead Sea that swallows all Virtues. Be active in Business, that Temptation may miss her Aim. The Bird that sits is easily shot. Here was ample preparation for the America that was to turn inexorably to urbanism and industrialization.

Politicians capitalized on the self-made man theme. Nineteenth-century candidates for office talked fast to explain why they had not risen from a log cabin, if such advantage had been denied them. They seized upon Franklin as a ready-made symbol linking eighteenth- and nineteenth-century ideology. A series of Franklin Lectures was instituted at Boston in 1830 "to encourage young men to make the most of their opportunities." Presently Franklin monuments appeared in city squares, and his likeness on stamps, coins, and medallions. His had been a fully satisfying American success story; he was worthy of imitation.

The same man who aided Washington helped Franklin. Parson Weems, who could spot a potential hero on a cloudy day without his glasses, turned his hierophancy on *Poor Richard's* creator in 1796. He asked Jefferson for Franklin stories "to be cooked up into a savoury dish for juvenile palates," and dashed off to do a life of Franklin. It went through eleven editions. Still, Franklin was overshadowed by that rip-roaring, coonskin-hatter from the West, the first poor boy to make the White House, Andrew Jackson.

Jackson can best be understood against the background of an America in which the value of manufacturing increased more than tenfold between 1810 and 1860. Coal, land, oil, power, and metals were plentiful. Come and get it! When Phineas Barnum

said that having more land than people in America meant that
anyone could make money, he was stating a truism. Old Hickory saw that with the new economic prosperity, democracy
would become militant. So he picked up his sword and fran-
chise, got in front of a group of voters, and said, "Follow me!"
They did—right to the White House lawn. On Jackson's inauguration day, hell-raising was advanced to a new level. A rough-
and-tumble, self-made man had become chief executive of our
nation. The political pattern for the next century had been set.

The swaggering, mythic mood of the Jacksonian period was
reflected in art, literature, and education as well as in politics.
Democracy was made into a secularized religion, with the self-
made man as high priest. A poor Virginia orphan named Henry
Clay, who became a Republican candidate for President, first
used the term "self-made man" in a Congressional debate on
February 2, 1832. Under different guises, and in other connections, it had already been understood throughout America. Such
men as Clay and Jackson rose not by revolution, but resolution. To a Creole aristocrat who saw Jackson for the first time
he looked like "an ugly old Kaintuck flat-boatman." To most
Americans he seemed like one of themselves magnified a few
times. Under him the perfumed gentry trembled, the national
bank collapsed, and the ambiguous phrase "equal opportunity
for all" meant something. Old Hickory said that if the job was
too hard for the man, you ought to get rid of the job. A fellow
could vote for an executive like that, and whoop at the privilege.

This new democracy was built squarely on the old morality
and on the self-made man cult. It scorned the bones of a buried
ancestry and determined to remove the political obstacles that
got in the hero's way. Success was the end point. Individual
success justified not only the man but also the institutions under which he served.

In the Age of Jackson a new mythic phrase surfaced—Manifest Destiny. Attributed to John L. O'Sullivan, who first used it
in the July 1845 issue of the *Democratic Review*, the phrase
dramatized our god-given mission "to overspread the continent allotted by Providence for the free development of our
multiplying millions." The heady words were matched by earthy

deeds. In character, volume, and rate of progress, the West-ward Movement in America is not fully paralleled in world his-tory. Nowhere else has an area of equal size been settled so quickly, almost entirely by individual initiative.

The people most responsible have become heroes, some-times myth-makers. I shall single one out for detailed analysis: Daniel Boone. Surely not the greatest American hero, he is nevertheless one of the most enduring and believable. The de-bunkers who have found fair game in George Washington, Thomas Jefferson, Abraham Lincoln, Franklin Roosevelt, and John Kennedy have found Boone's feet are not of clay. He was what he said he was, did what he said he did. He filled (in Malinowski's sense) a mythic need. He was (in Jung's sense) archetypal. In a sense, he was the Westward Movement, and Manifest Destiny. He was a land-locked Ulysses, moving west without chart or compass; Moses, leading us into the Promised Land. He carried not only his long rifle but also his *mythos* to the end of his long, illustrious life.

Few myth-makers have sought or accepted the role as reluc-tantly as Daniel Boone. Touted as the great Indian fighter, he claimed to have killed only one Indian, and that in self de-fense. A semiliterate, he had trouble writing his own name, let alone a book. An unsocial fellow uneasy with neighbors, he kept moving west. Yet he could not escape adulation and fame. In Boone we have the first outline of what became the amalgam hero of the New World—the Man of the West.[23]

Poeticized, lionized, and fictionalized, Boone was seen as America's archetypal trailblazer, a man of mythic proportions. Entering the forest with long rifle and coonskin hat, his myth merely changed costume to conquer new frontiers. No article of faith has gripped us like that which involves frontiers and their part in forming American character.[24]

Boone was the living personification of Jean Jacques Rous-seau's myth which had captivated the literary imagination and fired the Romantic Revolution. Like Rousseau himself, Boone spent his life fluctuating between a dream of solitude and ad-venture, between the lure of domesticity and security. Man, said Rousseau, was born free, and was everywhere in chains—Boone was the exception. In him, the Noble Savage and the Natural

Man merged. Tutored by the savages themselves, yet master of
them, Boone adapted himself to the virgin forest, Indianlike.
Like the aboriginals (who also captivated the civilized imagination), Boone was filled with the wild beauty of nature—a free
individual, living just outside civilization. What the European
romantic dreamed, the American actually experienced.[25]

Daniel Boone felt the ecstasy of complete possession of the
new country. Like God, he looked around at the world and
pronounced it good. Sensing this, the poet William Carlos Williams calls Boone, "A great voluptuary born to the American
settlements against the niggardliness of the damning puritanical tradition."[26] This updated the famous passage in Canto X
of Lord Byron's *Don Juan*:

> Boone lived hunting up to ninety;
> And what's still stranger, left behind a name
> For which men vainly decimate the throng
> Not only famous, but of that good fame
> Without which glory's but a tavern song—
> Simple, serene, the antipodes of shame.

There was something epical about Boone: long, lean, full of
unquenchable fire, as firm and true as the mountains on which
his mocassins trod. The Natural Man myth found other forms
in America—the Peddler, Riverboatman, Pirate, and Sod-Buster.
But it was the pioneer rifleman, exemplified by Boone, that took
first place. He became an admirable exemplar for the Jackson
Democrats. Pioneer anecdotes, in the hands of an Abe Lincoln
who split logs on the frontier, became a potent political weapon.
They carried Lincoln into the White House, where he became
a great (if not *the* greatest) president.

The sacred word *frontier* has come to epitomize any urgent
national need, perceived by people as different as Jefferson,
Lincoln, Wilson, Roosevelt, Kennedy, or Reagan. Roosevelt's
New Deal and Kennedy's New Frontier have given way to the
New Conservatism. In the 1980s, Ronald Reagan "came out of
the West," and returns there whenever he can, to don cowboy
clothes and ride a horse. The congealed idea of frontier still
sustains us in outer space—rite words in rote order. All this ties

in with the sinewy figure of Boone—compact and capable of incredible activity, symmetrical and instinctive in understanding.

He was *always on the move*. The mythic key is mobility. This restlessness, this willingness to challenge the gods, even if like Prometheus it costs him his liver, gives Boone an edge on many others. We are planters without roots, settlers who can't settle down. This has been true ever since Europeans came to the New World, and the cosmic restlessness seems to have increased in the twentieth century. Somehow Edna St. Vincent Millay speaks for us all when she says that when she sees a train she wants to take it—no matter what the destination.[27]

Substitute "path" for "train," and you have Boone's epigraph. The sixth son of Squire and Sarah Boone, Daniel was born in 1734. Seeking religious freedom, his grandfather left England to settle in Abingdon, fourteen miles north of Philadelphia.[28] But he soon moved to Berks County, Pennsylvania. The Boones were born wanderers, always answering the call just over the ridge. Young Daniel got little education even for that place and time. His mother made a slight attempt to improve his always highly individualistic handwriting. Uncle John Boone tried to guide Daniel in the ways of books, but gave up in despair. It was to John that Squire Boone made the well-known defense of his son: "Let the girls do the spelling, and Dan will do the shooting."

The boy learned to shoot as soon as he could handle a gun, and became familiar with the dense woods. He was expected to watch his father's cattle on ground located some miles from the main farm. The cattle were usually left to wander at will as did Daniel himself. He also became acquainted with the friendly Indians. These experiences left an indelible mark on the young boy's life.

Boone was fifteen when his parents headed for the Shenandoah Valley. For a year and a half they lived near Harrisonburg before moving to Rowan County, North Carolina. A nearby Virginian neighbor was John Lincoln; his great-grandson would share America's mythic supremacy with George Washington, whose ancestors were by now well established on the Northern Neck.

Legend has it that Daniel almost shot his wife-to-be. When

"firehunting," the hunter would flash a torch until he attracted a curious deer; the fire reflected in the animal's eyes showing the hunter his target. Boone caught sight of gleaming eyes and raised his rifle to shoot, but discovered just in time the figure of Rebecca. She rushed home to tell her father she had been chased by a panther. The whole tale conjures up classical mythology.

In 1759 the Boones moved on to Culpeper County where Daniel made his living hauling tobacco. This was no life for him, so he sold his property and left with six families and forty men for Kentucky. Attacked by Indians before they reached Cumberland Gap, six travellers were killed, including Boone's son James, who was to the rear of the main party.[29] In 1774 Boone was sent to warn the surveyors in the Kentucky territory of the impending danger of an Indian uprising. Boone was accompanied by "Big Mike" Stone, who shared with him amusing and thrilling adventures. They covered a distance of eight hundred miles in sixty-two days, going as far as the Falls of the Ohio. Boone was placed in command of Moore's Fort in the Clinch River Valley, and commissioned to carve out the Wilderness Road to Boonesborough, where he built a fort. He returned for his family and brought them to Boonesborough. At Sycamore Hollow on May 23, 1775, Boone sponsored the last three of nine laws adopted for the infant colony:

For establishing courts of jurisdiction and regulating the practice thereof; for regulating a militia; for the punishment of criminals; to prevent profane swearing and Sabbath breaking; for writs of attachment; for ascertaining clerks' and sheriffs' fees; to preserve the range; for improving the breed of horses; for preserving the game.[30]

Boone was the leader in the rescue of his daughter Jemima and the Calloway girls, kidnapped by the Indians while canoeing on the Kentucky river. Daniel himself was captured by Indians at Blue Licks and adopted by the Shawnees, receiving the tribal name "Big Turtle." Finally he escaped in time to warn his comrades at Fort Boone of an Indian attack. He was always on the run.

Boone did little of historical importance in his later life. His chief concern was contesting the loss of various pieces of land. Deprived of all his holdings, Boone left the Kentucky which was later to consider him a special saint, pushing on to present-day Missouri, where his son lived. There he became magistrate of the district. Once again his holding was voided by the United States land commissioner. Back in Kentucky to pay off his debts, he ended up with fifty cents to his name and stayed only long enough to transact his business, then headed West.

Why did he prefer to live on the cutting edge of the frontier? He felt too crowded back East and had to have more elbow-room. The tranquility of his later years did not diminish Boone's earlier achievements. In his autobiography, *The Life of John James Audubon*, Audubon said that the stature and general appearance of this wanderer approached the gigantic; and that the very motion of his lips brought the impression that whatever he uttered was strictly true. This observation is remarkable when we recall that Boone was only five-feet-eight-inches tall. Audubon viewed Boone as a mythical as well as an historical figure.

The component parts of the saga were a demi-paradise west of the mountains; land-hungry families who pictured it as a new Eden; a stalwart leader to lead the people westward; a lone wanderer guiding his generation on a God-sanctioned trek into the virgin forest. That scores of people had preceded Boone into Kentucky did not damage the legend. Their achievements were laid at his feet; he received the esteem due others. Through his life, contemporaries' feats and accomplishments are funneled. In the case of Boone "popular fancy was granted opportunity for unrestrained imagination in creating myth, which age so hallowed that even well trained historians have hesitated to submit it to scientific analysis."[31]

Boone got along reasonably well with his neighbors; he was no misanthrope. With his native capacity for leadership, he was an unmachined man. These qualities appeal to the twentieth century, when machines and bombs bring on perplexing problems. Americans look with nostalgia at the image of a man most happy when he was miles from the nearest gadget, factory, or smokestack. The final word on Boone was penned by Mark Twain at the end of *Huckleberry Finn*: "But I reckon I got to light out for the territory ahead of the rest, because Aunt Sally she's going to adopt me and civilize me, and I can't stand it. I been there before."

Yet the essential myth preceded Twain. The foundation stones were laid by John Filson (1747–1788), the frontier's first notable writer. Born on a Pennsylvania farm, Filson basked in Rousseau-like fantasies. He moved west to take up land and became a Kentucky schoolteacher. In 1784 he published *The Discovery, Settlement, and Present State of Kentucky*. The appendix, "The adventures of Col. Daniel Boone," was the first authentic sketch. Although cast in Filson's and not Boone's idiom, it had a wide influence. Florid and pedantic, it purported to be an autobiography, although thoughts in "sylvan shades" about "the ruins of Persepolis or Palmyra" were about as familiar to the real Boone as arguments over the latest coiffures at Versailles. In fact, the book made much more of an impression at Versailles than at Boonesborough; when translated into Chateaubriand-like prose in 1785, it became popular among French intellectuals and courtiers. While later scholars have considered Filson's account pompous and inaccurate, it was twice endorsed by Boone himself as being the best account of his life and as "not having a lie in it."

The popularity of Filson's account can be seen from the number and variety of editions. A year after the first printing in Wilmington, Delaware, it appeared in Paris as *Histoire de Kentucke, Nouvelle Colonie a l'ouest de la Virginia*; two years later as the *Adventures of Colonel Daniel Boone, One of the Original Settlers of Kentucky*; and three years after that, in Leipzig, as *Reise nach Kentucke und Nachrichten von diser neu Angebauten Landschaft in Nordamerika*. Excerpts cropped up often in accounts of Western life. The book made an international figure of Boone and established his identity as *the* Natural Man. Filson later published the *Kentucky Gazette*. Ironically enough, the man who had so successfully described Boone's triumph over numerous Indians was himself a redskin's victim, being killed while traveling up the Little Miami River. In his life of Boone, he left behind an influential book about a man who was not educated enough to understand many passages Filson put into Boone's mouth.

In 1934 the Filson Club of Kentucky celebrated its semi-centennial and the sesquicentennial of Filson's account of Boone—

which the club's president rightly called "one of the most important in American pioneer history, the foundation of Boone's reputation."

Timothy Flint (1780–1840) spread Boone's myth. To Flint, history was a means of conveying moral ideas and edifying stories. Born in Massachusetts, Timothy Flint graduated from Harvard in 1800. Restless and adventurous, he too was always on the move. Chateaubriand was his favorite author, conjuring up romantic dreams of heroism:

There is a kind of moral sublimity in the contemplation of their adventures and daring . . . . They tend to reinspire something of that simplicity of manners, manly hardihood, and Spartan energy and force of character, which forms so conspicuous a part of the nature of the settlers of the western wilderness.[32]

Boone was Flint's favorite hero—"the Achilles of the West." Flint learned about Boone through Daniel's grandson, Albert Gallatin Boone. Despite inaccuracies in Flint's account, Albert Boone always maintained that Flint's vividness came from his romantic conception of what Boone actually represented—a walking embodiment of coonskin individualism. He imagined Boone (as he depicted William Weldon, the hero of his own *Shoshonee Valley*) "disgusted with social and civilized life," and anxious "to purge his soul by lonely treks into the interior." To cleanse his own spirit, Flint traveled thousands of miles, suffering from fever and ague. His was a life of endless wandering and adoration. Like the idolized Boone, mobility was his god.

Flint made much of Boone's killing a bear and subsequently carving on a birch tree, "D. Boon cilled a bar." With various localities claiming to have the very inscription, Flint constructed a national myth. How many trees have been subjected to real knives, and how many bears slain by imaginary Daniel Boones, we dare not guess. Without historical justification, Flint shows Boone slipping tartar emetic into the whiskey bottle of his Irish schoolmaster, making this the episode which ended Boone's brief schooling. In Flint's last chapter, Boone takes up the creed of the noble red men of the forest. "Such were the truth, simplicity, and kindness of his characters, there can be

but little doubt, had the gospel of the Son of God been proposed to him, in its sumblime truth and reasonableness, that
he would have added to all his virtues, the higher name of
Christian."[33] When some objected to such fabrication on Flint's
part, he replied that like Pindar's razor, the book was made to
sell, not to use.

And sell it did. Fourteen editions appeared between 1833 and
1868. Flint's stories were retold in other books and his imaginary Boone dialogues plagiarized, sometimes so blatantly that
typographical errors were copied without correction. The Boone
most people read about in the nineteenth century was one that
had been compounded in the brain of Timothy Flint; a Boone
that has been public property ever since.

Boone's virtues were displayed in literary as well as historical
accounts, in cantos and couplets as well as travel books and
biographies. Even while he was moving westward, Boone
seemed to his contemporaries a subject for an American *Odyssey* or *Aeneid*. A long epic poem by Daniel Bryan was published
in 1813 as *The Mountain Muse, Comprising the Adventures of Daniel Boone; and the Power of Virtuous and Refined Beauty*. Boone ca-
vorted with the fates; his mission was superhuman:

> O'er all the mazy complicated chain
> Of objects, which are link'd to the grand theme
> That with sublime sensation swell the soul;
> Boone now in all its forceful influence felt.[34]

The forces of evil confronted Boone, but the "sinewy sons of
Enterprise" prevailed. So did Boone's position as the ultimate
frontiersman.

Boone moved effortlessly out of history into folklore and fiction, aided by James Fenimore Cooper (1789–1851). Born in his
father's village of Cooperstown, New York, and raised near the
eighteenth-century frontier, Cooper became a leading American writer. William Thackeray thought Cooper's "Leatherstocking" was a better fictional figure than any invented by Sir Walter Scott; one that ranked with Uncle Toby, Sir Roger de Coverly,
and Falstaff. The boost Cooper gave Daniel Boone was inestim-
able, for Leatherstocking—like Hawkeye, Natty Bumppo, and
Deerslayer—was a thinly disguised Boone.

Of the five novels in the Leatherstocking Series, the first was *The Pioneers*. Cooper specifically acknowledged his debt to the Boone myth and based part of *The Last of the Mohicans* on Boone's rescuing his daughter and two other white girls from the Cherokees.[35] Cooper believed Boone moved on beyond the Mississippi "because he found a population of ten to the square mile inconvenient." While there is some question as to the extent to which Cooper drew directly from Boone's life, there is none about his using Boone as his model. Like Boone, Leatherstocking was vested with an historic mission. Both appealed to an America intoxicated with the heady wine of Manifest Destiny. Both demonstrated moral stamina, physical courage, indomitable will, and individualism. Cooper's hero even looked and dressed like Boone: tall, agile, leathery, quiet, and buckskin-clad, with coonskin cap sitting casually on his head. Cooper's model was not the actual but the mythic Boone.

Cooper's *Leatherstocking Tales*, all best sellers, were unsurpassed accounts of American empire-building and fortitude, of the dramatic struggle in the forests, of Manifest Destiny. Leatherstocking's consistency, nobility, and simplicity made him hard to forget. He demonstrated that a man need not talk, act, and dress fancily to be a hero. Cooper's contemporaries also used Boone's life as the theme for artistic creations. An 1824 play called *Daniel Boone, or the First Settlers of Kentucky*, was successfully produced. Judge James Hall's *Legends of the West* (1832) contained much Boone material, as does Robert Montgomery Bird's *Nick of the Wood* (1837). More important was the considerable use of Boone material by William Gilmore Simms.

A Boone prototype was also established in art by Horatio Greenough's statue of him in Washington, D.C.; it portrayed the contest between civilization and barbarianism as a death struggle between Boone and an Indian brave. Many painters have used the same figure, although only one of them painted Boone from real life. This was Chester Harding, who traveled to Missouri to see Boone in 1819. John J. Audubon, Thomas Sully, Alonzo Chappel, W. C. Allen, Reuben Macy, J. B. Langacre, and Y. W. Berry did Boone portraits; but the painter who best reflected his symbolic importance was George C. Bingham. His famous "Emigration of Daniel Boone" showed the hunter leading a group of settlers into a lush, Eden-like land.

Later on Walt Whitman (1819–1892) added to the growing myth of the pioneer. Himself a Long Islander, Whitman went west, where the frontier and the stories he heard about pioneer heroes made a deep impression as is evident in "The Song of the Pioneers," "Song of the Broad Axe," and "Pioneers! O Pioneers!"[36]

Whitman's words helped, but Dan Beard (1850–1941) got Boone back to the campfire and the woods. Beard's Boy Scout movement, which consciously drew from the Boone myth, sent millions of youngsters on the trail of Boone. Beard's own words confirm this:

I suggested a society of scouts to be identified with the greatest of all Scouts, and to be known as the Sons of Daniel Boone. Each "member" would have to be a tenderfoot before he attained the rank of Scout. I never realized that the Boy Scouts would sweep over much of the world and become my life's work.[37]

The Boy Scout movement depended on characteristically American symbols. In place of the lance and buckle, the American long rifle and buckskin clothes; in place of the plumed helmet, the coonskin cap. Beard's triumphant appearance in the White House, at the invitation of President Theodore Roosevelt, put the kind of official stamp on the Boone story that it has kept to this very day. Bicentennial activities and publications reawakened Boone memories in 1976.[38] Americans were still on the move; Boone was beckoning them on.

Boone was a doer, not a thinker; a shooter, not a sayer. Someone else would have to make of his saga a "thesis." That man was Frederick Jackson Turner (1861–1932), an historian who shaped a nation's thinking and mythology. Speaking before a convention of professional historians in Chicago, the thirty-two-year-old Turner proposed that the true point of view for our history is not from the Atlantic Coast, but from the Great West. Mobility was our god, Boone its patron saint. The thesis was applauded and accepted, soon becoming, in the words of Robert E. Riegel, "only slightly lower in the popular estimation than the Bible, the Constitution, and the Declaration of Independence."[39] No need to follow the extraordinary expansion of the

Turner thesis here.[40] Mobility has driven us not only to the west coast, but also back to the cities, and up to the moon. Turner saw our epic journey as psychological as well as geographical. Our culture was not monolithic but mythic; a land of untapped potential, to be conquered and colonized, forming the basis for greater epics than the Greeks and Romans ever dreamt of.[41]

While the Turner thesis was reshaping mythology, John C. Van Dyke put forth his own in a book called *The Money God* (1908). It too dealt with the myth tree and the growth of sturdy branches. "It is money that the new generation expects to win," Van Dyke wrote, "and it is money that the parents want them to win. The boy will make it, and the girl, if she is not a goose, will marry it. They will get it one way or another."[42]

True, perhaps, but certainly not new. Van Dyke stated bluntly what Americans had known all along: money talks. Success succeeds. The best kind of mobility is up—the Ladder of Success. Our pillar has rungs like a ladder. Eventually it stretched not just across America, but around the globe. What was America, if not the land of Golden Opportunity? Like heaven itself, were not its streets paved with gold?

Studying long-dead myths, scholars stress their dependence on invention and imagination, fantasy and wish-fulfillment. But if you study current American myths you will find they are firmly rooted in reality: our legal tradition, history, economy, and heroes. The Success Myth, fueled by the Self-Made Man, occupies the center of American mythology.

However, they have both emphasized and inherited it. "Success," Aeschylus wrote in ancient Greece, "is man's god." What was unique in America was the scope of the success; the ability of poor and unpromising people to achieve it. What makes success both a process and a myth is the "Rags to Riches" framework.

That frame was mass produced by Horatio Alger, Jr. (1832–1899). His own story, more intriguing than those of most of his heroes, reveals much about American life. Born of old Yankee stock in Massachusetts, Horatio was the first son of a stern Unitarian minister who was a walking blue law. He damned human activities leading to enjoyment and prescribed as remedies generous portions of piety. His son became known at Gates

Academy and Harvard College as "Holy Horatio." Indignantly, Horatio changed his Harvard lodgings when his landlady appeared in her negligee. "I might have seen her bare, but I did not look," he wrote in his 1850 diary.

Confused and unhappy, he persuaded his parents to let him journey to Paris, where he learned things which the Unitarians had never stressed. He looked. His 1852 Paris diary contains two lines more worthy of immortality than any others in the Alger canon: "I was a fool to have waited so long. It is not nearly so vile as I had thought."

Back home, he reformed and became a Unitarian minister. In 1866 he moved to New York to launch his literary career, writing juveniles for William Adams ("Oliver Optic"). His pose was Byronic; since there were no Alps close at hand, he took refuge in the stormy metropolis. Political biographies being in demand, he turned out three with titles-of-the-times: *Webster: From Farm Boy to Senator*; *Lincoln: The Backwoods Boy*; and *Garfield: From Canal Boy to President*. He finished the last in thirteen days to get it to the publisher before Garfield died. But biography was not his medium; he needed the freedom of fiction. Alger turned out 135 novels which sold at least 20 million copies. The books were not carefully constructed or written. Yet they became dicta for generations of rising Americans. This is the story he always told—my version of the myth he brought to fruition:

I am a sturdy lad. I know I can climb the golden ladder with only my talent and talons to sustain me. Nothing can stop me, because I have both pluck and luck. True enough, my father has been killed, and my dear mother takes in washing. As an honorable son I sell papers.

I could seek better prospects; but being a sturdy lad, I cannot desert my ailing mother. Then the tide turns. One day I find a wallet which a Rich Man has dropped. Innate honesty makes me take it to the Rich Man's house. The door is opened by his lovely blue-eyed daughter, an imperial young lady. I love her from that moment forward—though she is Far Above me.

As I back away from the house (she must not see the patch on the seat of my pants) her father comes in. His face lights with joy as he sees the wallet. "I'll start you up the ladder of success," he says. "Thank you, sir, but I must stay with my sick mother." This I do, until her gallant heart gives up over the scrubbing board, and she goes to her reward. "Take the Rich Man's job," she says with her dying breath. "Go up the Ladder!"

My chief competitor is a slick mustached fellow who wants not only the junior partnership but the boss's blonde daughter. I watch closely and discover (by pluck and luck) that he's a secret swindler. I confront him; he resists. In vain—I live clean, he smokes. So I get the credit, the promotion, and the girl. Up the ladder I go! I am a success.

Silly? Simplistic? Not to the millions who read and believed. How could a country specializing in Mom, apple pie, and Manifest Destiny challenge the Alger formula? And was it not confirmed daily in the newspapers and magazines? Hadn't Thomas A. Edison begun as a newsboy, Adolph S. Ochs as a printer's devil, and Andrew Carnegie as a messenger? Don't forget Phillip Armour, Jay Cooke, Jay Gould, Jim Fiske, Leland Stanford, and Cornelius Vanderbilt. (Weren't there even Stanford and Vanderbilt universities?) Wasn't someone moving up every day, with a little pluck and luck?

Alger made no apologies for his cookie-cutter pot-boilers. In the open marketplace, his books sold and sold and sold. Not only did his heroes get ahead—so did the author. You could sever God and Mammon at the same time—his royalty checks proved it. "I should have let go," Alger admitted. "But writing in the same vein becomes a habit, like sleeping on the right side. Try to sleep on the left side and the main purpose is defeated— one stays awake." While other writers did single volumes, Alger turned out whole series—the *Ragged Dick*, *Tattered Tom*, *Brave and Bold*, *Luck and Pluck*, *New World*, *Way to Success*, *Campaign*, *Atlantic*, and *Pacific*.

Because Alger customarily wrote two books simultaneously, he sometimes got his characters mixed. Hence, Grant Thornton disappears mysteriously from *Helping Himself* (chapter 9) only to pop up and thrash a bully in *Hector's Inheritance* (chapter 13). Did Alger's readers mind? Not in the least. To them an Alger novel was as much a part of the scheme of things as state fairs, Sunday, and the Declaration of Independence. He never let them down. Even as the novel was being written, some real-life American of Alger's day would be living the legend he heralded. James B. Duke was peddling his first tobacco; Henry Ford was moving up from his job polishing steam engines; and John D. Rockefeller, after a period of unemployment, was lining up a job. Their rises reaffirmed the nation's faith in laissez-faire capitalism and in Alger. The times not only made the novels, they also justified them.

None of the peaches and cream of his books spilled over into Alger's life. There is pathos in his tipping the Astor House desk clerk to point out celebrities, or his pounding the drum in newsboys' parades. A violent affair with a married woman, the antagonism of his family, and his failure to rid himself of despair lined the face of the plump, balding author and caused him to seek refuge in the Newsboys' Lodging House in New York City. To the end he wrote steadily, desperately, parodying his own earlier style, writing for boys because he couldn't write for men. Finally even the Sunday School teachers found it hard to read his little sagas with a straight face. The gilt in his style had long since worn off. At the century's end he died quietly in a drab dormitory room. Sometime before he had written, half in jest, his own epitaph. No one could have written a better one:

Six feet underground reposes Horatio Alger, Helping Himself to a part of the earth, not Digging for Gold or In Search of Treasure, but Struggling Upward and Bound to Rise at last In a New World—where it shall be said he is Risen from the Ranks.[43]

Alger benefited from existing conditions, and from the work of influential predecessors. One of these, William McGuffey (1800–1873) had, through his school textbooks, prepared millions of children for Alger's "message." McGuffey's First and Second Readers (written when Alger himself was just learning to read) had sold 7 million copies by 1850, 40 million by 1870, over 122 million by 1922. Henry Ford, a ladder-scaler if ever there was one, had the entire series reissued in 1925.[44] McGuffey's readers, mythic to the core, were a skillful synthesis of middle-class virtues and capitalistic maxims. They were carefully prepared "to exert a decided and healthful moral influence" over the reader, dealing with self-reliance, the advantages of industry, and the importance of well-spent youth. What McGuffey did for children, Alger did for adults. So it was that "Rags to Riches" became the national credo. Not even the lives of kings, saints, or martyrs touched off the American imagination like stories of impoverished lads who climbed up the magic ladder. Biographies were supplemented by manuals. One needed to know little or nothing about business or finance to write one; achieving wealth was a matter of moral character. Any red-blooded man could do it. (Women? They had a different task— to marry big money, then raise red-blooded boys). The key word? *Success.* During Alger's own lifetime, these books, and scores like them, saturated the American psyche: *The Foundations of Success* (1843), *Elements of Success* (1848), *Success in Business* (1867), *The Secret of Success in Life* (1873), *The Elements of Success* (1873), another *Success in Business* (1875), *Successful Folk* (1878), *How to Succeed* (1882), *What They Say of Success* (1883), *The Law of Success* (1883), and so on and on and on.[45] A century later, we have the same old song, in slightly different titles.

No one, in my opinion, has matched Alger's impact and influence. The closest contender might be Dale Carnegie, whose courses became a sort of American institution in their own right. Such a sturdy branch of the myth tree deserves special attention.

Born on a scraggly Missouri farm in 1888, young Dale rode to and from school on horseback, studying by lamplight after midnight, and feeding the pigs at 3 A.M. so as to free him for the morning dash for culture. After graduating, he sold correspondence courses, lard, and Armour Star bacon.

His thoughts turned to the big city; he went to New York and enrolled in the American Academy of Arts. Among the things that impressed him there was Carnegie Hall. He changed his name from the Missouri spelling of Carnegey to Carnegie. Jobless and despondent, he contemplated suicide, just as Horatio Alger had. To the manager of the 125th Street Y.M.C.A., who let him teach public speaking there, must go special credit for his surviving. By 1916 he was able to hire a hall—Carnegie Hall—for his speeches. With a Times Square office, an assistant, such unusual honorary degrees as B.Pd. and B.C.S., and a ghost writer to do research on famous men, he gained momentum.

Carnegie believed Americans respected historic successes and Niagara Falls for similar reasons: cubic tons of water and cubic tons of wealth are overwhelming. His *How to Win Friends and Influence People* (1937) went through seventeen printings in five months. Newspapers, advertisements, radio programs, and free demonstrations popularized his method. Carnegie moved from business to domestic problems, dispensing marital advice with a sincerity not evident when he declared himself a bachelor so as to avoid explaining his divorce after an unhappy marriage.

Sinclair Lewis defined Carnegism as "yessing the boss and making Big Business right with God." Two key rules in *How to Win Friends and Influence People* were: "Never tell a man he is wrong," and "Get the other persons saying 'yes, yes' immediately."

Opening schools, seminars, and conferences around the country, Carnegie was everywhere. His death in 1955 did not stop the flow of "yesses," and in the grim recession of the 1980s, Carnegism picked up steam. Old myths die hard—perhaps they are the most enduring thing that cultures produce.

The myth has, of course, had its challengers and defamers. Mark Twain's classic *The Adventures of Huckleberry Finn*, can be seen as a satire of Alger's world. Here the child's life is full of complexity and bitterness; the ladder can lead to hell. The rise of the Naturalists in literature—especially Theodore Dreiser (1871–1945)—was an even stronger rebuff. No happy ending here. The central protagonist in three of Dreiser's novels, Frank Cowperwood, got ahead not by returning the Rich Man's wallet, but by keeping it. Life to him was nasty, brutish, and short. His formula for survival was consecrated egotism.[46]

As a young boy Frank Cowperwood stood in front of a store window tank and watched as a lobster caught and devoured a squid. This was the whole lesson of the world around him. The lobster ate the squid by supreme natural right. He'd be the lobster, society the squid. Dreiser's heroes liked their Darwinism raw and did not mind a little blood on it.

Equally tough and amoral were the dozens of detective heroes modeled on Dashiell Hammett's Sam Spade. This is a world in which Darwinism is dished up raw—with a little blood on it. Women are well-oiled machines, waiting for copulation; men are punching bags, there to be beaten out of shape. Which of them survives? No one can say. Much of the erotica and violence is fortuitous. These people are like animals making their way through a jungle in which only the fittest survive; there is nothing personal about it. This is simply the way it is.

Another literary reaction to the Alger lad is the hero created by Ernest Hemingway (1889–1961) who *will not* get ahead and doesn't care. So to hell with you. A handsome fellow, a hunter, a lover, he is usually a newspaperman, always on the move; he writes novels by day and collects women and material by night. Bullfights intrigue him. Bourgeois values disgust him and he is drawn to primitive areas, particularly Africa. Because he knows the world is a shoddy place, he takes his fun in the company of the "initiated." He is quietly desperate, cheerfully dissipated, and highly entertaining.[47] He is the epitome of mobility—and in his own way, he is quite successful. He is yet another variation to hang on the myth tree.

Nor has the pure-and-simple guy, the kind popularized by Horatio Alger, been driven from the scene. He has a new name: Tom Swift, Tarzan, Luke Skywalker, or "E.T." Alger himself pales beside the production record of Edward Stratemeyer (1862–1930) and the Stratemeyer Syndicate. Using various pseudonymns and tried-and-true adventure formulas, Stratemeyer & Company turned out over 1,800 books, including more than 1,500 dime novels, retitled reprints, and revised editions. No one can be sure of the total sales figures—probably over 200 million copies. There's success for you![48]

My own childhood included literary trips into the worlds of Tom Swift, the Rover Boys, and the Hardy Boys. By pluck and luck—plus new technology—they managed to protect maidenhood, white supremacy, and Old Glory. Tom Swift personified Better Things for Better Living Through Science. He was Horatio Alger's Sturdy Lad with rockets. Like the heroes of *Star Wars* and *E.T.*, and like the astronauts whom Tom Wolfe writes about, they had the Right Stuff.[49]

So did Tarzan, born in the brain of Edgar Rice Burroughs (1875–1950)—ex-miner, rancher, and aluminum salesman. Knowing little and caring less about the real Africa, Burroughs invented his own continent where he controlled history, genetics, and language. Selling his first piece to *All-Story Magazine* in 1912, Burroughs went on to write twenty-four best-selling Tarzan novels, reinvigorating American mythology.

Tarzan, almost literally a self-made man, grew up among the wild animals of Africa, although he was actually the son of Lord Greystoke, an English nobleman. Instead of facing the problems of capitalism, he dealt with the primordial jungle. Suckled by a female gorilla, he befriended Tantor the elephant and feuded with Numa the lion. Leopard-women, ant-men, white renegades, and even men from Mars tried in vain to outwit him. He was a triumph of human brawn and instinct—and of superb restating and repackaging of the basic Mobility Myth. Celebrating his seventieth anniversary in 1982, Tarzan had a publication record that would make any man, woman, or ape envious: twenty-four novels in fifty-five languages, thirty-seven feature films, scores of animated cartoons, and a major television series. Still another movie, the 1984 version called *Lord Greystoke*, was widely acclaimed and drew large audiences. Viewing all this, Erling B. Holtsmark considers the Tarzan series an artful and sophisticated modern epic.[50] Russel B. Nye concludes that "except for Mickey Mouse, Tarzan is undoubtedly the best-known fictional character in the world."[51]

With this in mind, Gary Harmon has set out to "decode Tarzan as a hero," using a structuralist analysis. Tarzan's story is mythic—a narrative providing a large, controlling image that gives shape and expression to our collective hopes and dreams. The lost world, Utopian, and time-warp themes are all there. So, claims Harmon, is "the underlying order that helps the mythic analyst arrive at the fundamental structure of the unconscious mind."[52] We are back to Carl G. Jung and the basic premise on which *mythos* is built.

Thus we can confirm for the twentieth century what was true of every previous one: people live by the mythology of their time. What they believe is more closely related to fiction than to fact. As Ortega Y. Gasset points out (in *Ideas y Creencias*) these "fictions" claim a position for historians on a par with ideas. When half-conscious beliefs spread throughout a culture, they are powerful weapons. Mythology is psychology misread as history or biography.

At White Sulphur Springs, West Virginia, where the aristocracy of the Old South drank from both real and mythic springs, two contemporary Americans don clothes from the "Good Old Days" of the Confederacy—with watermelon in front of them and a small Greek temple topped by the goddess Hygeia behind them. Old South and Old Greece wrote a new chapter in the history of *mythos*. *Photo by the author.*

Misread, but never discarded. One can even argue that in contemporary America we have more myths, and more variations on them, than any other nation—because we have accepted and processed more immigrants. This has required us to invent and embellish symbols, slogans, deeds, and creeds. In this sense "Americanization" has itself become a kind of ritual, and a way of kindling the mythic process.

Americanized, but not homogenized. Black culture is still unique. Indians still perform their ancient rituals, dance their

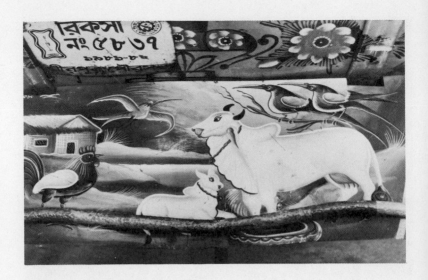

Most of the 4.7 billion people alive today are caught between their ancient *mythos* and that of the new Electronic Age. On the streets of Asia thousands of drawings portray the sacred animals—and thousands of young people choose motorcycles over buffaloes. *Photos by the author.*

timeless dances. Italian pizza, Polish sausage, Chinese chop suey, Mexican tacos, and French fries show that even our national menu is international. The result feeds popular culture.

The Greeks had their centaurs, the medievalists their saints, the *philosophes* their reason, the British their empire. We have our mobility—the road going out and the ladder going up. Today that road leads to the moon. And tomorrow?

With such prospects before us, who can possibly believe that mythology is dead? Some portions of the American version (such as the "Rags to Riches" myth) were badly shaken (even destroyed) by the Great Depression. Instead of expecting millions, people were singing songs like "Brother, Can You Spare a Dime?" and "Can I Sleep in Your Barn Tonight, Mister?" Leading writers—John Dos Passos, Theodore Dreiser, John Steinbeck, and many others—took sharp turns to the left. They pointed out that two interlocking premises—unlimited opportunity and boundless frontier—no longer applied to millions of Americans. For two decades the economic and political resurgence of World War II and the rosy aftermath seemed to be reviving Algerism. The American middle class had a dream, which became a reality after the Second World War. In 1960, newly elected President John F. Kennedy gave us (in his Inaugural Address) a vision of the world in which we would help the poor "break the bonds of mass misery" and "form a new alliance for progress." But only twenty years later Daniel Yankelovich would write: "So startling are the shifts . . . between the late 1960's and the present time that social historians of the future should have little difficulty in identifying the end of one era and the beginning of a new one."[53]

The documentation already exists in studies by Irving Howe and others.[54] But even as American leadership disappeared in field after field, as millions of Americans faced chronic unemployment, as debts got larger while dreams got smaller, the "Rags to Riches" memory lingered on. Two recent studies prove the point: Lucy Komisar's *Down and Out in the USA* and Celeste MacLeod's *Horatio Alger, Farewell: The End of the American Dream.*[55]

If our national experience proves anything, it is that we are often down but never out. Have we really said farewell to Horatio Alger or only to those plucky Protestant pink-skinned males for whom the ladder has become wobbly and unpredictable? "One can hazard a guess," writes an able young female scholar, "that our success mythology will endure and prevail; adapt itself to the hopes of women and blacks and Latinos and Indians and others for whom in its present state it is often a lie. For a culture's mythology is a mirror of its hopes and aspirations."[56]

In 1960, when youthful John F. Kennedy became president, we finally had a twentieth-century leader attuned to the jet age, the first of a new breed. Yet in 1980, with the election of Ronald Reagan, we faced the old breed again—a nineteenth-century man who openly preached Alger platitudes, trusted self-help rather than big government, and spent vacations riding horses on a ranch out West. Despite the disasters of Reaganomics, he ranks as one of the most persuasive and personally attractive leaders of the century. Some even revived the long-discarded word *charisma*. Is *this* the new breed, the new line? Are we back to pluck and luck?

Those who follow and update these contentions will have to say. Who, having seen the changes in this generation, would dare predict those of the next? America is not so much a product as a process. Our myths, like our history, are on the move. Both inner space and outer space beckon us forward. So we had best heed Emerson, and hitch our wagon to a star.

NOTES

1. Peter Burke, *Popular Culture in Early Modern Europe* (New York: Harper & Row, 1978). These ideas are explored in chapter 7, "The World of Carnival." See also Henri Delehaye, *Les Legendes Hagiographiques* (Brussels: Croniques, 1905) and Ian Donaldson, *The World Turned Upside Down: Comedy from Jonson to Fielding* (Oxford: Clarendon, 1970).

2. For a fuller picture see Friedrich Heer, *The Medieval World* (New York: Mentor, 1964); Richard W. Southern, *The Making of the Middle Ages* (New Haven: Yale University Press, 1953); and F. C. Copleston, *Medieval Philosophy* (New York: Harper, 1961).

3. F.J.C. Hearnshaw, *The Social and Political Ideas of Some Great Medieval Thinkers* (New York: Charles Scribner's, 1923).

4. This idea is documented in Burke, *Popular Culture.* It is also the central thesis in the case I attempt to make in *Common Culture and the Great Tradition* (Westport, Conn.: Greenwood Press, 1982).

5. The best short treatise is Roland H. Bainton's *The Age of the Reformation* (New York: Anvil, 1956). Max Weber's *The Protestant Ethic and the Spirit of Capitalism* (New York: Charles Scribner's, 1948) is an acknowledged classic, as is Jacob Burckhardt's *The Civilization of the Renaissance in Italy* (New York: Methuen, 1890).

6. John Crowe Ransom, *God Without Thunder* (New York: Knopf, 1930). Ransom was a leader of the Nashville Agrarians, whose manifesto is a landmark of conservative and anachronistic thinking: *I'll Take My Stand* (New York: Dutton, 1930). See also Louis Cowan, *The Fugitive Group: A Literary History* (Baton Rouge: Louisiana State University Press, 1959) and Marshall W. Fishwick, *Sleeping Beauty and Her Suitors* (Macon, Ga.: Southern Press, 1961).

7. A number of scholars are busy "discovering" classical myths in popular literature. One of the most successful is Erling B. Holtsmark, *Tarzan and Tradition: Classical Myth in Popular Literature* (Westport, Conn.: Greenwood Press, 1982).

8. See Albert Lord, *The Singer of Tales* (Cambridge: Harvard University Press, 1964); and C. G. Jung and C. Kerenyi, *Essays on a Science of Mythology* (Princeton, N.J.: Bollingen Press, 1959).

9. See for example Dorothy Eggan, "The Personal Use of Myth in Dreams," in *Myth: A Symposium*, ed. by Thomas Sebeok (Bloomington: University of Indiana Press, 1958), pp. 107–121; and Mircia Eliade, *Myths, Dreams, and Mysteries* (New York: Harper, 1960).

10. Victor Turner, "Symbols in Ndembu Ritual," in *The Forest of Symbols: Aspects of Ndembu Ritual* (Ithaca: Cornell University Press, 1967), p. 27.

11. Bronislaw Malinowski, "Myth in Primitive Psychology," in *Magic, Science, and Religion* (Garden City, N.Y.: Doubleday, 1954), p. 146.

12. Bronislaw Malinowski, *A Scientific Theory of Culture and Other Essays* (New York: Oxford University Press, 1960), p. 150.

13. Ibid., p. 221.

14. Among many recent articles and books on Jung, the two most helpful, from the viewpoint of popular culture, are Mary Louis von Frantz, *C. G. Jung: His Myth in our Time* (New York: G. P. Putnam's, 1976) and Laurens van der Post, *Jung and the Story of our Time* (New York: Pantheon, 1976). As for Jung's own work, I have found his *Four Archetypes: Mother, Rebirth, Spirit, Trickster* (Princeton, N.J.: Bollingen Press, 1969) especially helpful. This work is excerpted from *The Collected Works of C. G. Jung*, vol. 9, part 1, also published by the Bollingen Press.

15. Harold Schechter and Jonna Gormely Semeiks, eds., *Patterns in Popular Culture: A Sourcebook for Writers* (New York: Harper & Row, 1980). The book makes frequent reference to Jung's work and ideas.

16. Ibid., p. 65.

17. Joseph Campbell, *Hero with a Thousand Faces* (New York: World, 1956), p. 19.

18. Joseph Campbell, "Introduction," in *The Portable Jung* (New York: Viking, 1971), p. xxii. This is one of the best general introductions.

19. Ibid.

20. C. G. Jung, "Psychology and Literature," in *Modern Man in Search of a Soul* (New York: Harcourt, Brace & World, 1955), p. 166.

21. Mircia Eliade, *Myths, Dreams, and Mysteries: The Encounter between Contemporary Faith and Archaic Realities* (New York: Harper & Row, 1975), pp. 27ff.

22. See A. Whitney Griswold's doctoral dissertation, "The American Cult of Success" (1942), in Yale's Sterling Library; and George W. Pierson, *The Moving American* (New York: Knopf, 1973). Griswold and Pierson, who both taught me at Yale, are responsible for my interest and direction in this area, and I am happy to express my gratitude here. They not only explained the central theme of mobility, but also stressed that few if any societies have absorbed mobility as profoundly into their way of life as have Americans. This might be not only our strong Pillar, but also the central thesis of American popular culture.

23. This theme is developed by Henry Nash Smith in *Virgin Land: The American West as Symbol and Myth* (1950) and Thomas D. Clark in *Frontier America: The Story of the Westward Movement* (1959). See also John Seelye, "Buckskin and Ballistics," in *Journal of Popular Culture*, I, no. 1, Summer 1967.

24. So argues Bruce Catton in "Half-Horse, Half-Alligator," in *American Heritage*, December 1957, p. 109.

25. Perry Miller, "The Romantic Dilemma in American Nationalism and the Concept of Nature," in *Harvard Theological Review*, 48, October 1955, p. 188.

26. William Carlos Williams, *In the American Grain* (1925), p. 134.

27. Edna St. Vincent Millay, *Collected Poems* (New York: Harper & Row, 1956), p. 156.

28. John Bakeless, *Daniel Boone* (New York: William Morrow & Co., 1939), p. 1. The accounts of Boone's life are numerous, and in many details contradictory. The best bibliographical summary is Willard R. Jillson's *The Boone Narrative* (Louisville: Standard Printing Co., 1932). The publications of the Filson Club of Kentucky, along with the *Kentucky Process Magazine* and the *Register* of the Kentucky State Historical Association, contain many articles which deal with the small details of Boone's career and the legends which have grown up around it. I have also drawn from an unpublished paper by John Cole, "Daniel Boone, Pioneer Hero Symbol," with Dr. Cole's permission.

29. For details of these years, see J. P. Crump, "A Biographical Sketch of Daniel Boone," in *The Boone Family* (Rutland, Vt.: n.p., 1922).

30. J. T. Dorris, "Transylvania Colony," in *Kentucky School Journal*, 13, No. 1, September 1934, p. 29.

31. Clarence W. Alvord, "The Daniel Boone Myth," in *Journal of the Illinois State Historical Society*, 19, April 1926, pp. 16–30.

32. Reuben G. Thwaites, ed., *Early Western Travels, 1748–1846* (Cleveland, Ohio: A. H. Clark Co., 1904–1907), vol. 18, p. 27.

33. Timothy Flint, *Biographical Memoir of Daniel Boone, the First Settler of Kentucky* (Cincinnati: n.p., 1833), p. 263.

34. Daniel Bryan, *The Mountain Muse* . . . (Harrisburg, Penn.: Davidson and Bourne, 1813), p. 136.

35. The question of Cooper's specific use of Boone material, and of Leatherstocking's significance, is discussed in Smith, *Virgin Land*, chapter 6.

36. For more on Whitman's western travels, see Gay W. Allen, *The Solitary Singer: A Critical Biography of Walt Whitman* (New York: Macmillan, 1955).

37. Dan Beard, *Hardly a Man Is Now Alive: The Autobiography of Dan Beard* (New York: Dutton, 1939), p. 353.

38. See, for example, George M. Waller, *The American Revolution in the West* (Chicago: University of Chicago Press, 1976); Jerry E. Clark, *The Shawnee* (Lexington: University of Kentucky Press, 1977); Richard Stotkin, "Emergence of Myth: John Filson's 'Daniel Boone Narrative' and the Literature of the Indian Wars, 1638–1848" (Ph.D. dissertation, Brown University, 1967); and William Lofaro, "The Genesis of the Biographical Image of Daniel Boone" (Ph.D. dissertation, University of Maryland, 1975). Lofaro also wrote *The Life and Adventure of Daniel Boone* (Lexington: University of Kentucky Press, 1978).

39. Robert E. Riegel, "American Frontier Theory," in *Cahiers d'Histoire Mondiale*, 3, no. 2, 1956, p. 367.

40. From the vast library on Turner, George Roger Taylor's essays, *The Turner Thesis Concerning the Role of the Frontier in American History* (Boston: Heath, 1949) are a good entry point. Walter P. Webb, *The Great Frontier* (Boston: Little Brown & Co., 1952) tries to put the Turner myth into world perspective.

41. Some of this Turnerian mystique is picked up in books like C. R. Fish, *The Rise of the Common Man* (New York: Charles Scribner's, 1927), John G. Cawelti, *The Six-Gun Mystique* (Bowling Green, Ohio: Popular Press, 1970), and Russel B. Nye, *The Unembarrassed Muse* (New York: Dial, 1976).

42. Quoted in Irvin G. Wyllie, *The Self-Made Man in America: The Myth of Rags to Riches* (New York: Free Press, 1954), p. 4.

43. Quoted in Herbert R. Mayes, *Alger: A Biography Without a Hero* (New York: Dutton, 1928), p. 226. See also Richard Morris, "Rags to Riches—Myth and Reality," in *Saturday Review*, November 21, 1953, pp. 12ff.

44. Henry Ford, whose life stretched from Gettysburg to Hiroshima, makes a particularly interesting case study of the Success Myth. He not only believed and lived it, but also built an empire which made his one of the best-known names around the world. See Keith Sward, *The Legend of Henry Ford* (New York: World, 1948), and Allan Nevins (with Frank Ernest Hill) *Ford: The Times, the Man, the Company* (New York: Dutton, 1954).

45. All these, and many more, are not only listed but discussed in Wyllie, *Self-Made Man*. Two books with a special flare and influence are Phineas T. Barnum, *The Art of Money-Getting (Chicago: L. P. Miller, 1882) and Andrew Carnegie, The Gospel of Wealth* (1900). So many books have appeared since Wyllie's was published in 1954 that his fine work needs to be updated. For a start, see Madonna Marsden, "The American Myth of Success: Visions and Revisions," in Jack Nachbar, ed., *The Popular Culture Reader* (Bowling Green: Popular Press, 1978). Like me, Marsden is optimistic about the future of *mythos* in America.

46. Various aspects of Dreiser's philosophy are explored in John Lydenberg, ed., *Dreiser: A Collection of Critical Essays* (Englewood Cliffs, N.J.: Prentice-Hall, 1971). See also Dorothy Dudley, *Forgotten Frontiers: Dreiser and the Land of the Free* (New York: Arno Press, 1971).

47. The best biographer-critic of Hemingway is Carlos H. Baker. See his *Hemingway: The Writer as Artist* (Princeton: Princeton University Press, 1972), and Richard Hardy, *Hemingway: A Psychological Portrait* (Sherman Oaks: Banner Books, 1977).

48. In a labor worthy of Hercules, Deidre Johnson has compiled an annotated checklist of all known magazine stories, dime novels, series, and nonseries titles published from 1889 to 1981. The resulting volume is called *Stratemeyer Pseudonyms and Series Books: An Annotated Checklist of Stratemeyer and Stratemeyer Syndicate Publications* (Westport, Conn.: Greenwood Press, 1981).

49. Tom Wolfe, *The Right Stuff* (New York: Simon & Schuster, 1979). All Wolfe's books smack of the mythic. Is he well on the way to becoming the intellectuals' Kandy-Kolored Horatio Alger?

50. Erling B. Holtsmark, *Tarzan and Tradition*.

51. Nye, *Unembarrassed Muse*, p. 321.

52. Gary Harmon, "Tarzan of the Apes: A Structuralist Analysis." I am grateful to Professor Harmon for letting me read and quote from his unpublished essay.

53. Quoted by John Oliver Wilson, *After Affluence: Economics to Meet Human Needs* (New York: Harper & Row, 1980), p. 101.

54. Irving Howe, *The World of the Blue Collar Worker* (New York: Dissent Publishers, 1972). See also Patricia Cayo Sexton, *Blue Collars and Hard Hats: The Working Class and the Future of American Politics* (New York: Random House, 1971); Lillian B. Rubin, *Worlds of Pain: Life in the Working Class Community* (New York: Basic Books, 1976); and Alan A. Fisher, "The Problems of Teenage Unemployment," (U.S. Dept. of Commerce, NTIS, No. PB–223914, 1980).

55. Lucy Komisar, *Down and Out in the USA: A History of Public Welfare* (New York: Franklin Watts, 1977); and Celeste MacLeod, *Horatio Alger, Farewell: The End of the American Dream* (New York: Seaview Books, 1980). MacLeod shares my conviction that upward mobility was the essence of the American dream, and that Americans still have the highest expectations in the world. She sees the picture as bleak, but not hopeless, urging us to readjust our thinking to fit reality; to abandon obsolete beliefs; and not to try winning a sports-car race with a horse and buggy. Can't we do all these things, and dream on?

56. Marsden, "American Myth of Success," p. 50.

POSTLUDE _____

Here then are our Seven Pillars: *demos, ethnos, heros, theos, logos, eikons,* and *mythos*. Inspired first by Lawrence's *Seven Pillars of Wisdom*, which in turn went back to *Proverbs* ("Wisdom hath builded a house: she hath hewn out her seven pillars"), modeled more specifically on Seldes's *7 Lively Arts*, my study took me far beyond Arabia and Broadway. I have concluded that to survive, culture must always be popular. The pillars we have seen and described are the very foundations of human life.

Visible in the latest best-seller, film, commercial, or video game, they are also so ancient that we dare not even date them. Perhaps 5 million years ago a kind of "ape-man" began to stand erect, and use sticks and stones as weapons. Several million years later came "upright man," and eventually, human communication. With early cave paintings and writings *homo erectus* began to share his experience—and later to construct pillars. To me they are both symbolic and architectural—erected not only on mountains but also inside minds.

At the same time, it is helpful to visualize them as actual pillars, made of marble—like those which sustained the Parthenon at Athens, the Temple of Neptune at Paestum, the Pantheon in Rome, Grand Central Station in New York. Later pillars were made of concrete, steel, plastic. They served not only as platform but also as synthesis—another Greek word, combining *syn*—together—and *tithenai*—to place: what is involved is the continuous adaptation of traditional forms to changing circumstances and contemporary life. Culture is constantly being reintegrated and reassimilated: but is it, in basic ways, being changed?[1] Are the alterations circular, not linear? Can we say, with T. S. Eliot, that our end is our beginning?

Some truths never change. Words must be symbolic, leaders heroic, and memories mythic. When they express, enhance, and exalt, they set hearts (and viewer ratings) soaring. Joyfully we go to the Realms of Gold, to escape the tinny clang of the commonplace and the glum news on A.P. Our own lives are often like receiving a sack-full of mail: most of it fourth class peppered with computer card bills. Never mind: a festival or film is coming; there will be new faces, new celebrities, new pleasures. The show must go on; we will be there, to applaud.[2]

The best of popular culture not only will survive but also will be accepted later on as high or elite culture. Hasn't the literature of the folk epic always used prefabricated material? Springing from the collective subconscious of the *demos*, much of it must have been crude, repetitive, and sentimental. Only the very greatest—such as the *Iliad* and the *Odyssey*—survived . . . distillations of countless others were not worth preserving. Might not that same process be going on now? Can we speculate on the idea that at some future time the best current television series could be studied as Folk Epic?[3] Doesn't genius always overcome media?

But let us not overestimate what we see before us—much is not worth comment, much less preservation. Thus has it always been. As in every culture and every clime, ineradicable diseases such as a long strain of perennial "isms" (racism, sexism, chauvinism, provincialism, narcissism, etc.) continue to plague and discourage us. They will always be the enemy, whatever subjects or areas (popular or otherwise) we study. Another perennial problem is the drawing of artificial lines or barriers between *demos, mythos*, nations, and subjects. Hardly a people anywhere on earth (as we noted in our *ethnos* chapter) have not felt themselves superior to their neighbors. Why this obsession with being "Number One"? Why not one among several, or even many? Must we continue to stand in line and have our "brows" (high, middle, and low) measured and calibrated? "To erase the boundaries created by snobbery and cultism that have so long divided us," Russel B. Nye writes, "means in the long run greater understanding for all."[4]

Differences in audiences, Nye goes on to point out, and in the artists' relationships with them, result in different methods and content. The popular artist's success or impact must be measured by his skill in operating within the boundaries set by majority will. He must develop certain specialized skills to accomplish this—and they are rare and important ones. That mass audiences exist, along with mass media, is an elementary fact of life.

Popular culture is committed to giving the public what it wants, which will not always agree with what the artist may feel to be the most aesthetically significant. Satisfying a large audience involves no less skill than pleasing a smaller or more sophisticated one; popular artists can and do develop tremendous expertise and real talent. Nor need popularity alone condemn what popular artists do as useless or inferior. A best-selling paperback is not *ipso facto* bad; a song is not necessarily worthless because people hum it; a painting is neither bad because many look at it with pleasure, nor good because few do.

If this be pragmatism (another word from a Greek root— *pragma*—meaning a thing done, business), then so be it. This particular "ism," founded by Americans C. S. Peirce and William James, holds that the function of thought is as a guide to action, and that the truth is preeminently to be tested by practical consequences. Does this not fit popular culture as a glove fits a hand?

Once again, we move forward by looking backward. We must learn from the Greeks, who showed how to discuss contemporary events under a mythological metaphor; and from the Romans, who adopted biographical archetypes among the gods. In the Middle Ages the lives of the saints fulfilled the same function. For Modern Man an immense new variety of types and themes has poured forth, as from a cornucopia. Writes Deric Regin:

We cannot see the contours of the great currents of our own time: we are too much inside the streams to chart their flow and volume. We are confronted with inner and outer historical surfaces. Of these, only the outer surfaces are accessible to historical knowledge.[5]

This inability to see the contours—to read the meaning of our time—is a central dilemma of popular culture. If we insist on living and thinking in "Now Time," how can we link up with the past? But if we only study the past, how can we cope with where and what we are?

And what about the media, which Tony Schwartz characterizes as "The Second God"? The media is everywhere and nowhere, "a disembodied entity occupying no space and all space at the same time." Using such words, Schwartz, "Merlin of the Media," sounds more like a medieval theologian than a modern communicator.

Media are not so much part of the new environment as the environment itself. Growing up in a postliterate environment, children receive vast amounts of visual information, unrelated to reading and writing. How will we teach them to by-pass many old constraints of print?

Two of the most far-ranging and radical critics of American media have been Canadians—Harold Adams Innis and Marshall McLuhan. Less given to the behavioral and quantitative methods that are hallmarks of many American scholars, they dared to range far afield in time and space, looking "in" on America somewhat the way Russians examined nineteenth-century Western Europe, and ex-Confederates the industrialized Robber Baron Yankee North. Despite his flamboyance and overkill, no critic has stimulated me as much as McLuhan; his urging me to attempt the Seven Pillars has been a constant stimulus. He, more than anyone else, saw that much scorned as "crass" and "commercial" reflects the true native culture of contemporary America. Only through this channel can we effect meaningful contacts with past cultures, and make our contribution to the Global Village. The quality of anybody's relations with the minds of the past is exactly and necessarily determined by the quality of his contemporary insights.

Our popular culture, and the electronic media which are now so crucial in transmitting it, are full of dialectical tensions. Those media use the airwaves—but they can't manufacture content out of thin air. Not the media, but the content, is the message. That content and its creators are the key to many dilemmas and doubts; and media content is becoming ever less American, ever more international. In music, for example, reggae, ska, punk, and salsa flourish. Hollywood and Nashville may hype stars and trends but, as Daniel Czitrom notes, "denial of the authenticity at the core of much popular music grossly simplifies the complex tensions existing within our popular culture."[6]

We have come to expect too much too soon from the new technology. Public access channels, "docutainment," two-way hook-ups, video telephones, talking computers, space shuttles: how much are they changing our lives and in what way? In a world of increasing scarcity and depression, how much more is affordable? Have we merely substituted the Electronic City for the Heavenly City—and who can say, in either case, that the streets are paved with gold?

With software so far behind hardware—the capacity to program so far ahead of quality programming—can and will we take advantage of the new devices? Or will broadcasting evolve into narrowcasting? John Cawelti is both fascinated and frightened by new radical cultural transformations. "At times they seem to hold out the promise of a revitalization of our culture," he writes. "At other times I wonder whether it is not simply an evasion of cultural responsibility."[7]

Following Cawelti's lead, we must unearth the fantasy that holds the popular arts together; find the formulas, then use them as creatively as the best scientists and mathematicians use theirs. Indeed, our most promising models may well be in the sciences: look what has been done within a single lifetime in cybernetics, genetics, bionics, decision-theory, linear programming, computer graphics, queuing and information theory. How such advances can be used by the humanities in general and popular culture in particular is bewildering, fascinating, and challenging.

It is not only by looking at the novel and untried that we shall go forward. The essential answers may well be buried in the past; our greatest hope is still our history. We are so wedded to the Greco-Roman tradition (as this book clearly demonstrates) that we do not look to more distant cultures (like those of Africa or Asia) for ways to adapt traditional form to modern life. As George Lewis has demonstrated, traditional peoples have been highly successful at such adaptation—what he calls "reintegrated or assimilated culture." His examples from West Africa include elite use of popular music; new patterns of Kente cloth by the Ashanti people of Ghana; and slogans appearing on the backs of African "Mammy Wagons"—neither a form of traditional culture nor an artifact of Western popular culture. Still another example is rickshaw paintings in Bangladesh.[8] The Western cult of change, and ever greater acceleration, may be blinders that hold us back. Sing a song of cycles. *Plus ça change, c'est plus la même chose.* Are not our changes more circular than linear? Once we remove the gadgetry, is not *Star Wars* another American Western—"Wagon Train in the Sky"? Is not all that we know of life (in biology, as well as culture) a series of cycles, of deaths and rebirths? Those of us raised in the Judeo-Christian tradition may do well, in a time of universalism, to study what other great systems, like Hinduism and Buddhism, have to teach on these issues. Hinduism, Carl Sagan points out in *Cosmos*, is "the only religion in which the time scales correspond to those of modern scientific cosmology."[9] Yet how many of us know about Hindu cycles, some as short as one calendar day, others as long as 8.65 billion years? Have the historians of the Western World in general, especially American historians, been so myopic as to miss larger patterns and meanings? What we don't see often shapes the entire way we look at human events. This blindness, William I. Thompson observes, may result not from inferior but superior eyesight: the expertise of the specialist causes him to squint into a microscope and blind himself to everything else around him. Held in tenure by temples, academics, or universities, we work for tunnel vision with peripheral blindness.[10]

This tendency towards overspecialization plagues popular culture studies and obscures the Seven Pillars. So does our obsession with external growth and the quantitative fallacy. Sixty cable television networks aren't necessarily twenty times better than three—expecially if most of them are showing reruns of *I Love Lucy* and *M.A.S.H.* This is not the road to reenchantment, but to disenchantment.

Among the original thinkers of our time who have sensed this are Mircea Eliade and George Kubler. Eliade calls for our collective regeneration through repetition of ancient myths and ceremonies, "leaving to possible future studies the detailed examination of each separate mythico-ritual complex."[11] Kubler believes lines of communication originated as signals, "which become commotions emitting further signals in an unbroken alternating sequence of event, signal, recreated event, renewed signal, etc."[12] Celebrated events have undergone the cycle millions of times each instant throughout their history, as when Jesus's life is commemorated in myriads of daily prayers. Today *celebrities* institute *celebrated* events; when one of the Beatles says his group "is better known than Jesus," it is conceivably true that for a certain group of people, in a narrow time-frame, that is the case. To put it differently, Kubler's "lines of communication" might for some lead more directly to the Lads from Liverpool than to the Carpenter from Nazareth. Blasphemy or historicity?

The scholar's task is to test and verify the evidence, not concerned with the signals other than as evidences or with the commotions they produce. In this domain the traditional problems arise which lace together the history of things. We are raising neither an *aesthetic* nor a *religious* question when we compare lines of communication opened by the Beatles and Jesus. Since an historical happening requires only an event together with its signals and a person capable of reproducing the signals, we have a *real* problem on our hands.[13] Now we must get busy and find the real solutions.

Beset by such dilemmas and the ever-growing complexities of modern living, what voices, what leaders shall we follow? Who are the wise men in our midst? If few dare list six immortal authors of today, one can name with assurance six for tomorrow: Homer, Virgil, Plato, Dante, Shakespeare, and Faulkner. They cut across barriers of time, place, and culture. They speak to mankind. The future of popular culture (whether it rests on seven or seventy pillars) is rooted in the dimly perceived past: folk rituals, founding fathers, sacred objects, mythic memories, enduring truths. The more we know what lay behind us, the more confident we can be about what is ahead.

Amidst all ominous signs—wars and rumors of war—I opt for optimism. Our legacy will be a worldwide popular culture, anchored in the past but adapted to the present. Our descendants will praise its solid purpose and technical perfection. It will have its own historical justification.

It is commonplace among certain scholars (especially in the social sciences) to claim that science and progress are in command—that homo sapiens has "come of age."[14] Secularism reigns. Nonsense. As Mary Douglas has pointed out, our modern "secular" society is anything but secular—being secularized only in respect to what was previously sacred.[15] The best scientists are beginning to explore the mystical; most people of the world are finding religion, not science, their hope and salvation. The archetype that best catches the spirit of the waning twentieth century is that of rebirth.

Every age invents, then enthrones, its own myths. We lie with the myth of the Mythless Society, unaware that the success of a Michael Jackson partakes of the mythic. The new videos raise questions about being—the *logos* of reality. Some formulas never change. Power plus structure always equals life-style.

We may be reaching a magic moment—a prophetic moment—when a new mythology is born. Popular culture can share in, even help shape, that moment. The *demos* will merge events with myth, as they have done time and again in the past. If so, we can infuse the minute and technical with the poetic and probing spirit; we can erect on our eternal pillars an enduring city.

NOTES

1. George H. Lewis raises the question in his article, "Assimilated Culture: The Ashanti People of Ghana," in *Michigan Sociological Review*, 5, Fall 1978; as did Alan Gowans in *The Unchanging Arts* (Philadelphia: J. P. Lippincott, 1971). My own thoughts on these matters are summed up in *Common Culture and the Great Tradition* (Westport, Conn.: Greenwood Press, 1982).

2. Specifics of how archetypes will be revised, again and again, to meet new needs is demonstrated by Harold Schechter and Jonna Gormely Semeiks, *Patterns in Popular Culture: A Sourcebook for Writers* (New York: Harper & Row, 1980).

3. Ibid. For a closer look at the kind of collaboration and cooperation that prevails today, see Robert C. Toll, *The Entertainment Machine: American Show Business in the Twentieth Century* (New York: Oxford University Press, 1981); and Michael Arlen, *Thirty Seconds* (New York: Penguin, 1981) which tells the story of what is involved in making a

single thirty-second commercial in the 1980s: scores of participants, two years of talk, millions of dollars, months of intensive filming, and over 10,000 feet of film.

4. Russel B. Nye, *The Unembarrassed Muse* (New York: Dial, 1976), p. 347. Past president of both the American Studies Association and the Popular Culture Association, Nye has done much to bridge the gaps of which he writes. No one has been more helpful to me as a scholar and a friend in the work which I have undertaken.

5. Regin, *Culture and the Crowd*, (New York: Chilton Book Co., 1968), p. 375.

6. Daniel J. Czitrom, *The Media and Man* (Chapel Hill: University of North Carolina Press, 1984), p. 192.

7. Cawelti, *Adventure, Mystery and Romance* (Chicago: University of Chicago, 1976), p. 134.

8. Lewis, "Assimilated Culture." A new journal, *International Popular Culture*, is attempting to expand this kind of comparative study. For details write Professor R. G. Powers, 130 Stuyvesant Place, Staten Island, N.Y. 10301.

9. Carl Sagan, *Cosmos* (New York: Random House, 1980), p. 258.

10. William Irwin Thompson, *Darkness and Scattered Light* (New York: Doubleday, 1978), p. 108. Thompson suggests that the coming world culture might be shaped far more by the contemplative traditions of the East than the exhausted intellection of the West. I agree.

11. Mircea Eliade, *The Myth of the Eternal Return* (New York: Pantheon Books, Bollingen Series XLVI, 1954), chapter 2.

12. George Kubler, *The Shape of Time: Remarks on the History of Things* (New Haven, Conn.: Yale University Press, 1962), p. 21.

13. Ibid.

14. See, for example, Stanley Diamond, *In Search of the Primitive* (New Brunswick, N.J.: Transaction Books, 1974).

15. One of the clearest statements of her argument is in Mary Douglas's essay on "Advertising and the Media: The Cultural Origins of Modern Myth and Ritual," in Richard Stivers, ed., *Evil and Modern Myth and Ritual* (Athens: University of Georgia Press, 1982).

BIBLIOGRAPHY ⸻

Agard, Walter R. *Classical Myths in Sculpture* (Madison: University of Wisconsin Press, 1953).

Alvord, Clarence W. "The Daniel Boone Myth," *Journal of the Illinois State Historical Society*, April 1926.

Amory, Cleveland. *Who Killed Society?* (New York: Harper & Row, 1960).

Andrist, Ralph K. *George Washington, A Biography in His Own Words* (New York: Newsweek Books, 1972).

Aptheker, Herbert. *A Documentary History of the Negro People in the United States* (New York: Citadel Press, 1951).

Arendt, Hannah. *The Human Condition* (Chicago: University of Chicago Press, 1958).

Arlen, Michael. *Thirty Seconds* (New York: Penguin, 1981).

Ashton, Dore. *The New York School: A Cultural Reckoning* (New York: Viking Press, 1972).

Bainton, Roland H. *The Age of the Reformation* (New York: Anvil, 1956).

Bakeless, John. *Daniel Boone* (New York: William Morrow & Co., 1939).

Baker, Carlos H. *Hemingway: The Writer as Artist* (Princeton, N.J.: Princeton University Press, 1972).

Bandinelli, Ranuccio Bianchi. *Rome: The Late Empire* (New York: George Braziller, 1971).

Banks, Louis Albert. *The Story of the Hall of Fame* (New York: Harpers, 1902).

Banks, Martha B. *Heroes of the South Seas* (New York: Macmillan, 1896).

Banton, Michael. *The Idea of Race* (London: Tavistock, 1977).

Barenholtz, Bernard, and McClintock, Inez. *American Antique Toys, 1830–1900* (New York: Harry N. Abrams, 1980).

Barth, Fredrick, ed. *Ethnic Groups versus Relativism in Language and Thought* (The Hague: Mouton Publishers, 1976).

Bartlett, Vernon. *The Colour of Their Skin* (London: Chatto and Windus, 1969).

Beane, Wendall C., and Doty, William G. *Myths, Rites, Symbols: A Mircea Eliade Reader* (New York: Harper & Row, 1976), Vol. 2.

Beard, Dan. *Hardly a Man Is Now Alive: The Autobiography of Dan Beard* (New York: Dutton, 1939).

Beauroy, Jacques, ed. *Popular Culture in France* (Saratoga, Calif.: Anma Libri & Co., 1976).

Belazs, Bela. *Theory of Film* (London: Dennis Dobson, 1952).

Benedict, Ruth. *Patterns of Culture* (Boston: Houghton Mifflin, 1959).

Benz, Ernst. *The Eastern Orthodox Church* (New York: Anchor Books, 1963).

Bercovitch, Sacvan. *Puritan Origins and the American Self* (New Haven, Conn.: Yale University Press, 1975).

Berger, John. *Ways of Seeing* (New York: Penguin, 1980).

Bigsby, C.W.E., ed. *Approaches to Popular Culture* (Bowling Green, Ohio: Popular Press, 1976).

———. *Superculture: American Popular Culture and Europe* (Bowling Green, Ohio: Popular Press, 1975).

Billington, Ray Allen. *Westward Expansion: A History of the American Frontier* (New York: Macmillan, 1952).

Bindy, Thomas H. *The Oecumenical Documents of the Faith* (London: Methuen, 1950).

Bloy, Myron. *The Crisis of Cultural Change* (Cambridge: MIT Press, 1965).

Boas, Franz. *Primitive Art* (New York: Dover, 1955).

Boas, George. *The History of Ideas: An Introduction* (New York: Charles Scribner's, 1969).

Bode, Carl. *Anatomy of American Popular Culture: 1840–61* (Berkeley: University of California Press, 1959).

———. *The Half World of American Culture: A Miscellany* (Carbondale: Southern Illinois University Press, 1965).

Boehn, Max von. *Dolls*, trans. by Josephine Nicoll. (New York: Dover, 1972).

Bogle, Donald. *Toms, Coons, Mulattoes, Mammies, and Bucks: An Interpretive History of Blacks in American Film* (New York: Viking, 1975).

Boorstin, Daniel J. *The Image: A Guide to Pseudo-Events in America* (New York: Atheneum, 1975).

———. *The Image; or, What Happened to the American Dream* (New York: Atheneum, 1962).

———. "The Mythologizing of George Washington." Chap. 6 in *The Americans: The National Experience* (New York: Random House, 1967).

Booth, Wayne C. *Modern Dogmas and the Rhetoric of Assent* (Notre Dame, Ind.: University of Notre Dame Press, 1966).

Boyce, George K. *Corpus of the Lararia of Pompeii* (Rome: American Academy, 1968).

Brackman, Arnold C., and Kamal El Mallakh. *The Gold of Tutankhamun* (New York: Newsweek Books, 1982).

Bradford, Roark. *John Henry* (New York: Harper and Brothers, 1931).

Brand, Oscar. *The Ballad Mongers* (New York: Funk & Wagnalls, 1962).

Broderick, Francis L. *W.E.B. DuBois, Negro Leader in a Time of Crisis* (Stanford: Stanford University Press, 1967).

Browne, Ray. *Objects of Special Devotion: Fetishes and Fetishism in Popular Culture* (Bowling Green, Ohio: Popular Press, 1981).

———. *Rituals and Ceremonies in Popular Culture* (Bowling Green, Ohio: Popular Press, 1980).

Browne, Ray, and Fishwick, Marshall, eds. *The Hero in Transition* (Bowling Green, Ohio: Popular Press, 1983).

———, eds. *Icons of America* (Bowling Green, Ohio: Popular Press, 1978).

———, eds. *Icons of Popular Culture* (Bowling Green, Ohio: Popular Press, 1970).

Browne, Ray; Grogg, Sam, Jr.; and Landrum, Larry, eds. *Theories and Methodologies in Popular Culture* (Bowling Green, Ohio: Popular Press, 1979).

Brunvand, Jan Harold. *Folklore: A Study and Research Guide* (New York: St. Martin's Press, 1976).

———. *The Study of American Folklore: An Introduction* (New York: Norton, 1968).

Bryan, Daniel. *The Mountain Muse . . .* (Harrisonburg, Va.: Davidson and Bourne, 1813).

Buel, James W. *Heroes of the Dark Continent* (London: Faber, 1890).

Burckhardt, Jacob. *The Civilization of the Renaissance in Italy* (London: Methuen, 1890).

Burke, Kenneth. "Rhetoric—Old and New," in *Journal of General Education*, 5, April 1951.

Burke, Peter. *Popular Culture in Early Modern Europe* (New York: Harper & Row, 1978).

Burland, C. A. *Gods and Heroes of War* (New York: G. P. Putnam's, Sons, 1974).

Burlingame, Roger. *Henry Ford* (New York: Holt, Rinehart & Winston, 1948).

Butcher, Margaret Just. *The Negro in American Culture* (New York: World, 1956).

Butler, Bill. *The Myth of the Hero* (London: Rider, 1979).

Cady, John F. *Thailand, Burma, Laos, and Cambodia* (Englewood Cliffs, N.J.: Prentice-Hall, 1966).

Cairns, David. *The Image of God in Man* (London: SCM Press, 1953).

Calas, Nicolas, and Calas, Elena. *Icons and Images of the Sixties* (New York: Dutton, 1971).

Calder, Jenni. *Heroes: From Byron to Guevara* (London: Hamish Hamilton, 1977).

Campbell, Joseph. *The Hero with a Thousand Faces* (New York: World, 1956; paperback ed., Meridian, 1956).

———. "Introduction," in *The Portable Jung* (New York: Viking, 1971).

Carnegie, Andrew. *The Gospel of Wealth, and Other Timely Essays* (New York: Century Co., 1900).

Carpenter, Edmund. *Explorations in Communication* (Boston: Beacon Press, 1960).

Casty, Alan. *Mass Media and Mass Man* (New York: Holt, Rinehart & Winston, 1968).

Catton, Bruce. "Half-Horse, Half-Alligator," in *American Heritage*, December 1957.

Cawelti, John G. *Adventure, Mystery and Romance: Formula Stories as Art* (Chicago: University of Chicago Press, 1976).

———. *The Six-Gun Mystique* (Bowling Green, Ohio: Popular Press, 1970).

Chaffee, Mary Law. "William E. B. Dubois's Concept of the Racial Problem in the United States," in *Journal of Negro History*, 41, July 1956.

Chametzky, Jules, and Sidney Kaplan, eds. *Blacks and White in American Culture* (New York: William Morrow & Co., 1969).

Chappell, Louis W. *John Henry* (Jena, Germany: Walter Biederman, 1933).

Childs, James Francis. *The English and Scottish Popular Ballads*, 5 vols. (Boston: Houghton Mifflin, 1882–1898).

Chu, Godwin C. *Popular Media in China: Shaping New Cultural Patterns* (Honolulu: University of Hawaii Press, 1978).

Clark, Jerry E. *The Shawnee* (Lexington: University of Kentucky Press, 1977).

Clark, Ronald Edison. *The Man Who Made the Future* (New York: Methuen, 1977).

Clark, Thomas D. *Frontier America: The Story of the Westward Movement* (New York: Charles Scribner's, 1959).

Cleaver, Eldridge. *Souls on Ice* (New York: McGraw-Hill, 1968).

Clemon, Wolfgang. *The Development of Shakespeare's Imagery* (Cambridge, Mass.: Harvard University Press, 1950).

Cleveland, Reginald M., and Williamson, S. T. *The Road Is Yours: The Story of the Automobile and the Men Behind It* (New York: Greystone Press, 1951).

Clevenger, Theodore, Jr., and Matthews, Jack. *The Speech Communication Process* (Glenview, Ill.: Scott, Foresman & Co., 1971).

Clymer, Joseph F. *Treasury of Early American Automobiles, 1877–1925* (New York: McGraw-Hill, 1950).

Coakley, Mary L. *Sex, Sisterhood, and Self-Consciousness: What's Happening to Women's Magazines* (New York: World, 1980).

Coffin, Tristram P., and Cohen, Henning, eds. *The Parade of Heroes: Legendary Figures in American Lore* (New York: Dutton, 1978).

Collier, Daniel M., Jr. "The Impact of American Subcultures on the Polity as a Model for Development," in *Protagonists of Change: Subcultures in Development and Revolution*, ed. by Abdul A. Said (Englewood Cliffs, N.J.: Prentice-Hall, 1971).

Cook, Joan Marble. *In Defense of Homo Sapiens* (New York: Dell, 1975).

Coon, Carleton S. *The Origin of Races* (New York: Knopf, 1962).

Cooper, Douglas. *The Cubist Epoch* (London: Phaedon Press, 1970).

Copleston, F. C. *Medieval Philosophy* (New York: Harper, 1961).

Cort, David. *Revolution by Cliche* (New York: Funk & Wagnalls, 1970).

Cowan, Louis. *The Fugitive Group: A Literary History* (Baton Rouge: Louisiana State University Press, 1959).

Cox, Harvey. *The Secular City: Urbanization and Secularization in Perspective* (New York: Macmillan, 1965).

————. *Religion in the Secular City: Toward a Postmodern Theology* (New York: Simon and Schuster, 1984).

Crawford, Hubert H. *Crawford's Encyclopedia of Comic Books* (Middle Village, N.Y.: Village Press, 1978).

————. *Thor*, vol. 1, no. 319, May 1982.

Cripps, Thomas. *Black Films as Genre* (Bloomington: Indiana University Press, 1978).

————. "Paul Robeson and Black Identity in American Movies," in *Massachusetts Review*, Summer 1970.

————. *Slow Fade to Black: The Negro in American Film* (New York: Oxford University Press, 1977).

Cruse, Harold. *The Crisis of the Negro Intellectual* (New York: William Morrow & Co., 1967).

Cunliffe, Marcus. *George Washington: Man and Monument* (New York: Mentor, 1958).

Cunningham, Adrian, ed. *The Theory of Myth* (London: Sheed and Ward, 1973).

Czitrom, Daniel J. *The Media and Man* (Chapel Hill: University of North Carolina Press, 1984).

Dauner, Louise. "Myth and Humor in the Uncle Remus Tales," *American Literature*, 20, May 1948).

Davidson, John. *Oration Delivered at Plainfield, N.J., February 22nd, 1867, before the Washington Monument and Historical Association.* (Plainfield, N.J., 1867).

Davis, Charles T., and Walden, Daniel, eds. *On Being Black* (New York: Fawcett, 1970).

DeCosta, B. F. "The Traditional Washington Vindicated," in *Magazine of American History*, 5, August 1880.

Deiss, Joseph J. *Herculaneum: A City Returns to the Sun* (New York: Crowell, 1966).

Delehaye, Henri. *Les Legendes Hagiographiques* (Brussels: Croniques, 1905).

DeMott, Benjamin. "Vonnegut's Otherworldly Laughter," in *Saturday Review*, May 1, 1971.

———. *Supergrow* (New York: Dutton, 1969).

Demus, Otto. *Byzantine Mosaic Decoration: Aspects of Monumental Art in Byzantium* (Boston Books, 1955).

Denisoff, R. Serge. "Urban Folk 'Movement Research': Value Free?" *Western Folklore*, 27, no. 3, July 1969.

Dennis, Everette E. *The Media Society: Evidence about Mass Communication in America* (Dubuque, Iowa: Wm. C. Brown, 1978).

Diedrich, Maria. *Kommunismus in Afroamerikanischen Roman* (Stuttgart, F.R.G.: Metzler, 1977).

Dietz, Lawrence. *Soda Pop: The History, Advertising, Art, and Memorabilia of Soft Drinks in America* (New York: Chelsea House, 1973).

Dobie, J. Frank. *In the Shadow of History* (Detroit: Folklore Associates, 1971).

Donaldson, Ian. *The World Turned Upside Down: Comedy from Johnson to Fielding* (Oxford, U.K.: Clarendon, 1970).

Dorris, J. T. "Transylvania Colony," in *Kentucky School Journal*, 13, no. 1, September 1934.

Dorsey, George. *The Story of Civilization: Man's Own Show* (New York: Halcyon, 1931).

Dorson, Richard. *American Folklore and the Historian* (Chicago: University of Chicago Press, 1971).

———. *American Negro Folktales* (Bloomington: Indiana University Press, 1967).

———. *Journal of American Folklore*, 72, September 1959.

Douglas, Jack B. *The Technological Threat* (Englewood Cliffs, N.J.: Prentice-Hall, 1971).

Dover, Cedric. *American Negro Art* (New York: Graphic Society, 1960).

DuBois, W.E.B. *Autobiography* (New York: International, 1968).

———. *The Negro* (New York: Oxford University Press, 1970).

Dudley, Dorothy. *Forgotten Frontiers: Dreiser and the Land of the Free* (New York: Arno Press, 1971).

Dundes, Alan. *The Study of Folklore* (Englewood Cliffs, N.J.: Prentice-Hall, 1965).

Dygert, James H. *The Investigative Journalist: Folk Heroes of a New Era* (Englewood Cliffs, N.J.: Prentice-Hall, 1976).

Eagleton, Terry. *Marxism and Literary Criticism* (New York: Methuen, 1976).

Eco, Umberto. *A Theory of Semiotics* (Bloomington: University of Indiana Press, 1976).

Eggan, Dorothy. "The Personal Use of Myth in Dreams," in *Myth: A Symposium*, ed. by Thomas Sebeok (Bloomington: University of Indiana Press, 1958), pp. 107–121.

Ehninger, Douglas. *Contemporary Rhetoric* (Glenview, Ill.: Scott, Foresman & Co., 1972).

El Mallakh, Kamal, and Brackman, Arnold C. *The Gold of Tutankhamen* (New York: Newsweek Books, 1982).

Eliade, Mircea. *Myths, Dreams and Mysteries* (New York: Harper and Brothers, 1960).

———. *Myths, Dreams, and Mysteries: The Encounter between Contemporary Faith and Archaic Realities* (New York: Harper & Row, 1975).

———. *The Myth of the External Return* (New York: Pantheon Books, Bollingen Series XLVI, 1954).

Eliot, T. S. *Essays Ancient and Modern by T. S. Eliot* (New York: Harpers, 1936).

Ellison, Ralph. *Invisible Man* (New York: Penguin, 1965).

Emery, Edwin. *The Press and America* (Englewood Cliffs, N.J.: Prentice-Hall, 1972).

Emery, Noemie. *Washington, A Biography* (New York: G. P. Putnam's Sons, 1976).

English, T. H. "The Twice-Told Tale and Uncle Remus," in *Georgia Review*, 2, Winter 1948.

Ewen, David. *All the Years of American Popular Music* (Englewood Cliffs, N.J.: Prentice-Hall, 1977).

Fairlie, Henry. "Too Rich for Heroes," in *Harper's* (November 1978), pp. 33ff.

Feiffer, Jules. *The Great Comic Book Heroes* (New York: Basic Books, 1965).

Fell, John L. *A History of Films* (New York: William Morrow & Co., 1979).

Ferguson, Rowena. *Editing the Small Magazine* (New York: Columbia University Press, 1976).

Fiedler, Leslie A. *The Inadvertent Epic.* (New York: Simon & Schuster, 1970).

———. *The Inadvertent Epic: From Uncle Tom's Cabin to Roots* (New York: Simon & Schuster, 1979).

Finch, Christopher. *The Art of Walt Disney* (Burbank, Calif.: Walt Disney Productions, 1973).

———. *Pop Art* (New York: Vista, 1968).

Fish, C. R. *The Rise of the Common Man* (New York: Charles Scribner's, 1927).

Fisher, Alan A. "The Problems of Teenage Unemployment" (U.S. Dept. of Commerce, NTIS, No. PB–223914, 1980).

Fisher, Walter R. "Rhetorical Fiction and the Presidency," *Quarterly Journal of Speech,* 66, April 1980.

Fishwick, Marshall W. *American Heroes: Myth and Reality* (Washington, D.C.: Public Affairs Press, 1954).

———. *Art and Life in Black America* (Wilmington, Del.: American Studies Institute, 1970).

———. *Common Culture and the Great Tradition* (Westport, Conn.: Greenwood Press, 1982).

———. *Contemporary Black Artists* (New York: Sandak, 1970).

———. *The Hero, American Style* (New York: David McKay, 1969).

———. *Heroes of Popular Culture* (Bowling Green, Ohio: Popular Press, 1972).

———. *Lee After the War* (New York: Greenwood Press, 1963).

———. "The Man in the White Marble Toga," *Saturday Review,* February 20, 1960.

———. *New Journalism* (Bowling Green, Ohio: Popular Press, 1975).

———. *Sleeping Beauty and Her Suitors* (Macon, Ga.: Southern Press, 1961).

———. *Springlore in Virginia* (Bowling Green, Ohio: Popular Press, 1979).

———. "Humane Communication," *Virginia Tech Magazine,* Fall 1977.

———. "The Cowboy: America's Contribution to the World's Mythology," *Western Folklore,* 11, April 1952.

———. *Zebras of the World, Disunite* (Wilmington, Del.: Wemyss Foundation, 1968).

———, ed. *Remus, Rastus Revolution* (Bowling Green, Ohio: Popular Press, 1972).

Fiske, John. *American Revolution* (Boston: Houghton Mifflin, 1897).

———. *The Critical Period of American History 1783–1789* (Boston: n.p., 1888).

Flanagan, John T., and Hudson, Arthur Palmer. *Folklore in American Literature* (Evanston, Ill.: Row, Peterson, 1958).

Flint, Timothy. *Biographical Memoir of Daniel Boone, The First Settler of Kentucky* (Cincinnati: n.p., 1833).

Flippen, Charles E. *Liberating The Media: The New Journalism* (Washington, D.C.: Acropolis Press, 1974).

Foner, Philip S. *DuBois: Speeches and Addresses* (New York: Pathfinder Press, 1970).

Ford, James L. C. *Magazines for Millions* (Carbondale: Southern Illinois Press, 1969).

Forkosch, Morris D. "Who Are the 'People' in the Preamble to the Constitution?" *Case Western Reserve Law Review*, 19, no. 3, April 1968.

Fotheringham, Allan. "A Lifetime of Rehearsals from Stagecoach to Stage," *Macleans*, July 28, 1980.

Fox, Ralph. *The Novel and the People* (New York: International Publishers, 1945).

Franklin, John Hope. *From Slavery to Freedom*. 3d ed. (New York: Knopf, 1967).

Fraser, Antonia. *A History of Toys* (London: Delacorte, 1966).

Freeman, Jo. *The Politics of Women's Liberation* (New York: David McKay, 1972).

Friar, Ralph E., and Friar, Natasha. *The Only Good Indian—The Hollywood Gospel* (New York: Drama Book Specialists, 1975).

Fuller, Melville W. *Address: Commemoration of the Inauguration of George Washington as First President of the United States Delivered Before the Two Houses of Congress, Dec. 11, 1889.* (New York: n.p., 1890).

Gabriel, Ralph H. *The Course of American Democratic Thought* (New York: Ronald Press, 1956).

Garreau, Joel. *The Nine Nations of North America* (Boston: Houghton Mifflin, 1981).

Gasset, Ortega Y. *The Modern Theme* (New York: Harper Brothers, 1961).
———. *The Revolt of the Masses* (London: Allen & Unwin, 1951).

Gayle, Addison, Jr. *The Black Situation* (New York: Horizon, 1970).
———, ed. *Black Expression: Essays by and About Black Americans in the Creative Arts* (New York: Weybright & Talley, 1970).

Geck, Elizabeth. *Johannes Gutenberg: From Lead Letter to the Computer* (Bad Godesberg, F.R.G.: Inter Natione Books, 1968).

Gelatt, Ronald. *The Fabulous Phonograph, 1877–1977* (New York: Dutton, 1977).

Gerhard, H. P. *The World of Icons* (New York: Harper & Row, 1971).

Gilborn, Craig. "Pop Iconology: Looking for the Coke Bottle," in *Icons of Popular Culture*, ed. by Ray Browne and Marshall W. Fishwick (Bowling Green, Ohio: Popular Press, 1970).

Glassie, Henry, ed. *Folksongs and Their Makers* (Bowling Green, Ohio: Popular Press, 1979).

Gleason, H. A. *An Interpretation to Descriptive Linguistics* (New York: Holt, Rinehart & Winston, 1961).

Golden, James L.; Berquist, Goodwin F.; and Coleman, William E. *The Rhetoric of Western Thought* (Dubuque, Iowa: Kendall/Hunt, 1968).

Gossett, Thomas F. *Race: The History of an Idea in America* (Dallas: Southern Methodist University Press, 1963).

Gouschev, Sergei. *Russian Science in the 21st Century* (New York: McGraw-Hill, 1961).

Gowans, Alan. *The Unchanging Arts* (Philadelphia: J. B. Lippincott, 1971).

Greene, Theodore P. *America's Heroes: The Changing Models of Success in American Magazines* (New York: Dutton, 1970).

Greenfield, Jeff. *Television: The First Fifty Years* (New York: Harry N. Abrams, 1977).

Gregory, Timothy E. *Vox Populi: Popular Opinion and Violence in the Religious Controversies of the Fifth Century A.D.* (Columbus: Ohio State University Press, 1979).

Griswold, A. Whitney. "The American Cult of Success" (Ph.D. dissertation, Yale's Sterling Library, 1942).

Grunig, James. *Decline of the Global Village* (Bayside, N.Y.: General Hall, 1976).

Gurr, Ted Robert. *Why Men Rebel* (Princeton, N.J.: Princeton University Press, 1970).

Guthrie, Lee. *Woody Allen: A Biography* (New York: Drake Publishers, 1978).

Hague, John A. *American Character and Culture in a Changing World* (Westport, Conn.: Greenwood Press, 1979).

Hall, William S., and Freedle, Roy O. *Culture and Language: The Black American Experience* (New York: John Wiley & Sons, 1975).

Handlin, Oscar, et al. *Harvard Guide to American History* (Cambridge, Mass.: Harvard University Press, 1954).

Hankins, Frank M. *The Racial Basis of Civilization* (New York: Knopf, 1926).

Hardy, Richard. *Hemingway: A Psychological Portrait* (Sherman Oaks, Calif.: Banner Books, 1977).

Harrington, Michael. *The Accidental Century* (New York: Macmillan, 1965).

Harris, Julia Collier. *The Life and Letters of Joel Chandler Harris* (New York: World, 1918).

Harris, Neil. "Iconography and Intellectual History: The Half-tone Effect," *New Directions in American Intellectual History*, ed. by John Higham (Baltimore: Johns Hopkins University Press, 1981).

Hart, James D. *The Popular Book: A History of America's Literary Taste* (Berkeley: University of California Press, 1963).

Hawes, William. *The Performer in Mass Media* (New York: Hastings House, 1978).

Hayes, Harold, ed. *Smiling Through the Apocalypse: Esquire's History of the Sixties* (New York: McCall's, 1969).

Hays, Robert P. "George Washington: American Moses," in *American Quarterly*, 21, no. 4, Winter 1969.

Hearnshaw, F.J.C. *The Social and Political Ideas of Some Great Medieval Thinkers* (New York: Charles Scribner's, 1923).

Heath, G. Louis, ed. *The Black Panther Leaders Speak* (Metuchen, N.J.: Scarecrow Press, 1976).

Heer, Friedrich. *The Medieval World* (New York: Mentor, 1964).

Heiddeger, Martin. *Introduction to Metaphysics* (New Haven, Conn.: Yale University Press, 1959).

  Hentoff, Nat. "Behold the New Journalism—It's Coming After You!" *Evergreen Review*, July 1968.

Hobsbawn, E. J. *Primitive Rebels* (Manchester, U.K.: University Press, 1959).

Hoellering, George, and Eliot, T. S. *Film of Murder in the Cathedral* (New York: Harcourt Brace and World, 1952).

Hoffman, Abbie. "Campus Activities," in *Parade*, February 20, 1983.

Holoein, Martin O. *Computers and Their Social Impact* (New York: John Wiley & Sons, 1977).

Holsaert, Eunice. *Outer Space* (New York: Holt, Rinehart & Winston, 1959).

Holtsmark, Erling B. *Tarzan and Tradition: Classical Myth in Popular Literature* (Westport: Greenwood Press, 1982).

Hook, Sidney. *The Hero in History* (New York: John Day, 1942).

Hopkin, Jerry. *Elvis: A Biography* (New York: Simon & Schuster, 1972).
———. *The Rock Story* (New York: Signet, 1970).

Hornback, Bert G. *Hero of my Life: Essays on Dickens* (Athens: Ohio University Press, 1981).

Howe, Irving. *The World of the Blue Collar Worker* (New York: Dissent Publishers, 1972).

Hoyt, James. "The Civil War; Nineteenth Century Turning Point," *The American Experience* (Washington, D.C.: U.S.I.S., 1976).

Hubbell, Jay. *The South in American Literature* (Durham, N.C.: Duke University Press, 1954).

Hudson, Kenneth. *The Jargon of the Professions* (New York: Macmillan, 1978).

Huggins, W. H., and Entwisle, Doris R. *Iconic Communication: An Annotated Bibliography* (Baltimore, Md.: Johns Hopkins University Press, 1974).

Hughes, Robert. *The Shock of the New* (New York: Random House, 1981).

Hussey, J. M. *The Byzantine World* (New York: Harper & Brothers, 1961).

Huxtable, Ada Louis. "Only the Phony is Real," in *New York Times*, May 13, 1973.

Inge, M. Thomas, ed. *Concise Histories of Popular Culture* (Westport, Conn.: Greenwood Press, 1982).

Innis, Harold A. *The Bias of Communication* (Toronto: University of Toronto Press, 1964).

Irving, John. *The World According to Garp* (New York: Dutton, 1978).

Isaacs, Susan. *Intellectual Growth in Young Children* (London: Routledge & Kegen Paul, 1930).

Jacobs, Norman. *Culture for the Millions? Mass Media in Modern Society* (Boston: Beacon Press, 1959).

Jessel, Levic. *The Ethnic Process: An Evolutionary Concept of Languages and Peoples* (The Hague: Mouton Publishers, 1978).

Jillson, Willard R. *The Boone Narrative* (Louisville, Ky.: Standard Printing Co., 1932).

Johnson, Alexander Bryan. *The Philosophy of Human Knowledge; Or, A Treatise on Language* (Utica, N.Y.: n.p., 1928).

Johnson, Deidre. *Stratemeyer Pseudonyms and Series Books: An Annotated Checklist of Stratemeyer and Stratemeyer Syndicate Publications* (Westport, Conn.: Greenwood Press, 1981).

Johnson, Lemuel A. *The Devil, the Gargoyle, and the Buffoon: The Negro as Metaphor in Western Literature* (New York: University Publications, 1971).

Johnson, Michael. *The New Journalism* (Lawrence: University of Kansas Press, 1971).

Jones, LeRoi. *Blues People* (New York: William Morrow & Co., 1963).

Jung, C. G. *The Collected Works of C. G. Jung*, 9 vols., (Princeton, N.J.: Bollingen Press, 1969).

————. "Psychology and Literature," in *Modern Man in Search of a Soul* (New York: Harcourt Brace & World, 1955).

Jung, C. G., and Kerenyi, C. *Essays on a Science of Mythology* (Princeton, N.J.: Bollingen Press, 1959).

Kahn, E. J. *The Big Drink* (New York: Random House, 1960).

Kato, Hidetoshi. "From Pantheon to Presley: Changes in Urban Symbolism" in *Communication and the City: The Changing Environment*, Paper 7 of the East-West Communication Institute, Honolulu, Hawaii, November 1973.

Kepes, Gyorgy, ed. *Sign, Image, Symbol* (New York: George Braziller, 1966).

Knowlton, K. C. *Computer-Produced Movies* (New York: Science, 150, 1965).

Kolker, Robert P. *A Cinema of Loneliness* (New York: Oxford University Press, 1980).

Komisar, Lucy. *Down and Out in the U.S.A.: A History of Public Welfare* (New York: Franklin Watts, 1977).

Kouwenhoven, John A. *American Studies: Words or Things?* (Wilmington, Del.: Wemyss Foundation, 1963).
————. *The Arts in Modern American Civilization* (New York: Dutton, 1960).
Krappe, Alexander H. *The Science of Folklore* (London: Methuen, 1930).
Kroc, Ray. *Grinding It Out: The Making of McDonald's* (Chicago: Henry Regnery Co., 1977).
Kubler, George. *The Shape of Time: Remarks on the History of Things* (New Haven, Conn.: Yale University Press, 1962).
Larkin, Oliver W. *Art and Life in America* (New York: Holt, Rinehart & Winston, 1960).
Larue, Gerald A. *Ancient Myth and Modern Man* (Englewood Cliffs, N.J.: Prentice-Hall, 1975).
Lasareff, Victor. *Russian Icons* (New York: UNESCO, 1962).
Laslett, Peter. *The World We Have Lost* (New York: Charles Scribner's, 1965).
Latourette, Kenneth Scott, *A Short History of the Far East*, 4th ed. (New York: Macmillan, 1964).
Laude, Jean. *La Peinture Francaise (1905–14) et 'l'art Negre* (Paris: Sorel, 1968).
Lax, Eric. *On Being Funny: Woody Allen and Comedy* (New York: Charter House, 1975).
Leakey, Richard, and Lewin, Roger. *People of the Lake* (New York: Anchor, 1978).
Leavis, F. R. *Mass Civilization and Minority Culture* (Cambridge, U.K.: Cambridge University Press, 1930).
————. *Nor Shall My Sword* (London: Macmillan, 1972).
Levine, Arthur. *When Dreams and Heroes Died: A Portrait of Today's College Student* (San Francisco: Jossey-Bass, 1980).
Levine, Jacob. *Motivation in Humor* (New York: Atherton Press, 1969).
Lewis, C. S. *Studies in Words* (Cambridge, U.K.: University Press, 1967).
Lewis, George H. "Assimilated Culture: The Ashanti People of Ghana," in *Michigan Sociological Review*, 5, Fall 1978.
Lewis, Jacob. *The Rise of the American Film* (New York: Mentor, 1968).
Lewis, R.W.B. *The American Adam* (Chicago: University of Chicago Press, 1955).
Ley, Willy. *Rockets, Missiles, and Men in Space* (New York: Viking, 1962).
Lifton, Robert Jay. "Protean Man," in *Partisan Review*, Winter 1968.
Lipsitz, George. *Class and Culture in Post War America* (New York: Praeger, 1981).
Locke, Allan. *The Negro: An Interpretation* (New York: Pyramid, 1925).
Lofaro, William. *The Life and Adventure of Daniel Boone* (Lexington: University of Kentucky Press, 1978).

L'Orange, H. P. *Art Forms and Civic Life in the Late Roman Empire* (Princeton, N.J.: Princeton University Press, 1965).

Lord, Albert. *The Singer of Tales* (Cambridge, Mass.: Harvard University Press, 1964).

Lossing, Benson J. *Washington and the American Republic*, 3 vols. (New York: Russell, 1870).

Lubin, Harold. *Heroes and Anti-Heroes* (San Francisco: Chandler Press, 1968).

Luedtke, Luther S. *The Study of American Culture: Contemporary Conflicts* (DeLand, Fla.: Everett Edwards, 1977).

Lundberg, Louis B. *Future Without Shock* (New York: Norton, 1973).

Lutwack, Leonard. *Heroic Fiction: The Epic Tradition and American Novels of the 20th Century* (Carbondale: Southern Illinois University Press, 1971).

Lydenberg, John, ed. *Dreiser: A Collection of Critical Essays* (Englewood Cliffs, N.J.: Prentice-Hall, 1971).

Lyman, Stanford M. *The Black American in Sociological Thought* (New York: G. P. Putnam's sons, 1972).

McCavitt, William E. *Radio and Television. A Selected, Annotated Bibliography* (Metuchen, N.J.: Scarecrow Press, 1978).

MacDonald, Dwight. *Against the American Grain* (New York: Random, 1962).

McLean, Albert F., Jr. *American Vaudeville as Ritual* (Lexington: University of Kentucky Press, 1965).

MacLeod, Celeste. *Horatio Alger, Farewell: The End of the American Dream* (New York: Seaview Books, 1980).

McLuhan, Marshall. *From Cliche to Archetype* (New York: Viking, 1970).

———. *The Gutenberg Galaxy: The Making of Typographic Man* (Toronto: University of Toronto Press, 1965).

———. *Understanding Media* (New York: McGraw-Hill, 1964).

McLuhan, Marshall, and Barrington, Nevitt. *Take Today: The Executive as Dropout* (New York: Harcourt Brace Jovanovich, 1972).

Madison, Charles A. *Book Publishing in American Culture* (New York: McGraw-Hill, 1966.

Magazine Industry Market Place. Annual. (New York: R. R. Bowker, 1980–).

Mailer, Norman. "The White Negro," *Dissent*, November 1957.

———. *Marilyn, A Biography* (New York: Warner Books, 1975).

Malcolmson, David. *Ten Heroes* (New York: Duell, 1939).

Male, Emily. *Hercules am Scheidewege und andere antike Bildstoffe in der neuron Kunst*, trans. by Dora Nussey (Leipzig, G.D.R.: B. G. Teubner, 1930).

Malinowski, Bronislaw. "Myth in Primitive Psychology," *Magic, Science, and Religion* (Garden City, N.Y.: Doubleday, 1954).

———. *A Scientific Theory of Culture and Other Essays* (New York: Oxford University Press, 1960).

Mapp, Edward. *Black in American Films: Today and Yesterday* (New York: World, 1972).

Margolies, Edward. *Afro-American Fiction, 1853–1976* (Detroit: Gale, 1979).

Marrou, H. I. *A History of Education in Antiquity*, trans. by George Lamb (New York: New American Library, 1964).

Marsden, Madonna. "The American Myth of Success: Visions and Revisions," *The Popular Culture Reader*, ed. by Jack Nachbar (Bowling Green, Ohio: Popular Press, 1978).

Mayes, Herbert R. *Alger: A Biography Without a Hero* (New York: Dutton, 1928).

Mayo, Bernard. "Washington 'Freedom's Myth' and 'More Than Man,' " in *Myths and Men* (New York: Harper & Row, 1959).

Mecklin, J. M. *The Passing of the Saint* (Chicago: University of Chicago Press, 1941).

Mellersh, H.E.L. *From Ape Man to Homer: The Story of the Beginnings of Western Civilization* (Westport, Conn.: Greenwood Press, 1962).

Miller, Elizabeth W. *The Negro in America: A Bibliography* (Cambridge, Mass.: Harvard University Press, 1966).

Miller, Perry. "The Romantic Dilemma in American Nationalism and the Concept of Nature," in *Harvard Theological Review*, 48, October 1955.

Moholy-Nagy, Sibyl. *Native Genius in Anonymous Architecture* (New York: Horizon, 1957).

Monaco, James. *Celebrity: The Media as Image Makers* (New York: Dell, 1978).

Mooney, Michael M. *The Ministry of Culture: Connections Among Art, Money, and Politics* (New York: Wyndham, 1980).

Moore, Charles. *George Washington's Rule of Civility and Decent Behavior* (Boston: Beacon Press, 1926).

Morin, Edgar. *The Stars: An Account of the Star System in Motion Pictures* (Evergreen Profile Book #7, 1960).

Morris, Richard. "Rags to Riches—Myth and Reality," in *Saturday Review*, November 21, 1953.

Moscowits, Samuel. *Explorers of the Infinitive* (Cleveland: World Publishing Co., 1963).

———. *Seekers of Tomorrow* (Cleveland: World Publishing Co., 1966).

Mott, Frank Luther. *Golden Multitudes* (New York: Macmillan, 1947).

————. *History of American Magazines*, 5 vols. (Cambridge, Mass.: Harvard University Press, 1930–68).

Muggeridge, Malcolm. *Christ and the Media* (London: n.p., 1977).

Muir, Dorothy T. *Mount Vernon: An Illustrated Handbook* (Mt. Vernon, N.Y.: Mt. Vernon Ladies Association, 1974).

————. *Presence of a Lady: Mount Vernon 1861–1868* (Mt. Vernon, N.Y.: Mt. Vernon Ladies Association, 1975).

Muir, Kenneth. "Shakespeare's Imagery, Then and Now," in *Shakespeare Studies*, 18 (1965).

Munsey, Cecil. *The Illustrated Guide to the Collectibles of Coca-Cola* (New York: Hawthorn Books, 1972).

Murray, Albert. *The Omni-Americans: Perspectives on Black Experience and American Culture* (New York: Vintage, 1983).

Murray, Henry A., ed. *Myth and Mythmaking* (Boston: Beacon Press, 1968).

Nachbar, Jack; Weiser, Deborah, and Wright, John L., eds. *The Popular Culture Reader* (Bowling Green, Ohio: Popular Press, 1978).

Nagai, Yonosuke. "The United States is Disintegrating," in *Psychology Today*, May 1972.

Neuburg, Victor E. *Popular Literature: A History and Guide* (Middlesex, U.K.: Penguin Books, 1977).

Nevins, Allan. *Ford: The Times, the Man, the Company* (New York: Dutton, 1954).

Newhall, Venetia J., ed. *Folklore Studies in the Twentieth Century* (Bury St. Edmunds, U.K.: St. Edmundsbury Press, 1980).

Noble, Peter. *The Negro in Films* (New York: Dutton, 1948).

Nocera, Joseph. "Tom Wolfe at the Keyboard," *Washington Monthly* (March 1980), pp. 20–26.

Nordham, George W. *George Washington, Vignettes and Memorabilia* (Philadelphia: Dorrance & Company, 1977).

————. *George Washington's Women: Mary, Martha, Sally and 146 Others* (Philadelphia: Dorrance & Company, 1977).

Norman, Dorothy. *The Hero: Myth, Image, Symbol* (New York: World Publishing Co., 1969).

Northrop, F.S.C. *The Meeting of East and West* (New York: Macmillan, 1945).

Nouwen, Henri. *Clowning in Rome* (New York: Doubleday Image, 1979).

Nye, Russel B. *The Unembarrassed Muse* (New York: Dial, 1976).

————, ed. *New Dimensions in Popular Culture* (Bowling Green, Ohio: Popular Press, 1972).

Oganov, Gregori. *Genuine Culture and False Substitutes* (Moscow, U.S.S.R.: Novosti Press, 1979).

O'Hallaren, Bill. "Hey, Katt, When Are You Going to Learn to Fly That Suit?" in *TV Guide* (July 24, 1982), pp. 28–31.

Oliphant, Pat. *Oliphant: An Informal Gathering* (New York: Simon & Schuster, 1978).

Oliver, Robert T. *Culture and Communication* (Springfield, Ill.: Charles C. Thomas, 1962).

O'Neill, William L. *Everyone Was Brave: The Rise and Fall of Feminism in America* (Chicago: Quadrangle, 1969).

Ong, Walter. *The Presence of the Word* (New Haven, Conn.: Yale University Press, 1967).

———. *Rhetoric, Romance, and Technology: Studies in Interaction of Expression and Culture* (Ithaca, N.Y.: Cornell University Press, 1971).

Oupensky, Leonid, and Lossky, Vladimir. *The Meaning of Icons* (Basel, Switzerland: Otto Walter, 1952).

Palmer, Myles. *Woody Allen: An Illustrated Biography* (New York: Proteus, 1980).

Panofsky, Erwin. *Hercules am Scheidewege und andere antike Bildstoffe in der neuron Kunst* (Leipzig, G.D.R.: B. G. Teubner, 1930).

———. *Studies in Iconology* (New York: Oxford University Press, 1939).

Park, Robert E. *Race and Culture* (Glencoe, Ill.: Free Press, 1973).

Park, Robert E., and Burgess, Ernest W. *Introduction to the Science of Sociology* (Chicago: University of Chicago Press, 1921).

Patai, Raphael. *Myth and Modern Man* (Englewood Cliffs, N.J.: Prentice-Hall, 1972).

Patterson, Lindsay. *The Afro-American in Music and Art* (Cornwallis Heights, Pa.: Publishers Agency, 1978).

Pearson, Catherine. *The Female Hero in American and British Literature* (New York: Bowker, 1981).

Peavy, Charles D. *Afro-American Literature and Culture Since World War II* (Detroit: Gale, 1979).

Pei, Mario. *Double Speak in America* (New York: Hawthorn Books, 1973).

Perates, John. *Twentieth Century American Icons* (Cincinnati: Cincinnati Art Museum, 1974).

Peterson, Merrill. *The Jefferson Image in the American Mind* (New York: Oxford University Press, 1960).

Peterson, Richard A. *The Production of Culture* (Beverly Hills: Sage Publications, 1976).

Peterson, Theodore. *Magazines in the Twentieth Century* (Urbana: University of Illinois Press, 1964).

Peterson, William. *The Background to Ethnic Conflict* (Leiden, Neth.: E. J. Brill, 1979).

Pettit, Charles. *The Concept of Structuralism* (Berkeley: University of California Press, 1975).

Phelan, John M. *Mediaworld: Programming the Public* (New York: Seabury Press, 1977).

Phelp, E. B. *Memoir of Washington Written for Boys and Girls* (Cincinnati: Day & Sons, 1874).

Pierce, J. R. *Symbols, Signals, and Noise: The Nature and Process of Communication* (New York: Harper Torchbook TB 574, 1965).

Pierson, George W. *The Moving American* (New York: Knopf, 1973).

Plank, Robert. *The Emotional Significance of Imaginary Beings* (Springfield, Ill.: Thomas, 1968).

Priestly, J. P. "Marilyn Monroe," *Saturday Evening Post*, April 27, 1963.

Pye, David. *The Nature and Art of Workmanship* (Cambridge, U.K.: Cambridge University Press, 1968).

Quarles, Benjamin. *The Negro in the Making of America* (New York: Dutton, 1964).

Rabecq-Maillard, M. *Histoire du Jouet* (Paris: Hachette, 1962).

Rank, Otto. *The Birth of the Hero and Other Essays* (New York: Vintage Books, 1964).

————. *The Myth of the Birth of the Hero: A Psychological Interpretation of Mythology* (New York: Robert Brunner, 1957).

Ransom, John Crowe. *God Without Thunder* (New York: Knopf, 1930).

Rao, Y. V. Laskhmana. *The Development of Communication* (Minneapolis: University of Minnesota Press, 1966).

Read, Herbert. *Icon and Idea* (Cambridge, Mass.: Harvard University Press, 1955).

Reagan, Ronald. "Unforgettable John Wayne," in *Reader's Digest*, October 1979.

Redding, Saunders. "The Black Revolution in American Studies," *American Studies: An International Newsletter*, 9, no. 1, Autumn 1970.

Reeves, Rosser. *Reality in Advertising* (New York: Knopf, 1960).

Regin, Deric. *Culture and the Crowd: A Cultural History of the Proletarian Era* (New York: Chilton Book Company, 1968).

————. *Culture and the Crowd: A Cultural History of the Proletarian Era* (Philadelphia: Chilton, 1968).

Reich, Charles. *The Greening of America* (New York: Random House, 1970).

Reichardt, Jasia. *Robots: Fact, Fiction and Prediction* (New York: Penguin, 1978).

Ribble, D. *The Martyrs, A Study in Social Control* (Chicago: University of Chicago Press, 1931).

Rice, David Talbot. *Byzantine Art* (Harmondsworth, U.K.: Penguin, 1968).

Richards, I. A. *The Philosophy of Rhetoric* (New York: Oxford University Press, 1965).

Richardson, Patrick. *Empire and Slavery* (London: Longmans, Green & Co., 1968).

Riegel, Robert E. "American Frontier Theory," *Cahiers d'Histoire Mondiale*, 3, no. 2, 1956.

Riesman, David. *The Lonely Crowd* (New Haven, Conn.: Yale University Press, 1950).

Ritter, Kurt. "Ronald Reagan and 'The Speech': The Rhetoric of Public Relations," *Western Speech*, Winter 1982.

Roback, A. A. *A Dictionary of International Slurs* (Cambridge, Mass.: Sci-Art Publishers, 1944).

Robbins, Thomas. *Even Cowgirls Get the Blues* (Boston: Houghton Mifflin, 1976).

Rogow, Arnold A. "The Revolt Against Social Equality," in *Dissent*, 4, Autumn 1957.

Rollin, Roger R. *Hero/Anti-Hero* (New York: n.p., 1973).

Rose, Peter I. *The Subject is Race* (New York: Oxford University Press, 1968).

Rosenberg, Harold. *Tradition of the New* (New York: Horizon, 1959).

Rouse, Irving. "The Strategy of Culture History," in *Anthropology Today* (Chicago: University of Chicago Press, 1958).

Rubin, Lillian B. *Worlds of Pain: Life in the Working Class Community* (New York: Basic Books, 1976).

Rude, George. *The Crowd in the French Revolution* (Oxford, U.K.: Clarendon Press, 1959).

———. *The Crowd in History: A Study of Popular Disturbances in France and England, 1730–1848* (New York: John Wiley & Sons, 1964).

Rudwick, Elliott. "The Niagara Movement," in *Journal of Negro History*, 42, July 1957.

———. "W.E.B. Dubois in the Role of Crisis Editor," in *Journal of Negro History*, 42, July 1957.

Russell, John, and Suzi Gablik. *Pop Art Redefined* (New York: Praeger, 1964).

Sagan, Carl. *Cosmos* (New York: Random House, 1980).

Salk, Erwin A. *A Layman's Guide to Negro History* (New York: McGraw, 1967).

Samuel, Richard. *Village Life and Labour* (London: Unwin, 1975).

San Anson, Robert. *Gone Crazy and Back Again: The Rise and Fall of the Rolling Stone Generation* (New York: Doubleday, 1981).

Sandford, Rich. *Heroes Die Young* (Chicago: Tower Books, 1979).

Schatz, Walter, ed. *The Directory of Afro-American Sources* (New York: R. R. Bowker Co., 1970).

Schauffler, Robert H., ed. *Washington's Birthday* (New York: Dodd, Mead & Co., 1926).

Schechter, Harold, and Semeiks, Jonna Gormely, eds. *Patterns in Popular Culture: A Sourcebook for Writers* (New York: Harper & Row, 1980).

Schechter, William. *The History of Negro Humor in America* (New York: Doubleday, 1972).

Schoener, Alon. *Harlem on my Mind: Cultural Capital of Black America, 1900–1968* (New York: Random House, 1968).

Schramm, Wilbur. *Men, Messages, and Media* (New York: Harper & Row, 1973).

Schroeder, Fred. "The Discovery of Popular Culture before Printing," *Journal of Popular Culture*, 11, Winter 1977.

———. *Five Thousand Years of Popular Culture* (Bowling Green, Ohio: Popular Press, 1980).

———. *Outlaw Aesthetics* (Bowling Green, Ohio: Popular Press, 1978).

Schwartz, Tony. *Media, The Second God* (New York: Doubleday, 1983).

Schweitzer, H. J. *Rural Sociology in a Changing Urbanized Society* (Urbana: University of Illinois Press, 1966).

Scully, Malcolm G. "John Lennon: 'The Whole Boat Was Moving,' " in *Chronicle of Higher Education*, December 15, 1980.

Seelye, John. "Buckskin and Ballistics," *Journal of Popular Culture*, 1, no. 1, Summer 1967.

Severn, James E. *Colt Firearms, 1836–1954* (Santa Ana, Calif.: Severn Press, 1954).

Sexton, Patricia Cayo. *Blue Collar Hard Hats: The Working Class and the Future of American Politics* (New York: Random House, 1971).

Shankar, Ravi. *My Music, My Life* (New York: Simon & Schuster, 1968).

Shapley, Harlow. *The View From A Distant Star* (New York: Basic Books, 1963).

Shay, Frank. *Here's Audacity! Legendary Heroes* (Jena, Germany: Biederman, 1933).

Shiner, Larry. *The Secularization of History* (New York: Basic Books, 1966).

Silver, Gerald A. *The Social Impact of Computers* (New York: Harcourt Brace Jovanovich, 1979).

Simkins, Francis B. *The South Old and New: A History 1820–1947* (New York: Knopf, 1947).

Sklar, Robert. *Movie-Made America: A Cultural History of American Movies* (New York: Vintage/Random House, 1976).

Slater, Philip. *The Pursuit of Loneliness* (Boston: Beacon Press, 1970).

Smelser, M. J. *Theory of Collective Behavior* (New York: Knopf, 1963).

Smith, Dwight La Vern. *Afro-American History: A Bibliography* (Santa Barbara, Calif.: ABC-Clio, 1974).

Smith, Henry Nash. *Virgin Land: The American West as Symbol and Myth* (Cambridge, Mass.: Harvard University Press, 1950).

Sontag, Susan. *Against Interpretation* (New York: Farrar, Straus & Giroux, 1969).

Spectorsky, A. C. *The Book of the Earth* (New York: Macmillan, 1957).

Spiller, Robert, et al., eds. *Literary History of the United States*, 1, 3d ed. rev. (New York: Macmillan, 1963).

Stafford, John. "Patterns of Meaning in Nights with Uncle Remus," *American Literature*, 18, May 1946.

Stearns, Marshall. *The Story of Jazz* (New York: Knopf, 1956).

Steinberg, S. H. *Five Hundred Years of Printing* (New York: Criterion Books, 1974).

Stivers, Richard. *Evil in Modern Myth and Ritual* (Athens: University of Georgia Press, 1982).

Strausz-Hupe, Robert. *The Zone of Indifference* (New York: G. P. Putnam's Sons, 1952).

Southern, R. W. *The Making of the Middle Ages* (New Haven, Conn.: Yale University Press, 1953).

Swados, Harvey. *The American Writer and the Great Depression* (New York: Bobbs-Merrill, 1966).

Swanberg, W. A. *Luce and His Empire* (New York: Charles Scribner's, 1972).

Sward, Keith. *The Legend of Henry Ford* (New York: World, 1948).

Sweeney, Louise. "Carl Sagan: Reviewing Our Sense of Wonder," in *Christian Science Monitor*, March 18, 1982.

Swiggett, Howard. *The Great Man: George Washington as a Human Being* (Garden City, N.Y.: Doubleday, 1953).

Taylor, George Roger. *The Turner Thesis Concerning the Role of the Frontier in American History* (Boston: Heath, 1949).

Tebbel, John W. *The American Magazine: A Compact History* (New York: Hawthorn, 1969).

Terkel, Studs. "The New Mood," *Parade*, October 11, 1981.

Thompson, Denys, ed. *Discrimination and Popular Culture* (Baltimore: Penguin, 1965).

Thompson, William Irwin. *Darkness and Scattered Light* (New York: Doubleday, Anchor Press, 1978).

Thornbrough, Emma L. "More Light on Booker T. Washington and the New York Age," *Journal of Negro History*, 43, January 1958.

Thwaites, Reuben G., ed. *Early Western Travels, 1748–1846*. 32 vols. (Cleveland, Ohio: A. H. Clark Co., 1904–7).

Tillyard, E.M.W. *The Elizabethan World* (New York: Vintage, 1959).

Toffler, Alvin. *Culture Consumers: A Study of Art and Affluence in America* (Baltimore: Penguin, 1964).
————. *The Eco-Spasm Report* (New York: Bantam, 1975).
————. *Future Shock* (New York: Macmillan, 1970).
Toll, Robert C. *The Entertainment Machine: American Show Business in the Twentieth Century* (New York: Oxford University Press, 1981).
Toole, John Kennedy. *A Confederacy of Dunces* (Baton Rouge: Louisiana State University Press, 1980).
Tow, Margaret. *George Washington—The Legend* (New York: Columbia University, unpublished, 1919).
Trachtenberg, Alan. *Democratic Vistas* (New York: George Braziller, 1970).
Trachtenberg, Marvin. *The Statue of Liberty* (New York: Viking, 1976).
Tunstall, Jeremy. *The Media are American* (New York: Columbia University Press, 1976).
Turner, Victor. "Symbols in Ndembu Ritual," *The Forest of Symbols: Aspects of Ndembu Ritual* (Ithaca, N.Y.: Cornell University Press, 1967).
Tuve, Rosemond. *Elizabethan and Metaphysical Imagery: Renaissance Poetic and Twentieth Century Critics* (Chicago: University of Chicago Press, 1947).
Twelve Southerners. *I'll Take My Stand* (New York: Dutton, 1930).
Unphlett, Wiley Lee. *Mythmakers of the American Dream: The Nostalgic Vision on Popular Culture* (Lewisburg, Pa.: Bucknell University Press, 1982).
Vacca, Roberto. *The Coming Dark Age* (New York: Doubleday, 1975).
Valdes, Joan, with Jeanne Crow. *The Media Reader* (Dayton, Ohio: Pflaum, 1975).
van der Post, Laurens. *Jung and the Story of Our Time* (New York: Pantheon, 1976).
von Frantz, Mary Louis. *C. G. Jung: His Myth in Our Time* (New York: G. P. Putnam's Sons, 1976).
Walker, Williston. *A History of the Christian Church* (New York: Charles Scribner's, 1959).
Waller, George M. *The American Revolution in the West* (Chicago: University of Chicago Press, 1976).
Ward, Barbara. *Spaceship Earth* (New York: Harper & Row, 1964).
Ward, John Williams. *Andrew Jackson: Symbol for an Age* (New York: Oxford University Press, 1962).
Warshaw, Robert. *Immediate Experience* (New York: Anchor, 1962).
Washington, George. *George Washington: A Biography in His Own Words* (New York: Harper & Row, 1972).
Washington, M. Bunch. *The Art of Romare Bearden: The Prevalence of Ritual* (New York: Harry N. Abrams, 1972).

Wavell, Bruce B. *The Living Logos: A Philosophico-Religious Essay* (Washington, D.C.: University Press of America, 1978).

Webb, Walter P. *The Great Frontier* (Boston: Little, Brown & Co., 1952).

———. *The Great Plains* (New York: Grosset, 1957).

Weber, Max. *The Protestant Ethic and the Spirit of Capitalism* (New York: Charles Scribner's, 1948).

Weber, Ronald. *The Reporter as Artist: A Look at the New Journalism Controversy* (New York: Hastings House, 1974).

Wecter, Dixon. *The Hero in America: A Chronicle of Hero-Worship* (New York: Charles Scribner's, 1941; reprint, Ann Arbor, Mich., University of Michigan Press, 1966).

Weems, Mason L. *The Life of Washington* (Cambridge, Mass.: Belknap Press of Harvard University Press, 1962).

Whannel, Paddy, and Hall, S. *Popular Arts* (New York: Pantheon, 1965).

Whetmore, Edward. *Mediamerica* (Belmont, Calif.: Wadsworth, 1978).

Whitcomb, Ian. *After the Ball: Pop Music from Rag to Rock* (Baltimore: Penguin, 1974).

Whittemore, Hank. "The Surprising Class of '83," *Parade*, February 20, 1983.

Wight, Robin. *The Day the Pigs Refused to be Driven to Market: Advertising and the Consumer Revolution* (New York: Random House, 1972).

Wilgus, Donald K. *Anglo-American Folksong Scholarship Since 1898* (Brunswick, N.J.: Rutgers University Press, 1959).

Williams, Denis. *Icon and Image* (New York: New York University Press, 1974).

Williams, Duncan. *To Be or Not To Be: A Question of Survival* (Oxford: Pergamon Press, 1974).

Williams, Raymond. *Culture and Society, 1870–1950* (New York: Harper & Row, 1959).

Williams, William Carlos. *In the American Grain* (New York: A. & C. Boni, 1925).

Williams, W. M. *The Country Craftsman* (London: Nicholson, 1958).

Wilson, Bryan R. *The Noble Savages: The Primitive Origins of Charisma and Its Contemporary Survival* (Berkeley: University of California Press, 1975).

Wilson, John Oliver. *After Affluence: Economics to Meet Human Needs* (New York: Harper & Row, 1980).

Wilson, William A. "Herder, Folklore, and Romantic Nationalism," *Journal of Popular Culture*, 6 (1973).

Wilson, Woodrow. *The New Freedom* (New York: Doubleday, 1913).

Winter, Gibson. *The New Creation as Metropolis* (New York: Knopf, 1963).

Wolfe, Tom. *The Kandy Kolored Tangerine Flake Streamline Baby* (New York: Simon & Schuster, 1965).

————. *The Painted Word* (New York: Farrar, Straus, & Giroux, 1975).

————. *The Right Stuff* (New York: Simon & Schuster, 1979).

Wolseley, Roland E. *The Changing Magazine: Trends in Readership and Management* (New York: Hastings House, 1973).

Woodward, W. E. *George Washington: The Image and the Man* (New York: Blue Ribbon Books, 1926).

Worthington-Williams, Michael. *Automobilia, A Guided Tour for Collectors* (New York: Hastings House, 1979).

Wright, Esmond. *Washington and the American Revolution* (New York: Methuen, 1957).

Wright, Richard. *Black Boy* (New York: Harper, 1945).

Wyllie, Irvin G. *The Self-Made Man in America: The Myth of Rags to Riches* (New York: Free Press, 1954).

Yacowar, Maurice. *Loser Take All: The Comic Act of Woody Allen* (New York: Frederick Unger, 1979).

Yeats, William Butler. *Collected Poems* (London: A. P. Watt, 1960).

Yeo, Eileen, and Yeo, Stephen, eds. *Popular Culture and Class Conflict, 1590–1914: Explorations in the History of Labour and Leisure* (Sussex, U.K.: Harvester Press, 1981).

Zinsser, William. *Pop Goes America* (New York: Harper & Row, 1966).

INDEX _____

About the Author

MARSHALL F. FISHWICK is Professor of Humanities and Communications Studies at Virginia Polytechnic Institute and State University. He has written many works on aspects of American history and popular culture, including *Common Culture and the Great Tradition* (Greenwood Press, 1982), *Icons of Popular Culture, Heroes of Popular Culture,* and *Around the World in Forty Years,* as well as more than two hundred articles.

Recent Titles in
Contributions to the Study of Popular Culture

Tarzan and Tradition: Classical Myth in Popular Literature
Erling B. Holtsmark

Common Culture and the Great Tradition: The Case for
Renewal
Marshall W. Fishwick

Concise Histories of American Popular Culture
M. Thomas Inge, editor

Ban Johnson: Czar of Baseball
Eugene C. Murdock

Putting Dell on the Map: A History of the Dell Paperbacks
William H. Lyles

Behold the Mighty Wurlitzer: The History of the Theatre Pipe
Organ
John W. Landon

Mighty Casey: All-American
Eugene C. Murdock

The Baker Street Reader: Cornerstone Writings about Sherlock
Holmes
Philip A. Shreffler, editor

Dark Cinema: American *Film Noir* in Cultural Perspective
Jon Tuska